ULTIMATE FANTASTIC FOUR

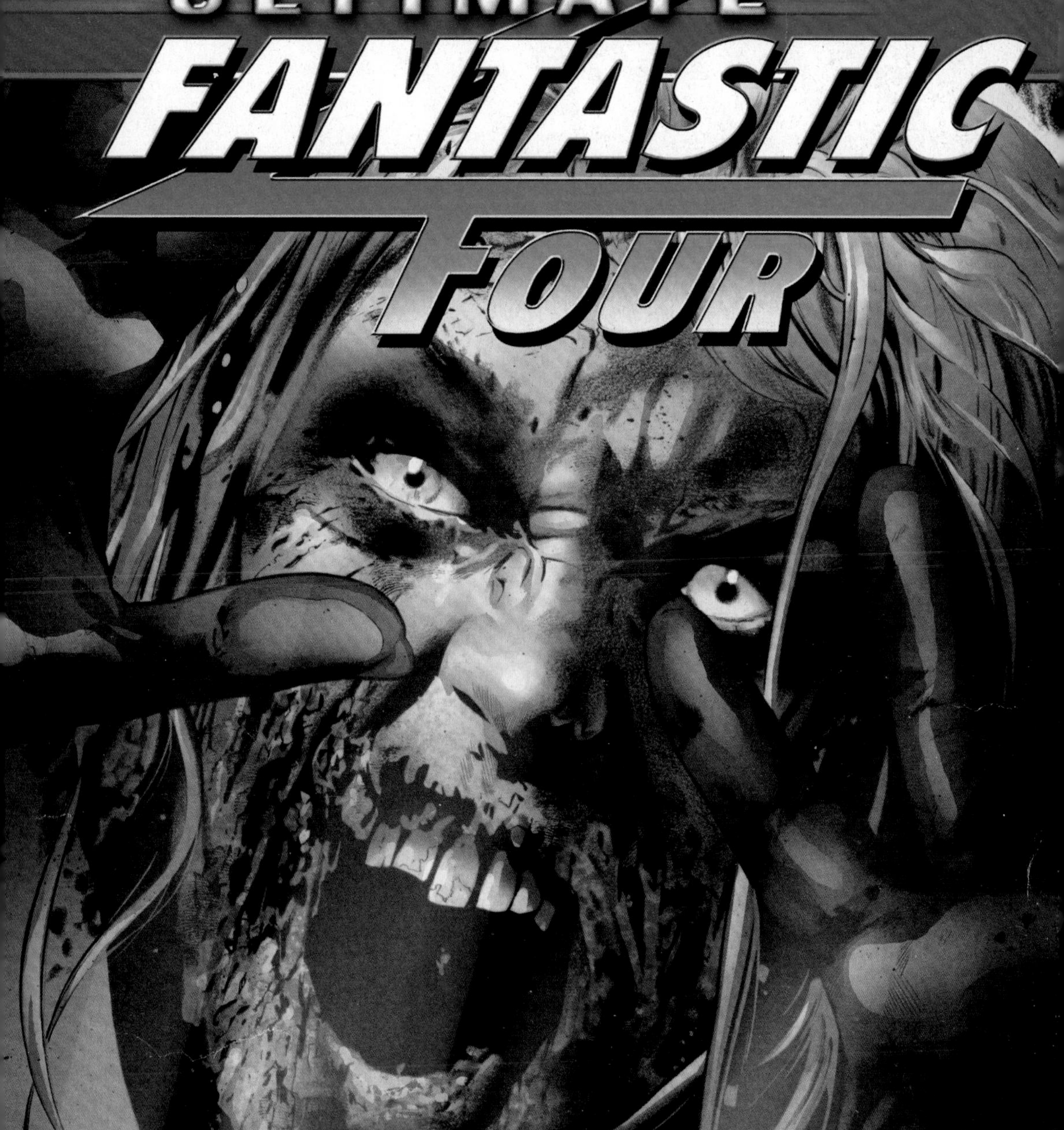

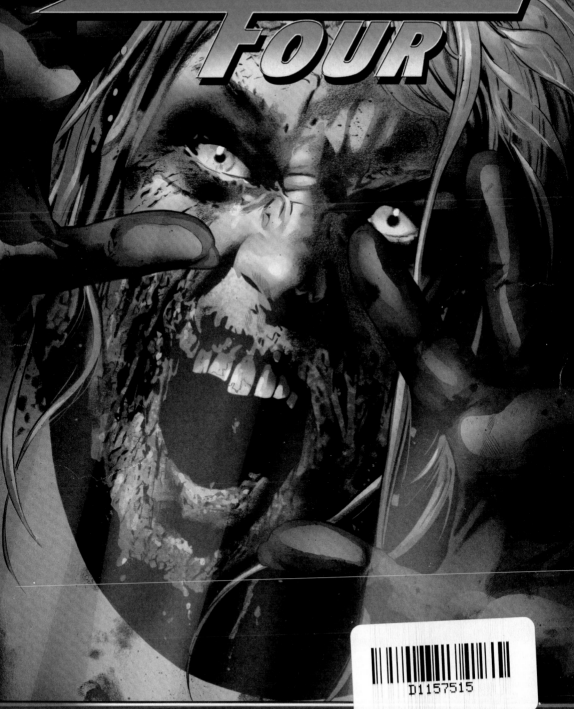

FRIGHTFUL

ULTIMATE FANTASTIC FOUR

FRIGHTFUL

writer:
MARK MILLAR

pencils:
GREG LAND

inks:
MATT RYAN

additional art:
MITCH BREITWEISER

colors:
JUSTIN PONSOR with JASON KEITH

letters:
VIRTUAL CALLIGRAPHY'S RANDY GENTILE

variant covers:
ARTHUR SUYDAM

assistant editor:
NICOLE BOOSE

associate editor:
JOHN BARBER

editor:
RALPH MACCHIO

collection editor:
JENNIFER GRÜNWALD

assistant editor:
MICHAEL SHORT

associate editor:
MARK D. BEAZLEY

senior editor, special projects:
JEFF YOUNGQUIST

vice president of sales:
DAVID GABRIEL

production:
**JERRON QUALITY COLOR
& JERRY KALINOWSKI**

vice president of creative:
TOM MARVELLI

editor in chief:
JOE QUESADA

publisher:
DAN BUCKLEY

PREVIOUSLY:

Reed Richards, handpicked to join the Baxter Building think tank of young geniuses, spent his youth developing a teleport system that transported solid matter into a parallel universe called the N-Zone. Its first full-scale test was witnessed by Reed, fellow think tank members Sue Storm and her brother Johnny, as well as Reed's childhood friend Ben Grimm.

There was an accident. The quartet's genetic structures were scrambled and recombined in a fantastically strange way. Reed's body stretches and flows like water. Ben looks like a thing carved from desert rock. Sue can become invisible. Johnny generates flame.

After returning from an alternate-universe Earth that had been conquered by zombies and battling the undersea super criminal called Namor, the young quintet is about to embark on their most amazing adventure yet...

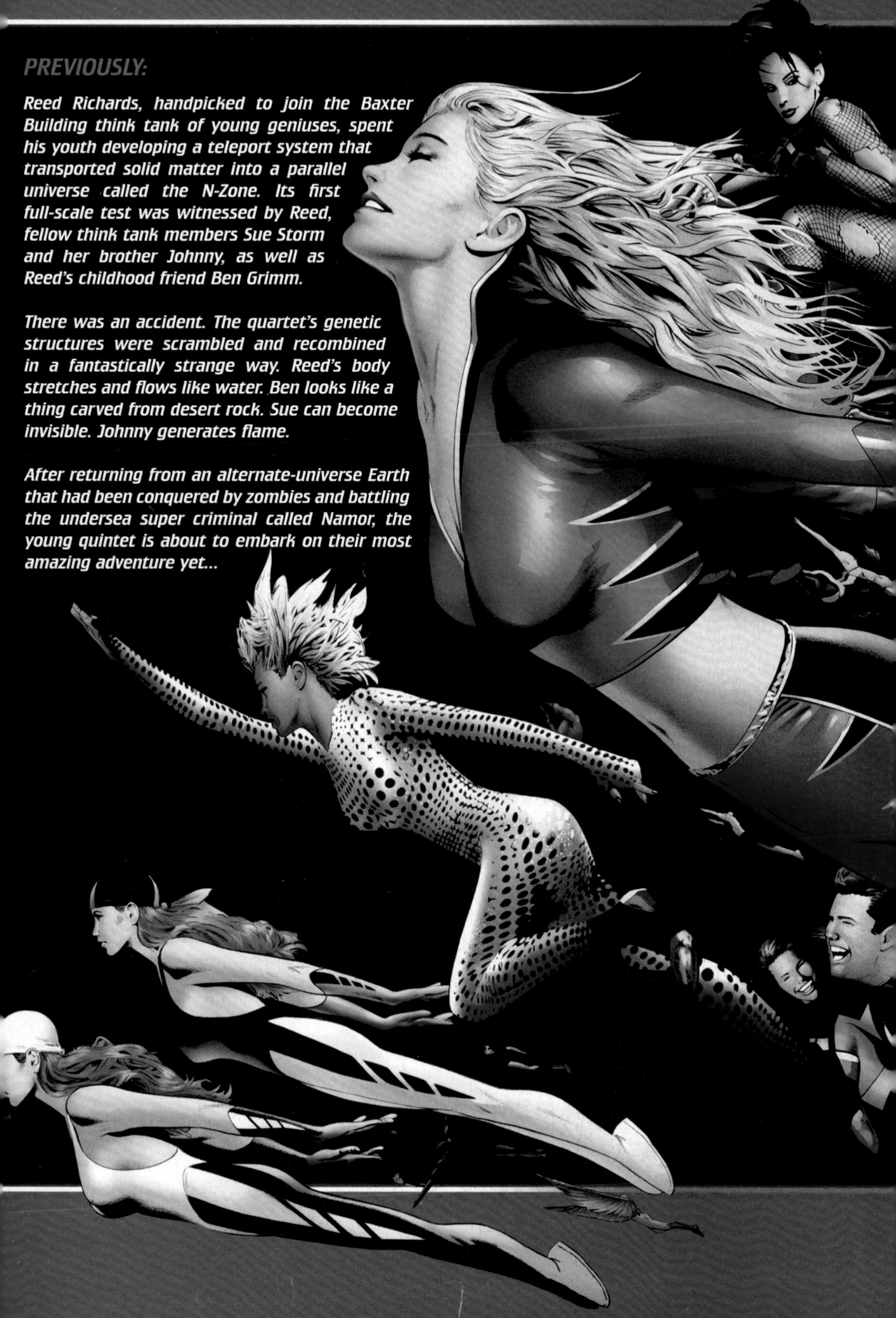

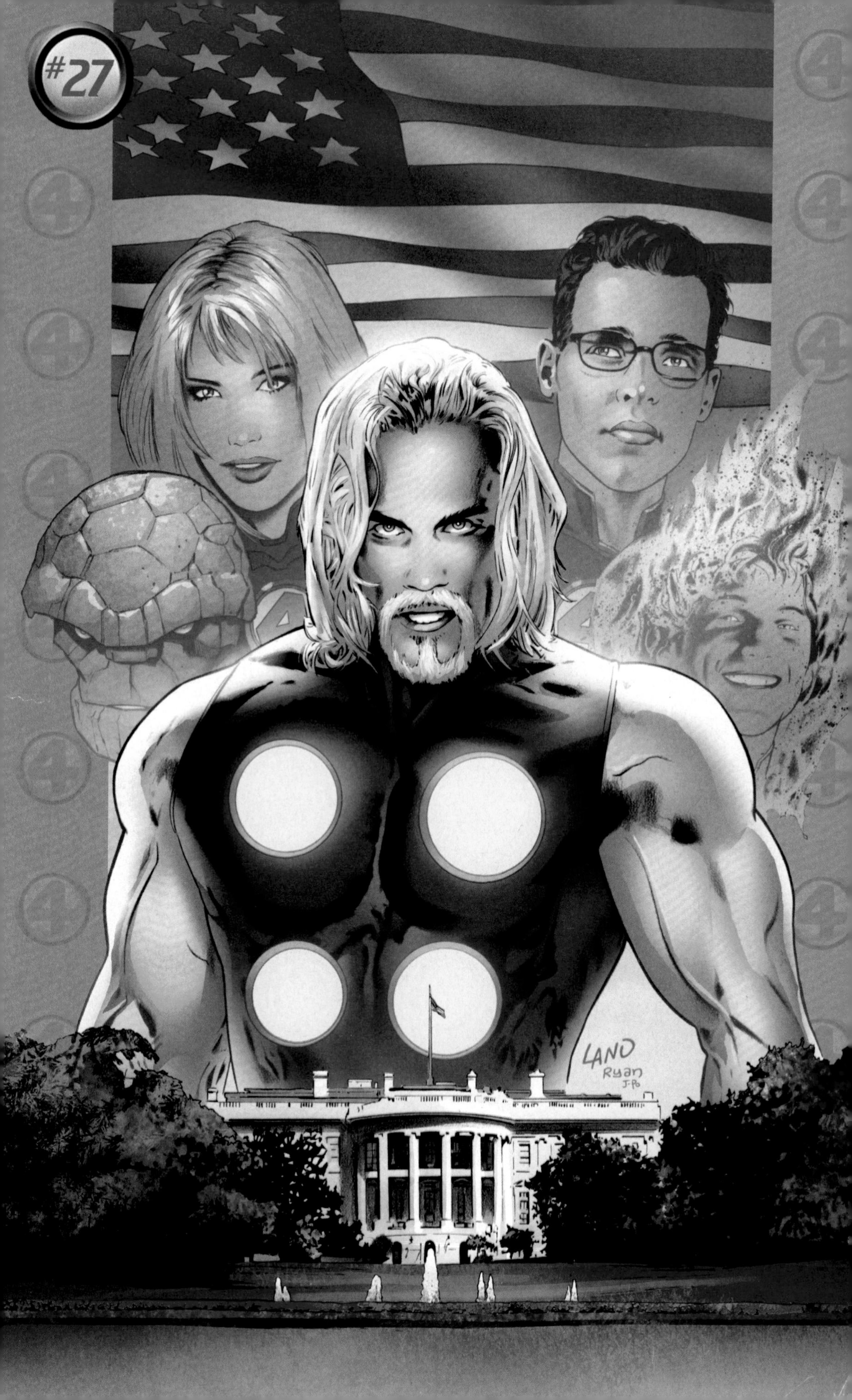
#27
LAND
Ryan
J-Po

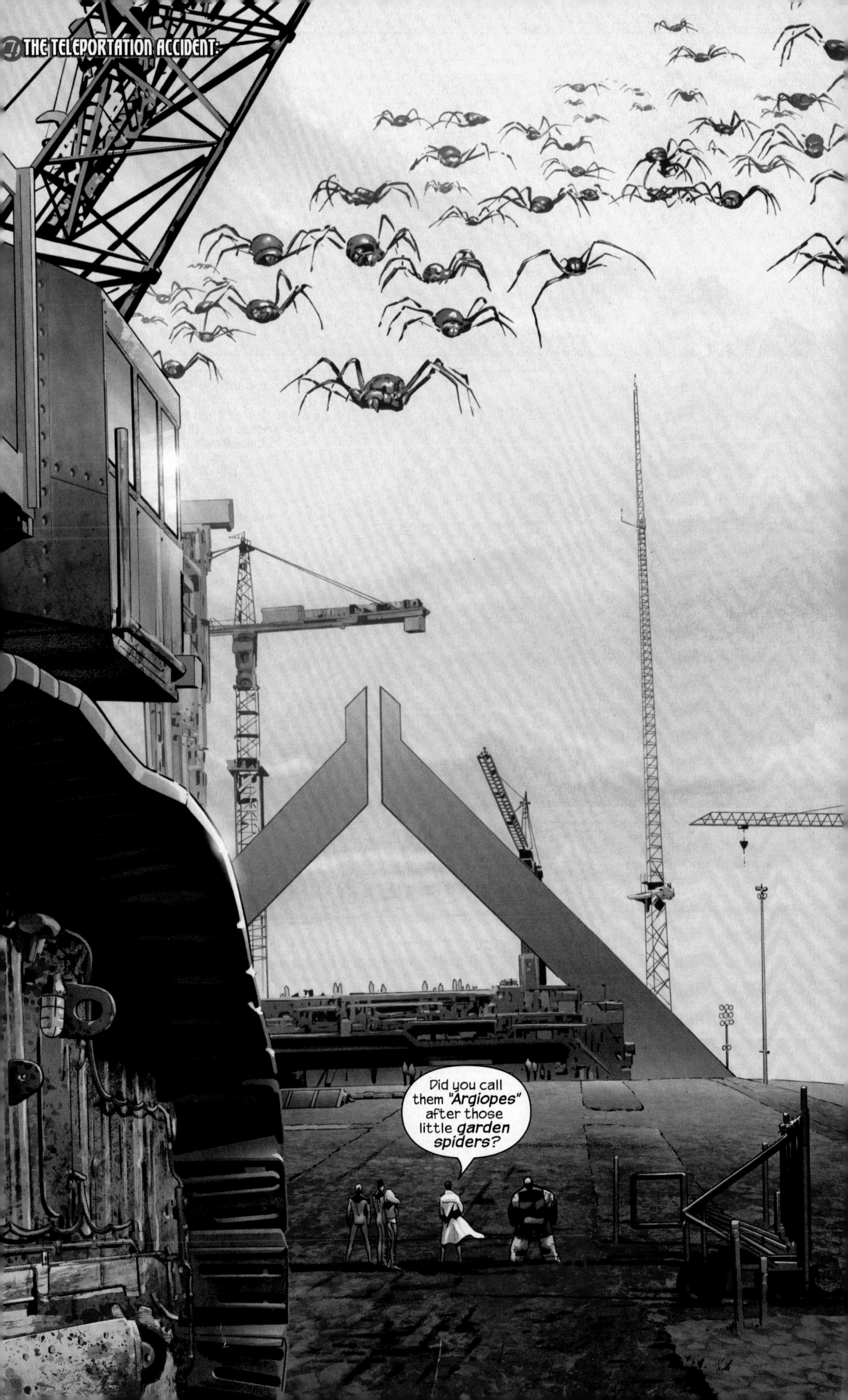
7) THE TELEPORTATION ACCIDENT:
Did you call them "Argiopes" after those little garden spiders?

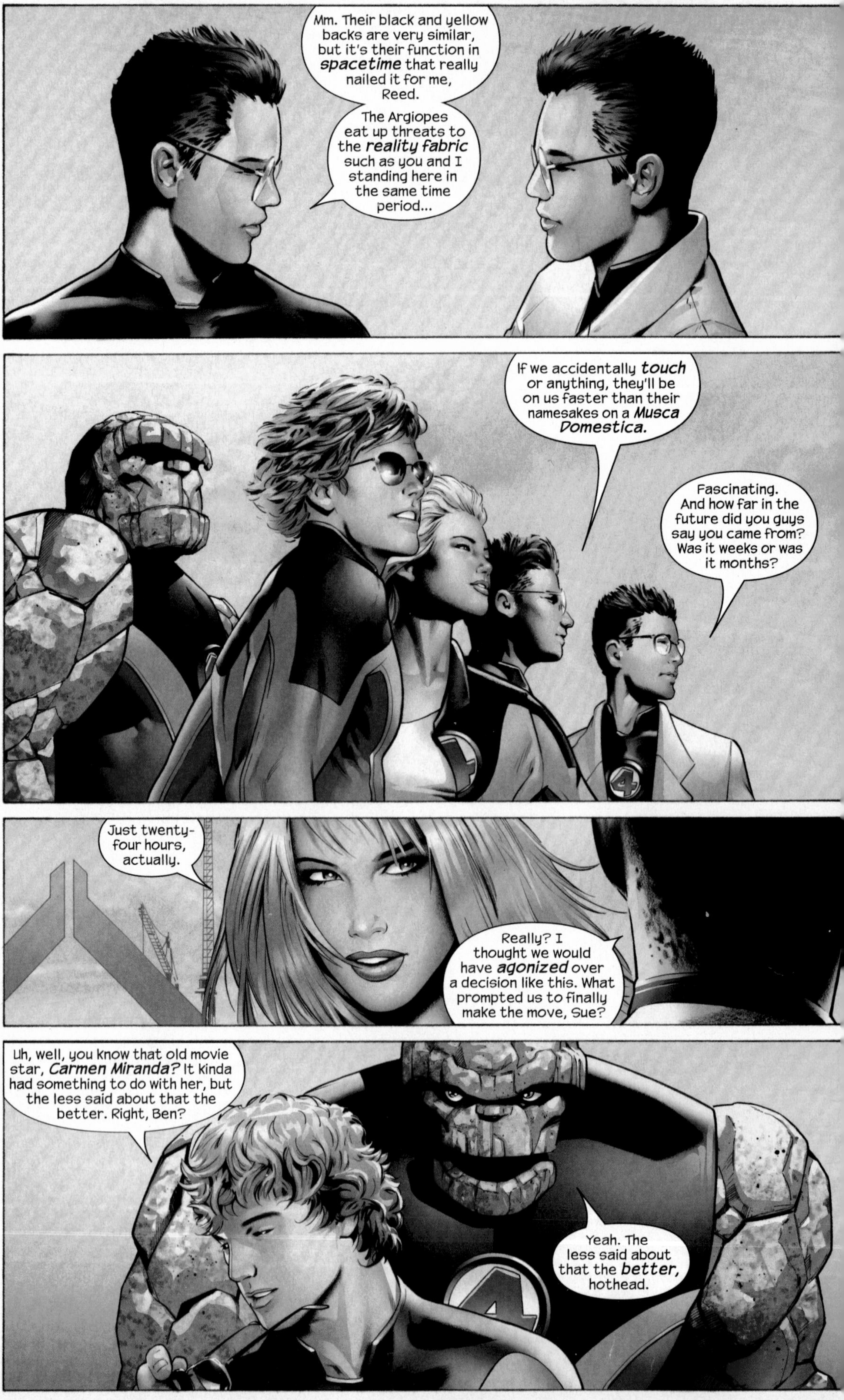
Mm. Their black and yellow backs are very similar, but it's their function in *spacetime* that really nailed it for me, Reed.
The Argiopes eat up threats to the *reality fabric* such as you and I standing here in the same time period...
If we accidentally *touch* or anything, they'll be on us faster than their namesakes on a *Musca Domestica.*
Fascinating. And how far in the future did you guys say you came from? Was it weeks or was it months?
Just twenty-four hours, actually.
Really? I thought we would have *agonized* over a decision like this. What prompted us to finally make the move, Sue?
Uh, well, you know that old movie star, *Carmen Miranda?* It kinda had something to do with her, but the less said about that the better. Right, Ben?
Yeah. The less said about that the *better,* hothead.

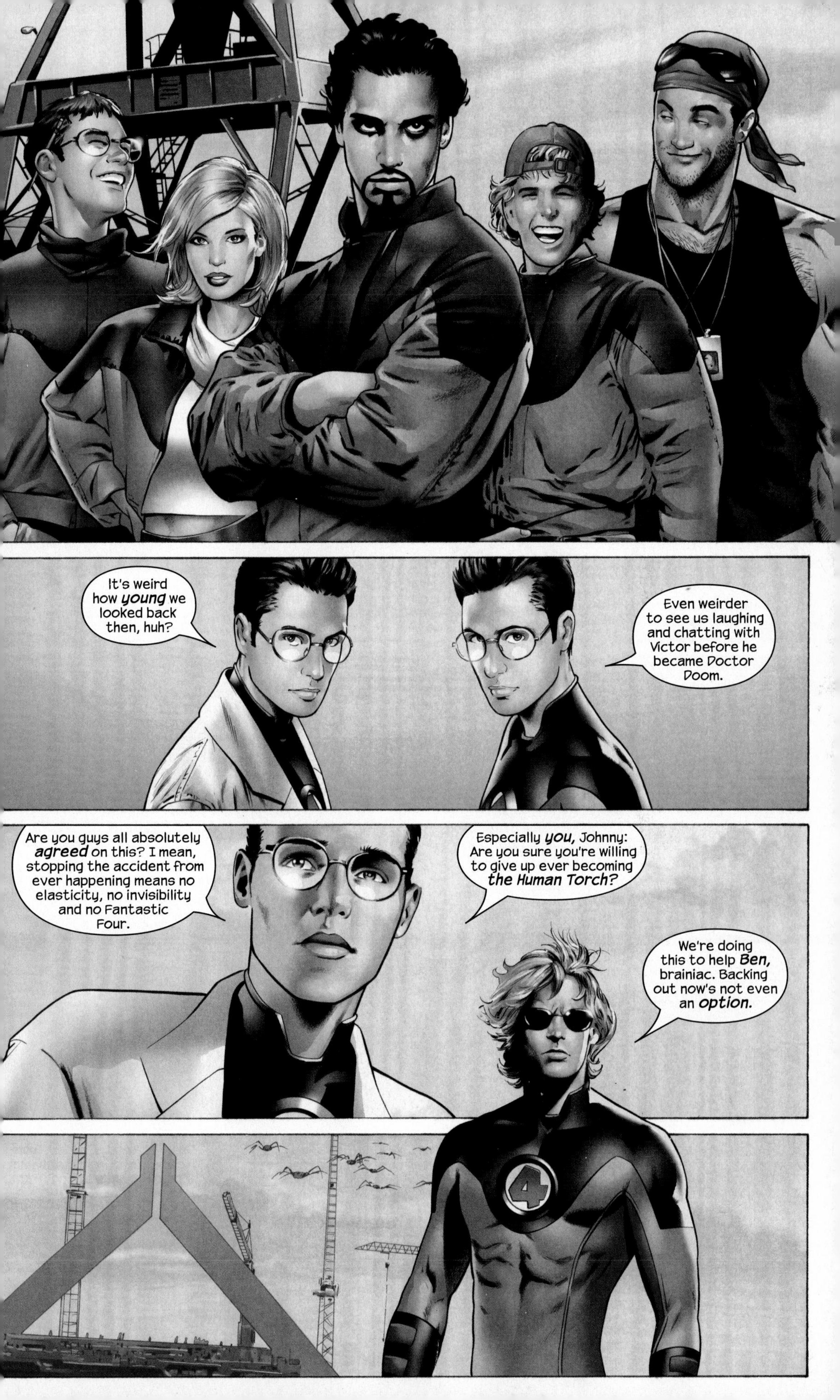
It's weird how young we looked back then, huh?
Even weirder to see us laughing and chatting with Victor before he became Doctor Doom.
Are you guys all absolutely agreed on this? I mean, stopping the accident from ever happening means no elasticity, no invisibility and no Fantastic Four.
Especially you, Johnny: Are you sure you're willing to give up ever becoming the Human Torch?
We're doing this to help Ben, brainiac. Backing out now's not even an option.

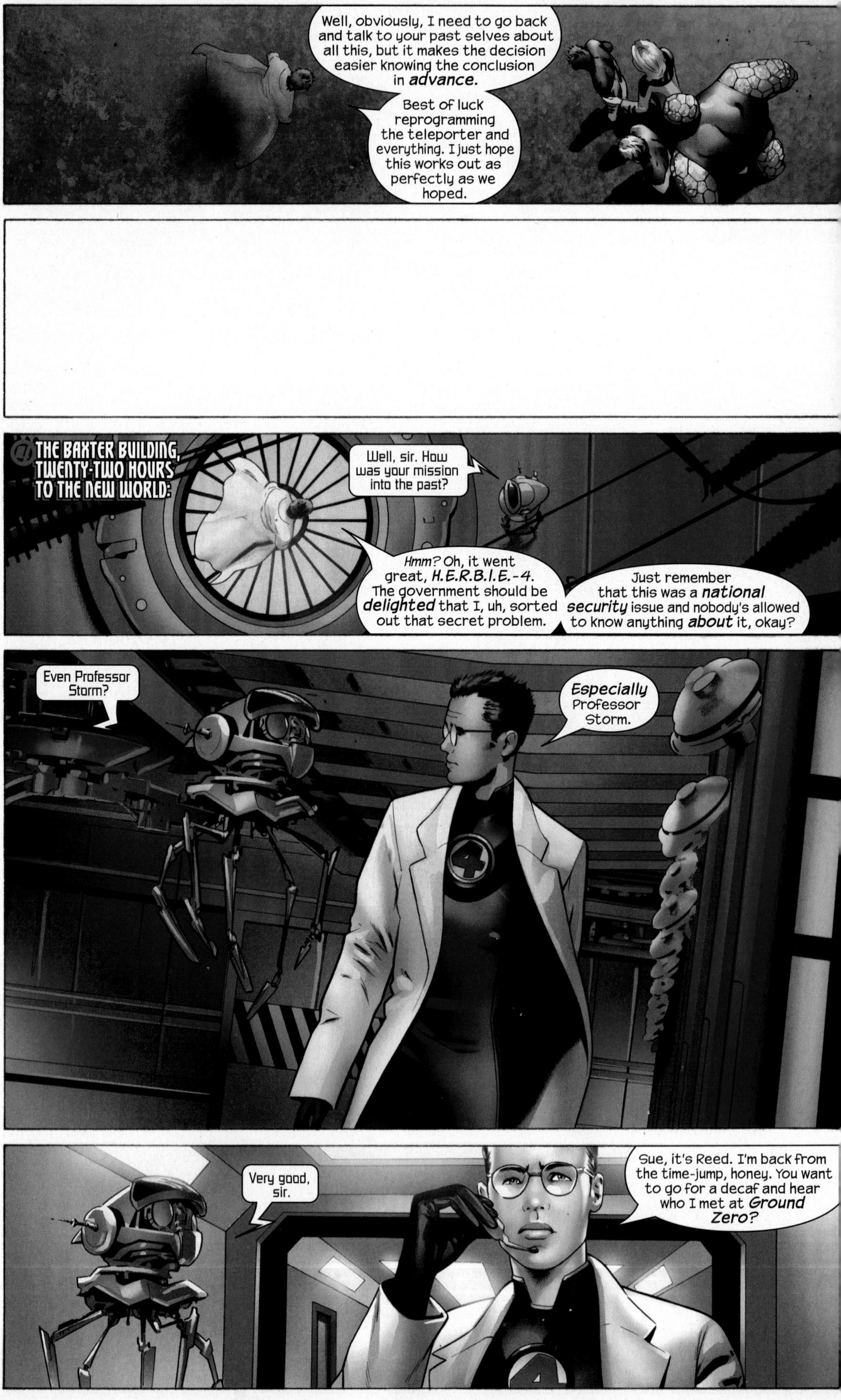
Well, obviously, I need to go back and talk to your past selves about all this, but it makes the decision easier knowing the conclusion in *advance.*
Best of luck reprogramming the teleporter and everything. I just hope this works out as perfectly as we hoped.
THE BAXTER BUILDING, TWENTY-TWO HOURS TO THE NEW WORLD:
Well, sir. How was your mission into the past?
Hmm? Oh, it went great, *H.E.R.B.I.E.-4.* The government should be *delighted* that I, uh, sorted out that secret problem.
Just remember that this was a *national security* issue and nobody's allowed to know anything *about* it, okay?
Even Professor Storm?
Especially Professor Storm.
Very good, sir.
Sue, it's Reed. I'm back from the time-jump, honey. You want to go for a decaf and hear who I met at *Ground Zero?*

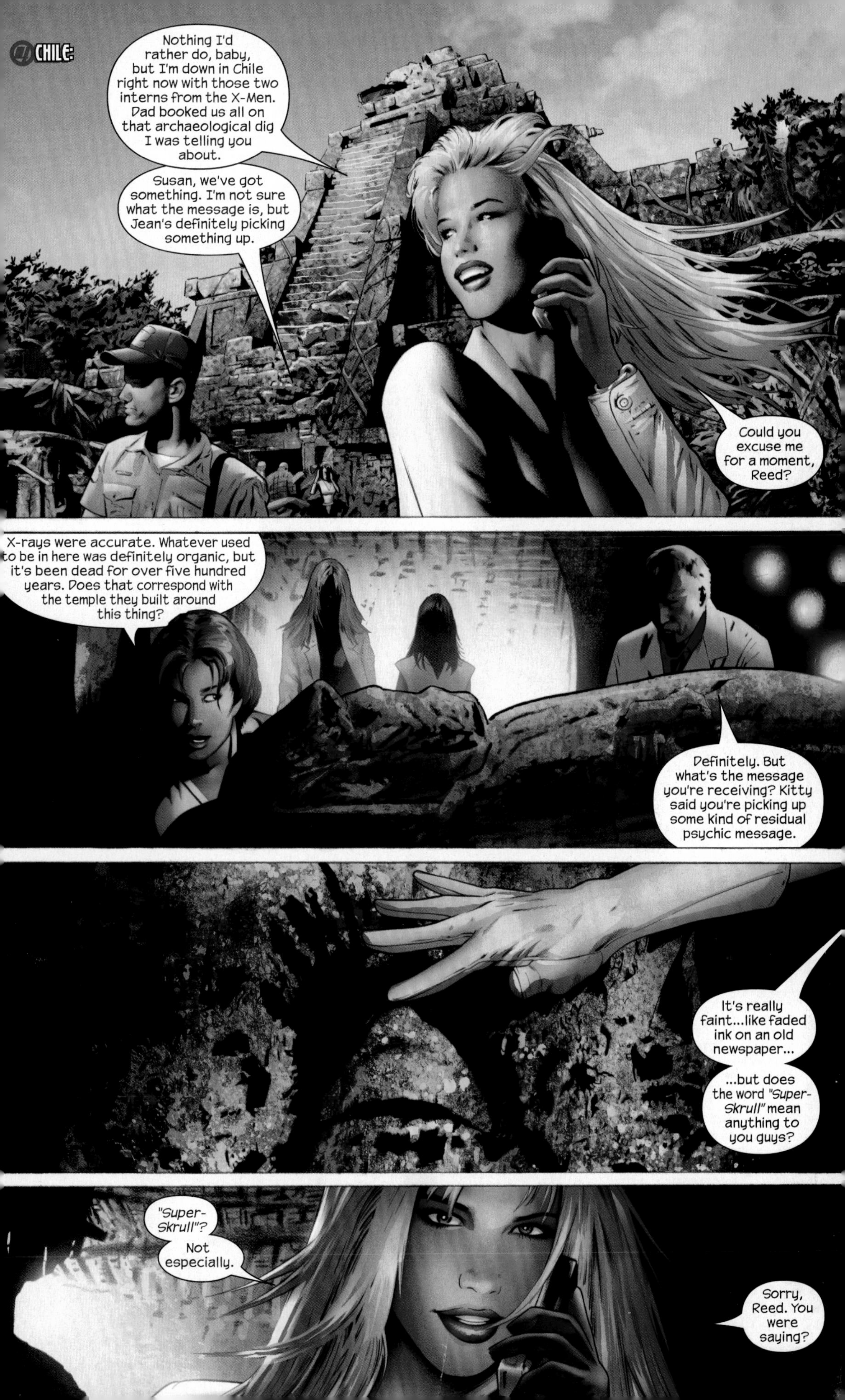
CHILE:
Nothing I'd rather do, baby, but I'm down in Chile right now with those two interns from the X-Men. Dad booked us all on that archaeological dig I was telling you about.
Susan, we've got something. I'm not sure what the message is, but Jean's definitely picking something up.
Could you excuse me for a moment, Reed?
X-rays were accurate. Whatever used to be in here was definitely organic, but it's been dead for over five hundred years. Does that correspond with the temple they built around this thing?
Definitely. But what's the message you're receiving? Kitty said you're picking up some kind of residual psychic message.
It's really faint...like faded ink on an old newspaper...
...but does the word "Super-Skrull" mean anything to you guys?
"Super-Skrull"? Not especially.
Sorry, Reed. You were saying?

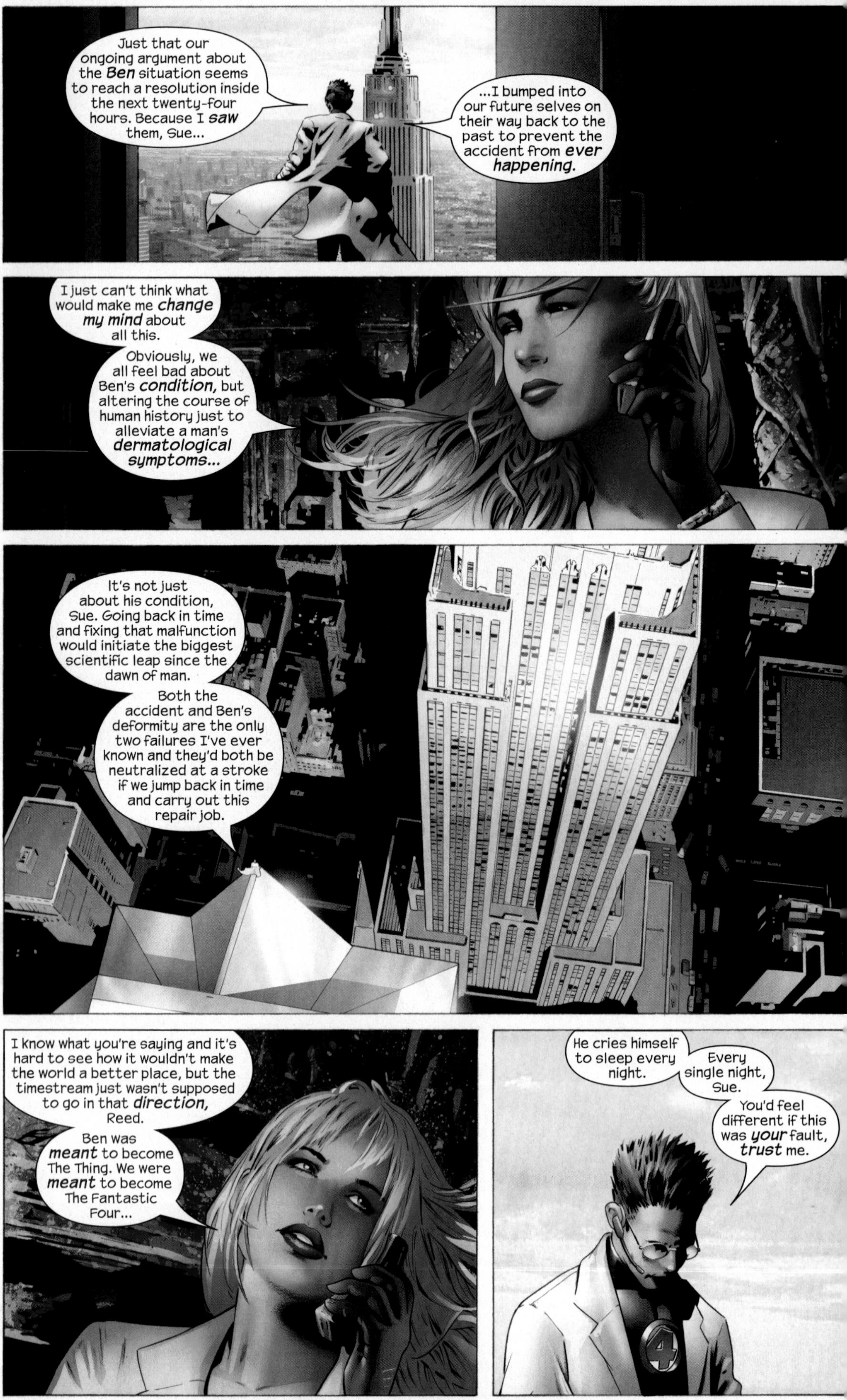
Just that our ongoing argument about the Ben situation seems to reach a resolution inside the next twenty-four hours. Because I saw them, Sue...
...I bumped into our future selves on their way back to the past to prevent the accident from ever happening.
I just can't think what would make me change my mind about all this.
Obviously, we all feel bad about Ben's condition, but altering the course of human history just to alleviate a man's dermatological symptoms...
It's not just about his condition, Sue. Going back in time and fixing that malfunction would initiate the biggest scientific leap since the dawn of man.
Both the accident and Ben's deformity are the only two failures I've ever known and they'd both be neutralized at a stroke if we jump back in time and carry out this repair job.
I know what you're saying and it's hard to see how it wouldn't make the world a better place, but the timestream just wasn't supposed to go in that direction, Reed.
Ben was meant to become The Thing. We were meant to become The Fantastic Four...
He cries himself to sleep every night.
Every single night, Sue.
You'd feel different if this was your fault, trust me.

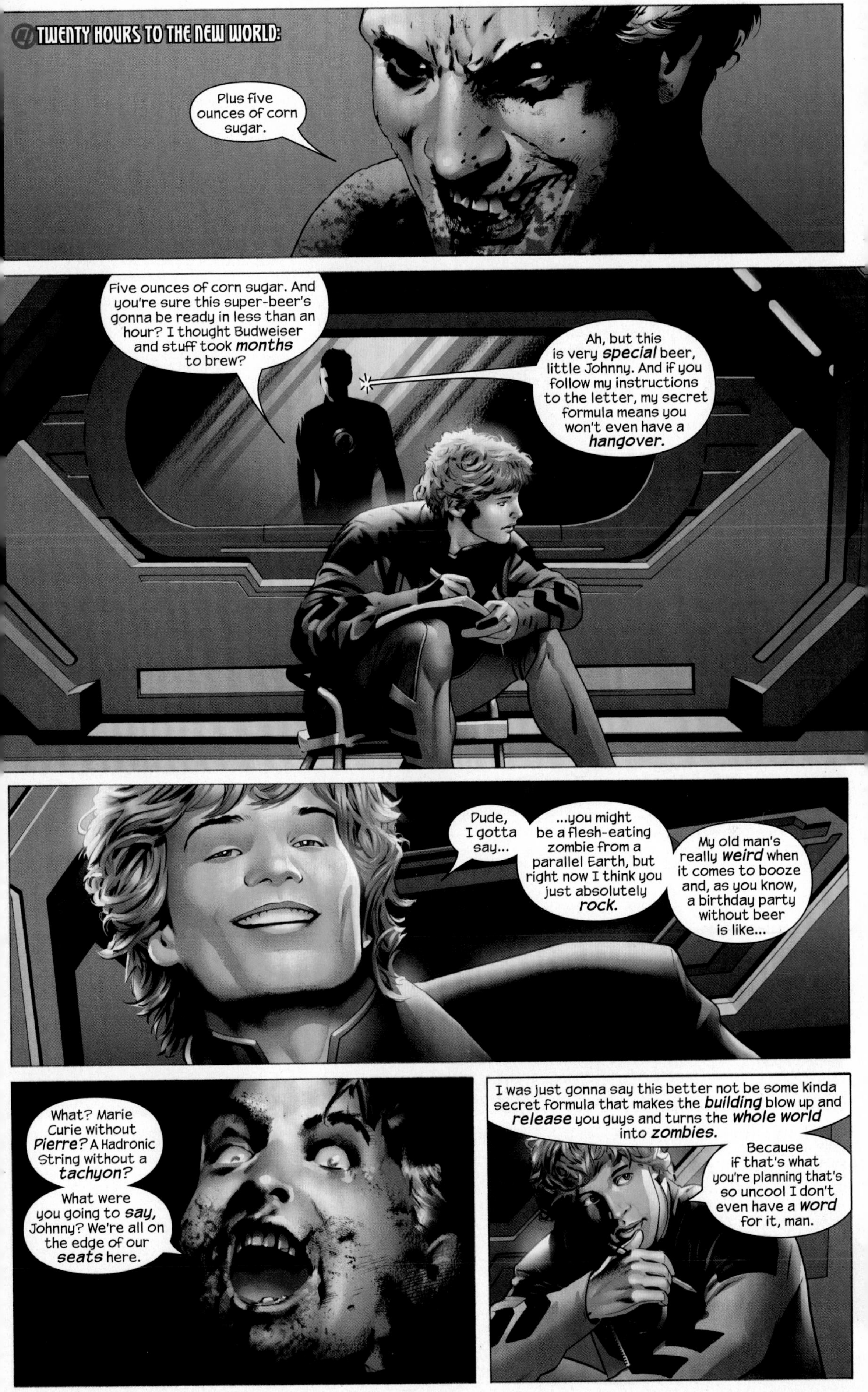
TWENTY HOURS TO THE NEW WORLD:
Plus five ounces of corn sugar.
Five ounces of corn sugar. And you're sure this super-beer's gonna be ready in less than an hour? I thought Budweiser and stuff took *months* to brew?
Ah, but this is very *special* beer, little Johnny. And if you follow my instructions to the letter, my secret formula means you won't even have a *hangover.*
Dude, I gotta say...
...you might be a flesh-eating zombie from a parallel Earth, but right now I think you just absolutely *rock.*
My old man's really *weird* when it comes to booze and, as you know, a birthday party without beer is like...
What? Marie Curie without *Pierre?* A Hadronic String without a *tachyon?*
What were you going to *say,* Johnny? We're all on the edge of our *seats* here.
I was just gonna say this better not be some kinda secret formula that makes the *building* blow up and *release* you guys and turns the *whole world* into *zombies.*
Because if that's what you're planning that's so uncool I don't even have a *word* for it, man.

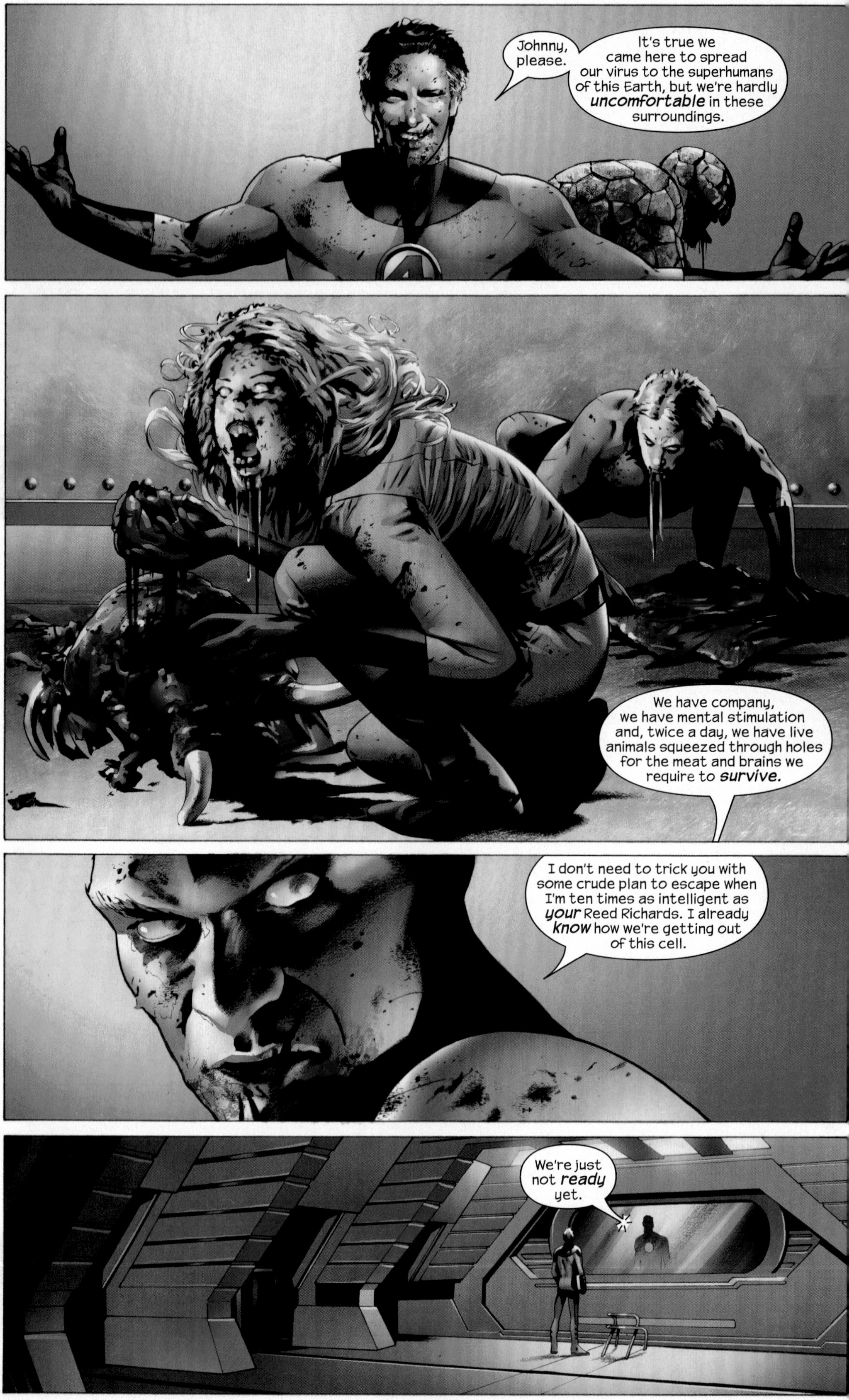
Johnny, please.
It's true we came here to spread our virus to the superhumans of this Earth, but we're hardly *uncomfortable* in these surroundings.
We have company, we have mental stimulation and, twice a day, we have live animals squeezed through holes for the meat and brains we require to *survive.*
I don't need to trick you with some crude plan to escape when I'm ten times as intelligent as *your* Reed Richards. I already *know* how we're getting out of this cell.
We're just not *ready* yet.

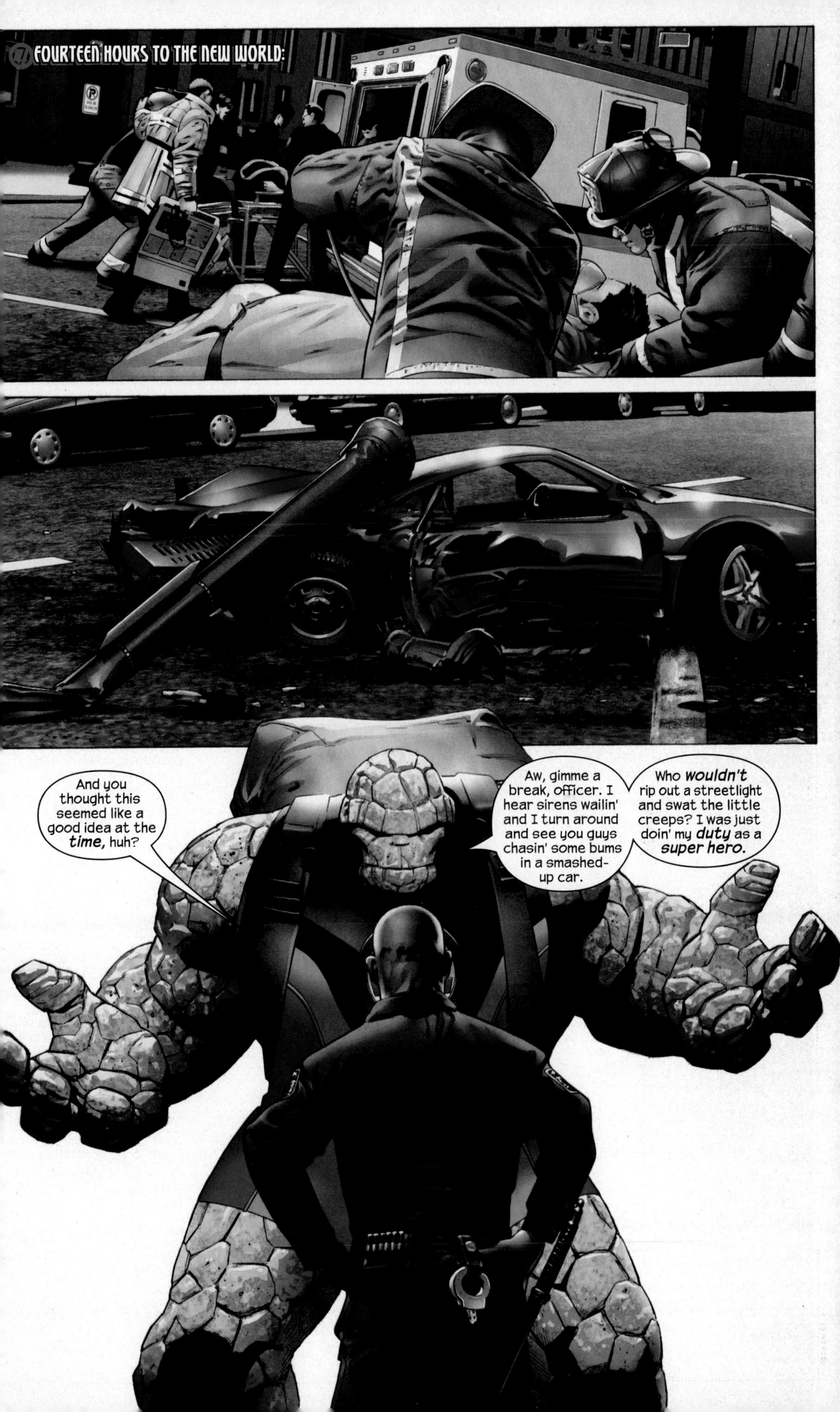
FOURTEEN HOURS TO THE NEW WORLD:
And you thought this seemed like a good idea at the *time,* huh?
Aw, gimme a break, officer. I hear sirens wailin' and I turn around and see you guys chasin' some bums in a smashed-up car.
Who ***wouldn't*** rip out a streetlight and swat the little creeps? I was just doin' my ***duty*** as a ***super hero.***

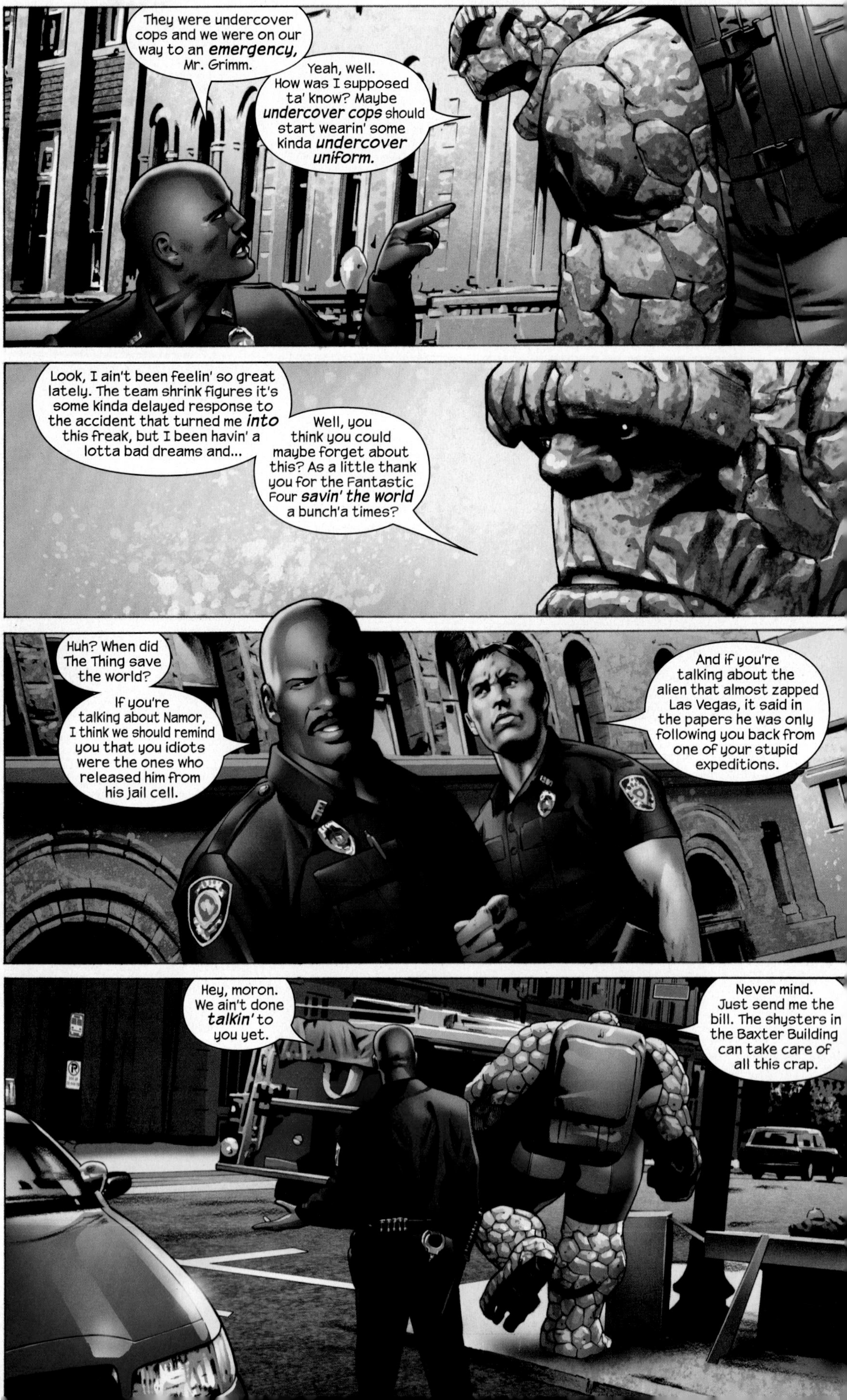
They were undercover cops and we were on our way to an *emergency,* Mr. Grimm.
Yeah, well. How was I supposed ta' know? Maybe *undercover cops* should start wearin' some kinda *undercover uniform.*
Look, I ain't been feelin' so great lately. The team shrink figures it's some kinda delayed response to the accident that turned me *into* this freak, but I been havin' a lotta bad dreams and...
Well, you think you could maybe forget about this? As a little thank you for the Fantastic Four *savin' the world* a bunch'a times?
Huh? When did The Thing save the world?
If you're talking about Namor, I think we should remind you that you idiots were the ones who released him from his jail cell.
And if you're talking about the alien that almost zapped Las Vegas, it said in the papers he was only following you back from one of your stupid expeditions.
Hey, moron. We ain't done *talkin'* to you yet.
Never mind. Just send me the bill. The shysters in the Baxter Building can take care of all this crap.

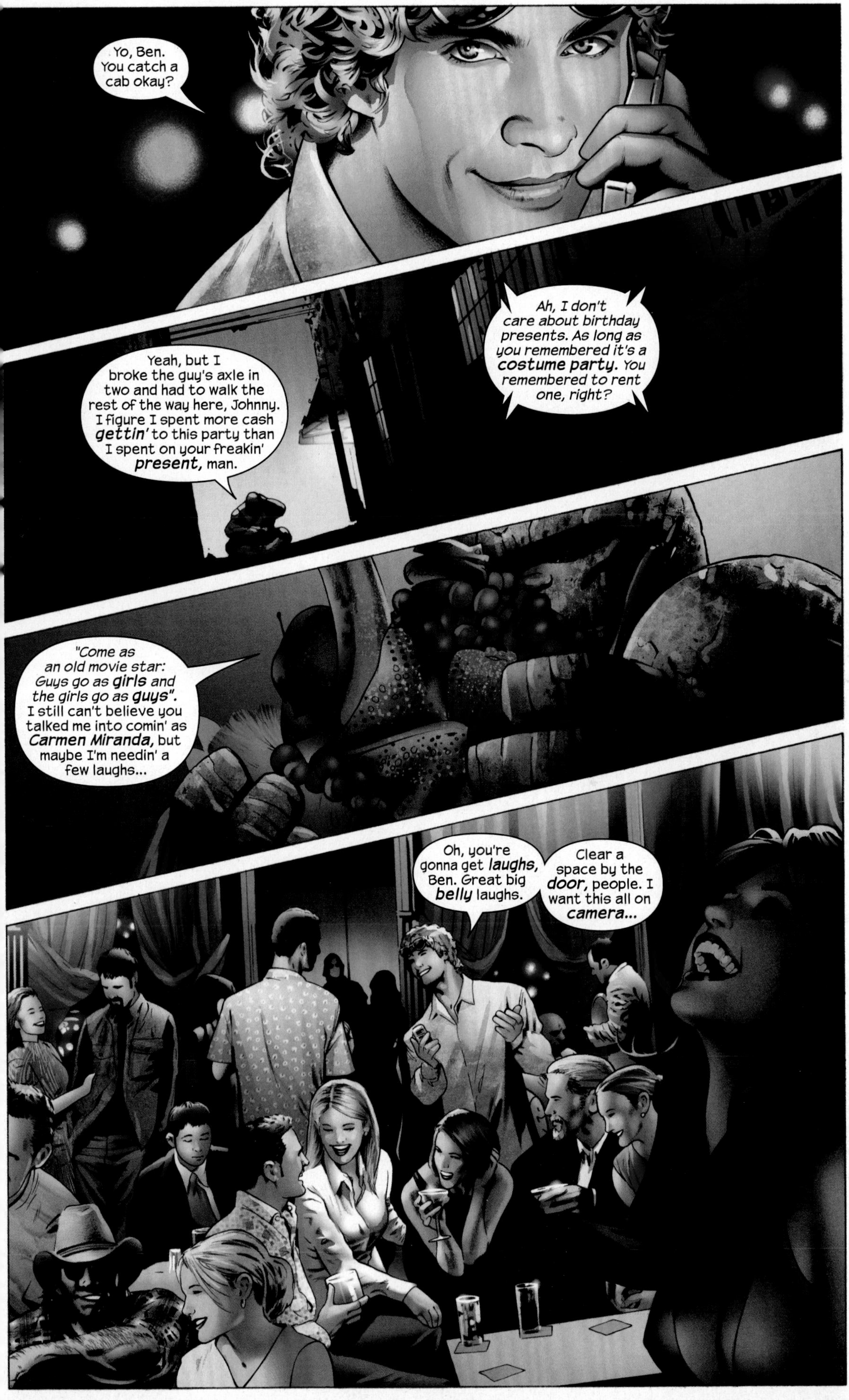
Yo, Ben. You catch a cab okay?
Yeah, but I broke the guy's axle in two and had to walk the rest of the way here, Johnny. I figure I spent more cash *gettin'* to this party than I spent on your freakin' *present,* man.
Ah, I don't care about birthday presents. As long as you remembered it's a *costume party.* You remembered to rent one, right?
"Come as an old movie star: Guys go as *girls* and the girls go as *guys*". I still can't believe you talked me into comin' as *Carmen Miranda,* but maybe I'm needin' a few laughs...
Oh, you're gonna get *laughs,* Ben. Great big *belly* laughs.
Clear a space by the *door,* people. I want this all on *camera...*

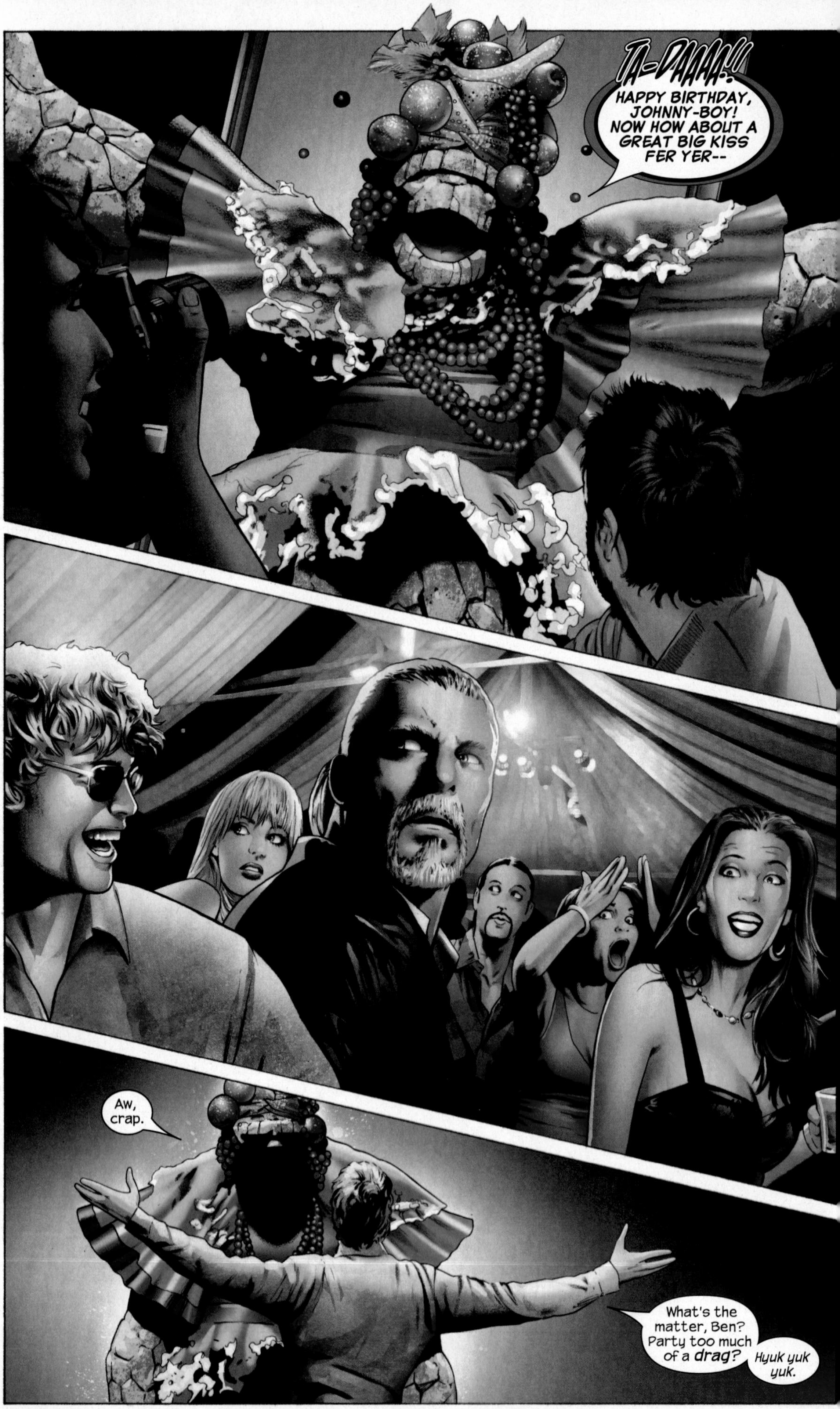
TA-DAAAA!!
HAPPY BIRTHDAY, JOHNNY-BOY! NOW HOW ABOUT A GREAT BIG KISS FER YER--
Aw, crap.
What's the matter, Ben? Party too much of a drag?
Hyuk yuk yuk.

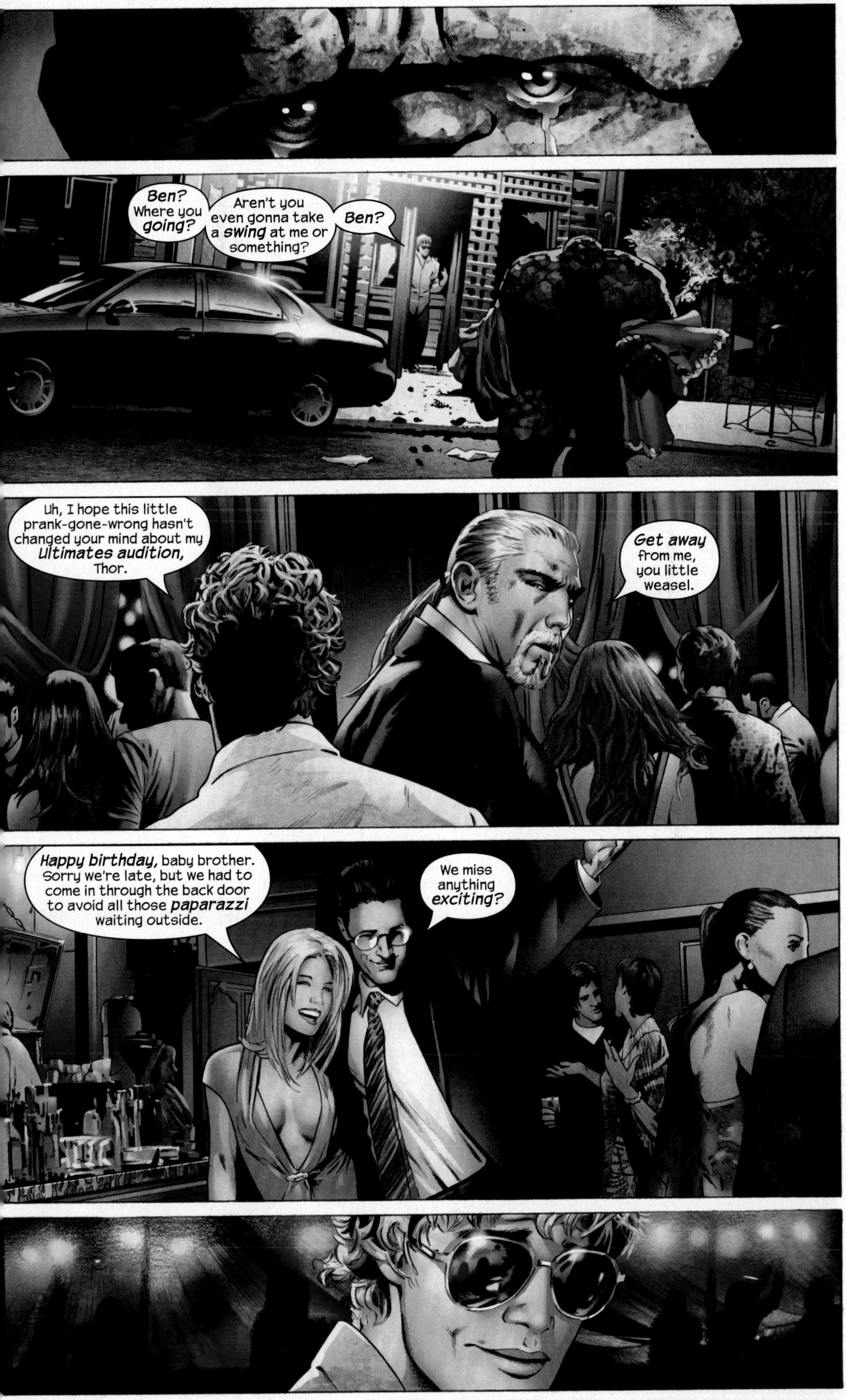
Ben? Where you going?
Aren't you even gonna take a swing at me or something?
Ben?
Uh, I hope this little prank-gone-wrong hasn't changed your mind about my Ultimates audition, Thor.
Get away from me, you little weasel.
Happy birthday, baby brother. Sorry we're late, but we had to come in through the back door to avoid all those paparazzi waiting outside.
We miss anything exciting?

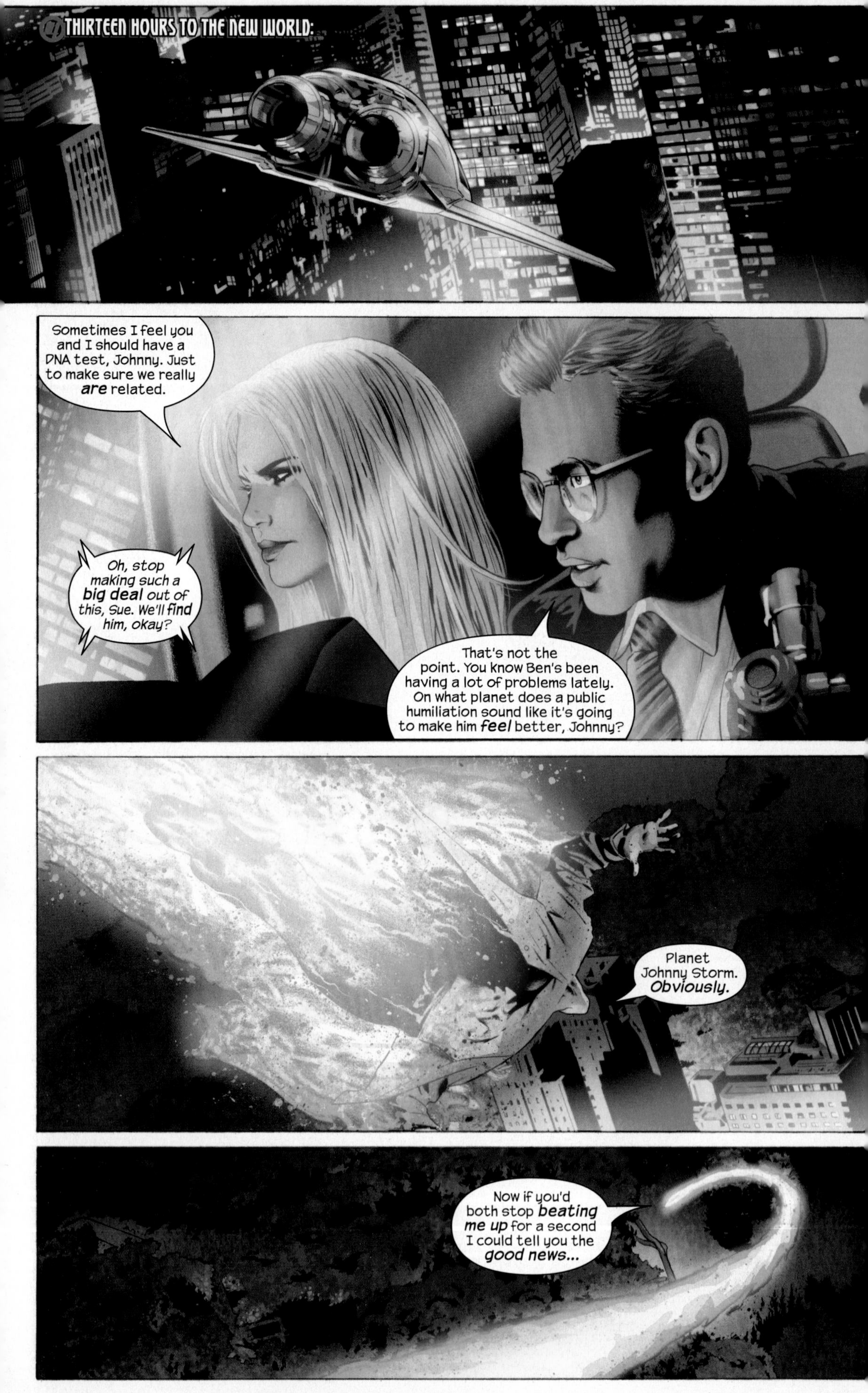
THIRTEEN HOURS TO THE NEW WORLD:
Sometimes I feel you and I should have a DNA test, Johnny. Just to make sure we really are related.
Oh, stop making such a big deal out of this, Sue. We'll find him, okay?
That's not the point. You know Ben's been having a lot of problems lately. On what planet does a public humiliation sound like it's going to make him feel better, Johnny?
Planet Johnny Storm. Obviously.
Now if you'd both stop beating me up for a second I could tell you the good news...

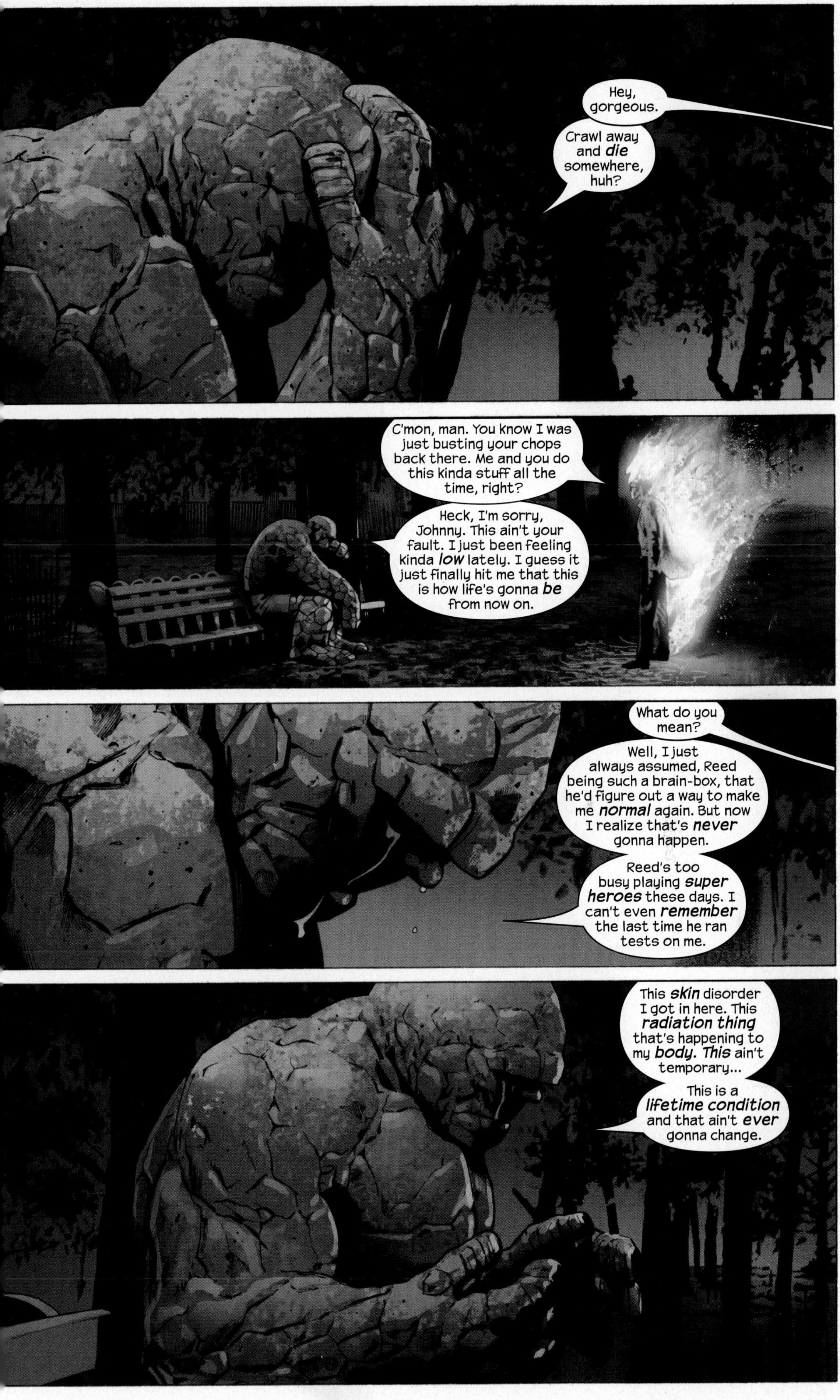
Hey, gorgeous.
Crawl away and *die* somewhere, huh?
C'mon, man. You know I was just busting your chops back there. Me and you do this kinda stuff all the time, right?
Heck, I'm sorry, Johnny. This ain't your fault. I just been feeling kinda *low* lately. I guess it just finally hit me that this is how life's gonna *be* from now on.
What do you mean?
Well, I just always assumed, Reed being such a brain-box, that he'd figure out a way to make me *normal* again. But now I realize that's *never* gonna happen.
Reed's too busy playing *super heroes* these days. I can't even *remember* the last time he ran tests on me.
This *skin* disorder I got in here. This *radiation thing* that's happening to my *body. This* ain't temporary...
This is a *lifetime condition* and that ain't *ever* gonna change.

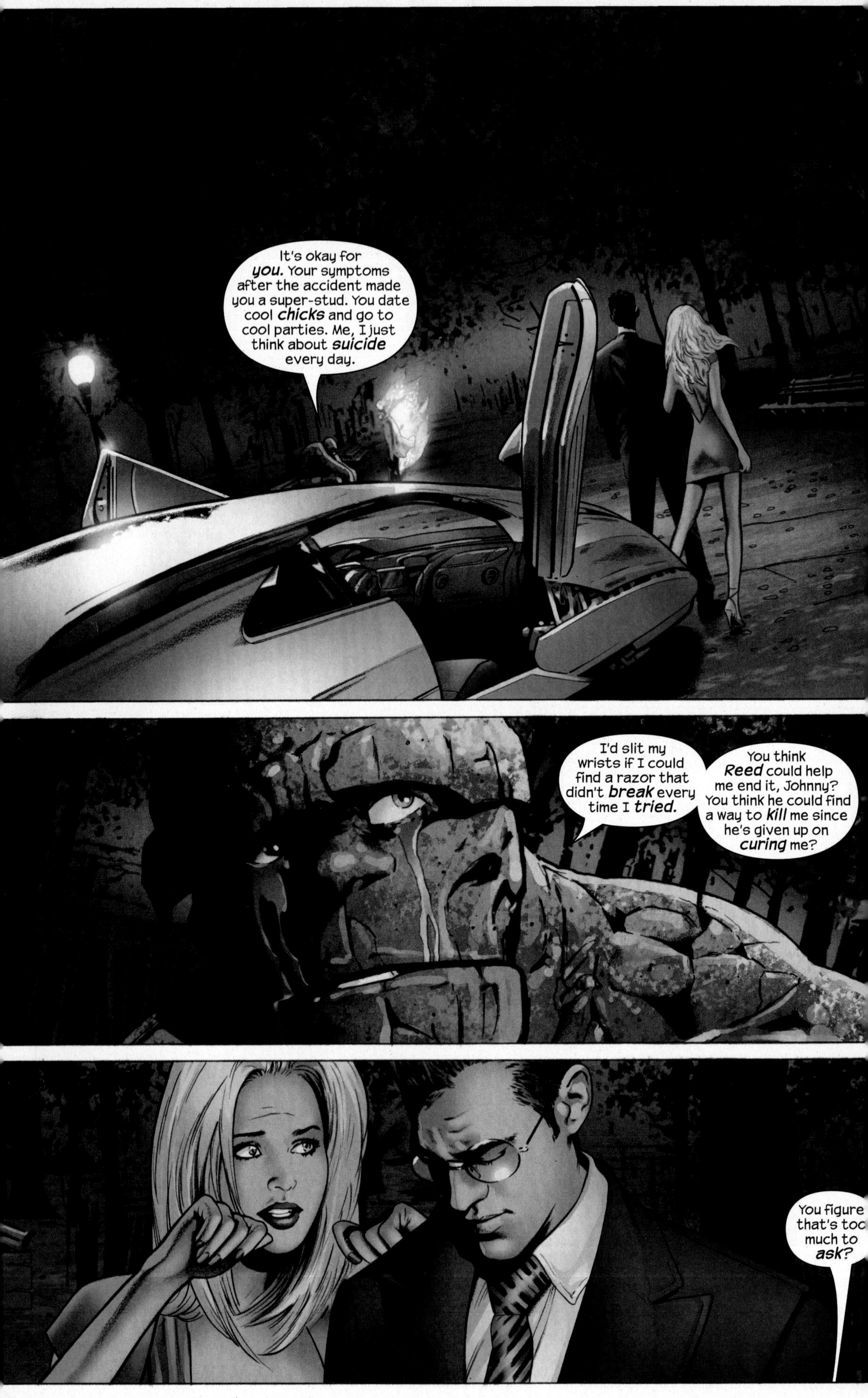
It's okay for you. Your symptoms after the accident made you a super-stud. You date cool chicks and go to cool parties. Me, I just think about suicide every day.
I'd slit my wrists if I could find a razor that didn't break every time I tried.
You think Reed could help me end it, Johnny? You think he could find a way to kill me since he's given up on curing me?
You figure that's too much to ask?

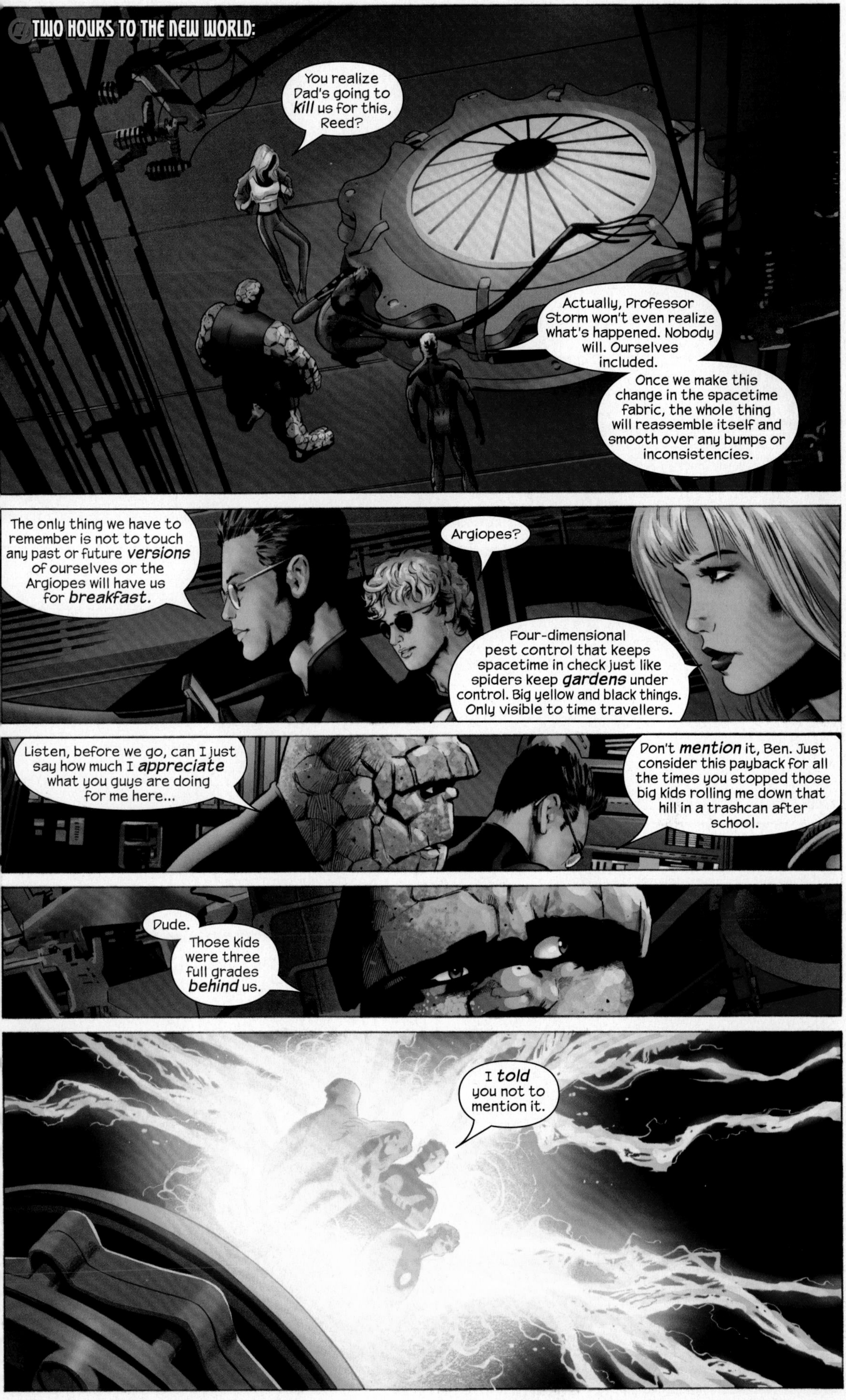
TWO HOURS TO THE NEW WORLD:
You realize Dad's going to kill us for this, Reed?
Actually, Professor Storm won't even realize what's happened. Nobody will. Ourselves included.
Once we make this change in the spacetime fabric, the whole thing will reassemble itself and smooth over any bumps or inconsistencies.
The only thing we have to remember is not to touch any past or future versions of ourselves or the Argiopes will have us for breakfast.
Argiopes?
Four-dimensional pest control that keeps spacetime in check just like spiders keep gardens under control. Big yellow and black things. Only visible to time travellers.
Listen, before we go, can I just say how much I appreciate what you guys are doing for me here...
Don't mention it, Ben. Just consider this payback for all the times you stopped those big kids rolling me down that hill in a trashcan after school.
Dude.
Those kids were three full grades behind us.
I told you not to mention it.

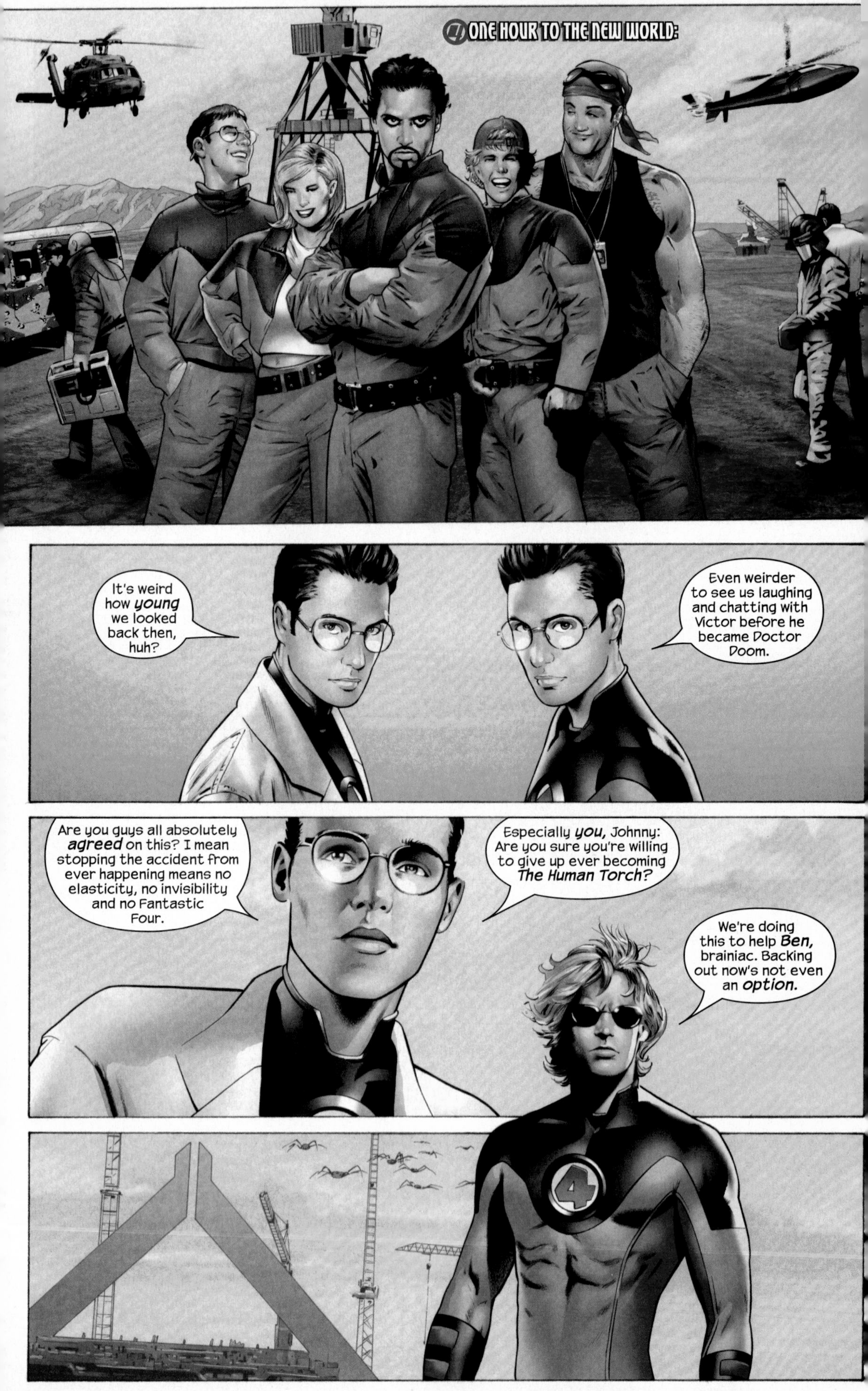
ONE HOUR TO THE NEW WORLD:
It's weird how young we looked back then, huh?
Even weirder to see us laughing and chatting with Victor before he became Doctor Doom.
Are you guys all absolutely agreed on this? I mean stopping the accident from ever happening means no elasticity, no invisibility and no Fantastic Four.
Especially you, Johnny: Are you sure you're willing to give up ever becoming The Human Torch?
We're doing this to help Ben, brainiac. Backing out now's not even an option.

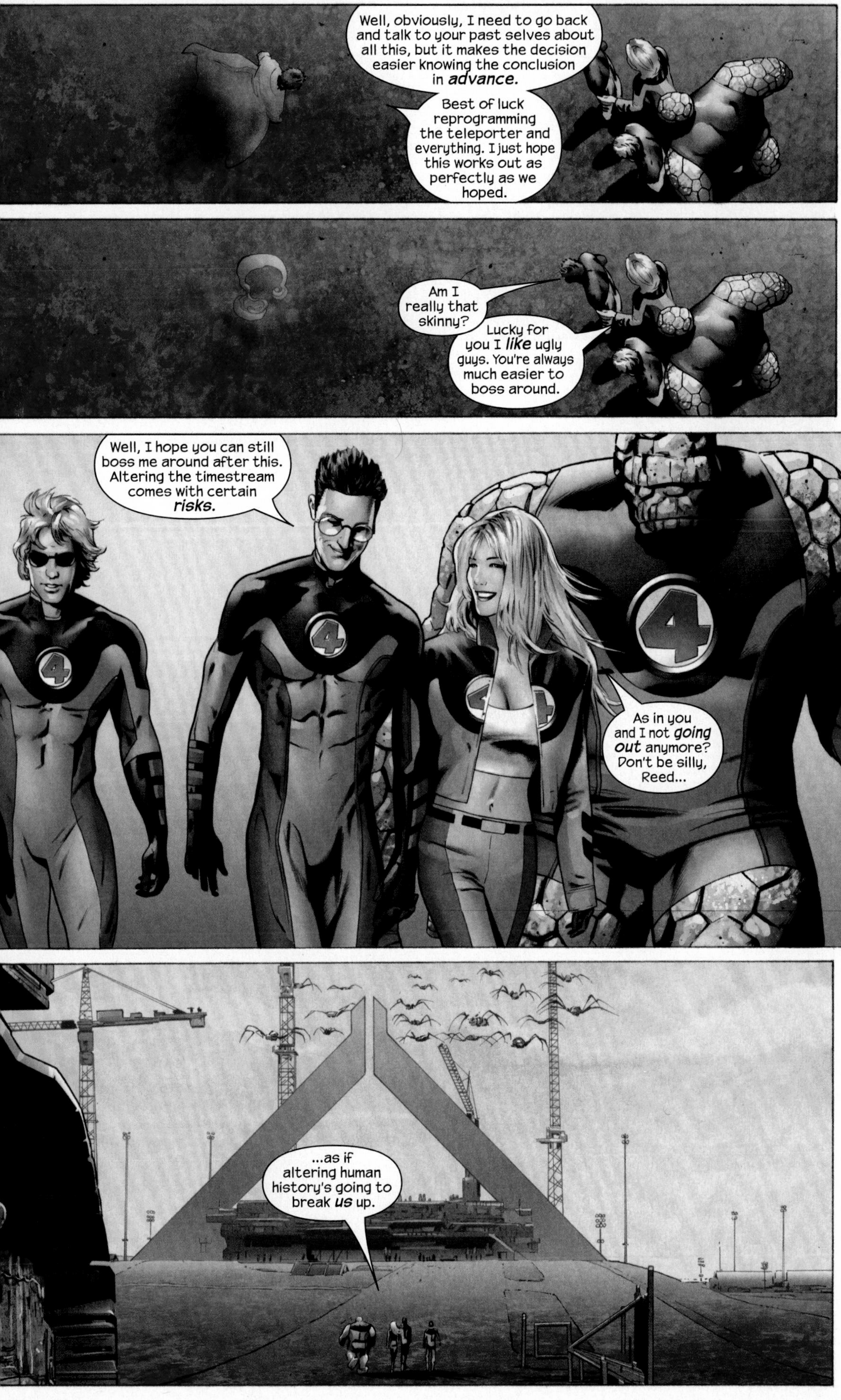
Well, obviously, I need to go back and talk to your past selves about all this, but it makes the decision easier knowing the conclusion in *advance.*
Best of luck reprogramming the teleporter and everything. I just hope this works out as perfectly as we hoped.
Am I really that skinny?
Lucky for you I *like* ugly guys. You're always much easier to boss around.
Well, I hope you can still boss me around after this. Altering the timestream comes with certain *risks.*
As in you and I not *going out* anymore? Don't be silly, Reed...
...as if altering human history's going to break *us* up.

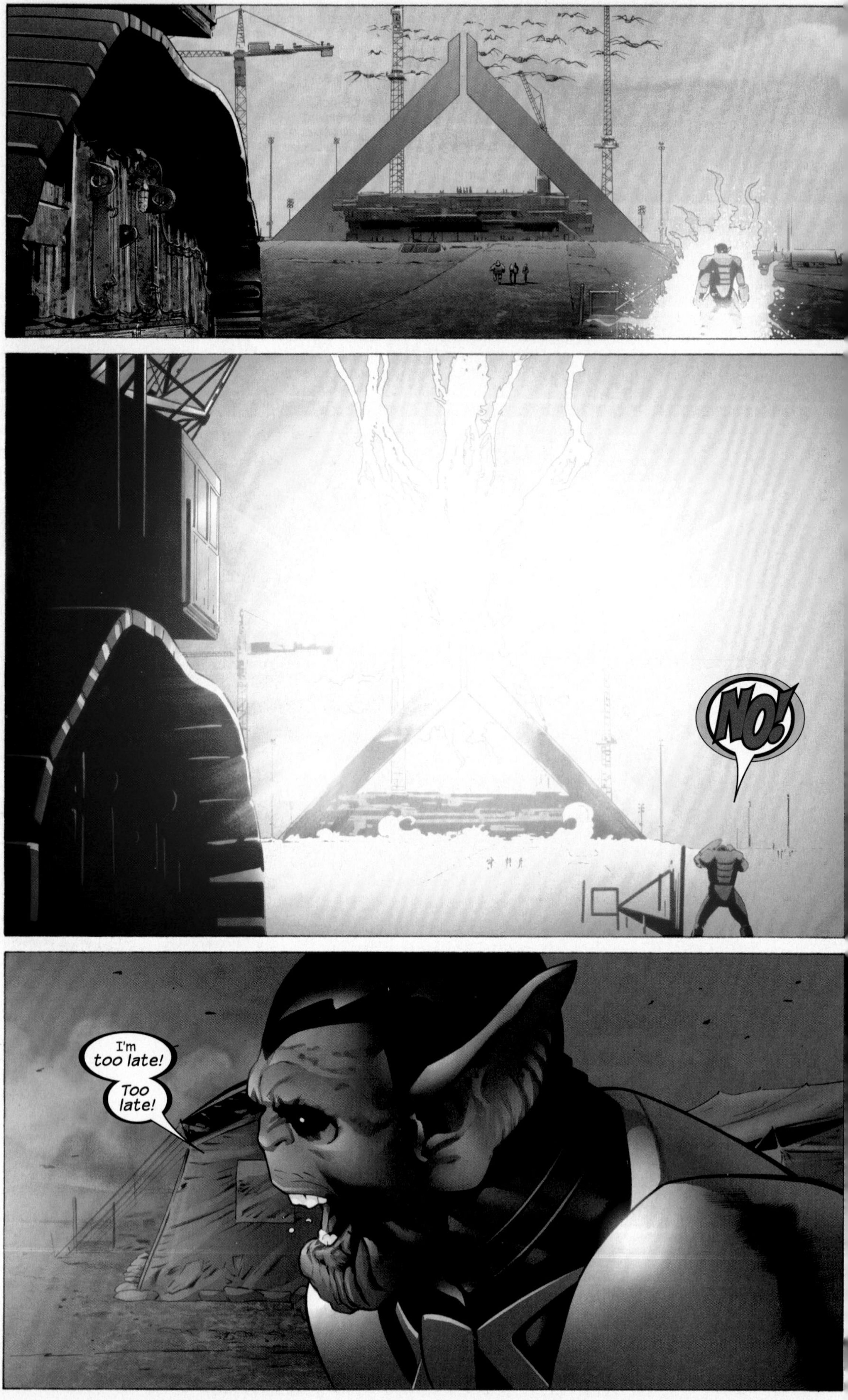
NO!
I'm too late!
Too late!

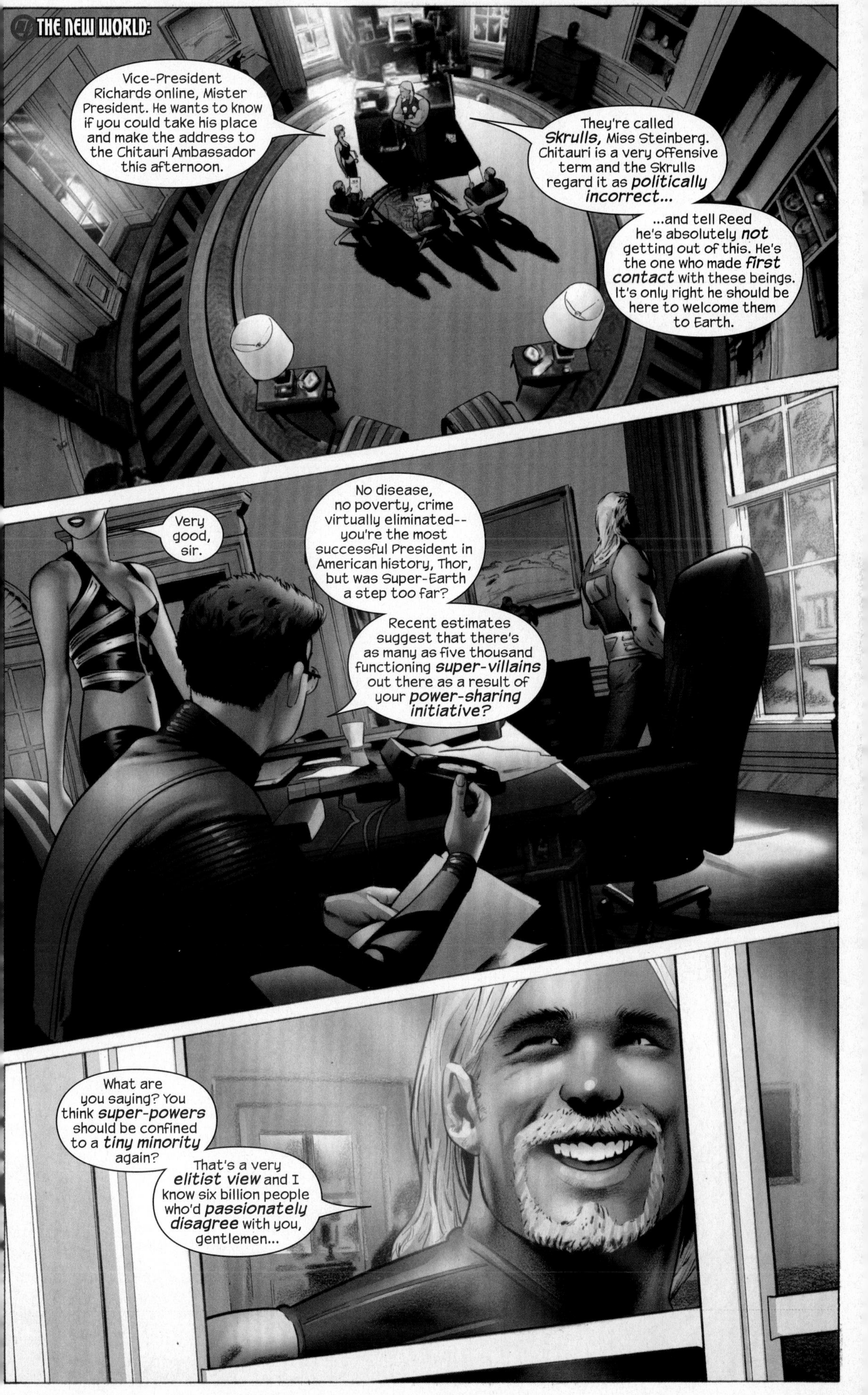
THE NEW WORLD:
Vice-President Richards online, Mister President. He wants to know if you could take his place and make the address to the Chitauri Ambassador this afternoon.
They're called Skrulls, Miss Steinberg. Chitauri is a very offensive term and the Skrulls regard it as politically incorrect...
...and tell Reed he's absolutely not getting out of this. He's the one who made first contact with these beings. It's only right he should be here to welcome them to Earth.
Very good, sir.
No disease, no poverty, crime virtually eliminated--you're the most successful President in American history, Thor, but was Super-Earth a step too far?
Recent estimates suggest that there's as many as five thousand functioning super-villains out there as a result of your power-sharing initiative?
What are you saying? You think super-powers should be confined to a tiny minority again?
That's a very elitist view and I know six billion people who'd passionately disagree with you, gentlemen...

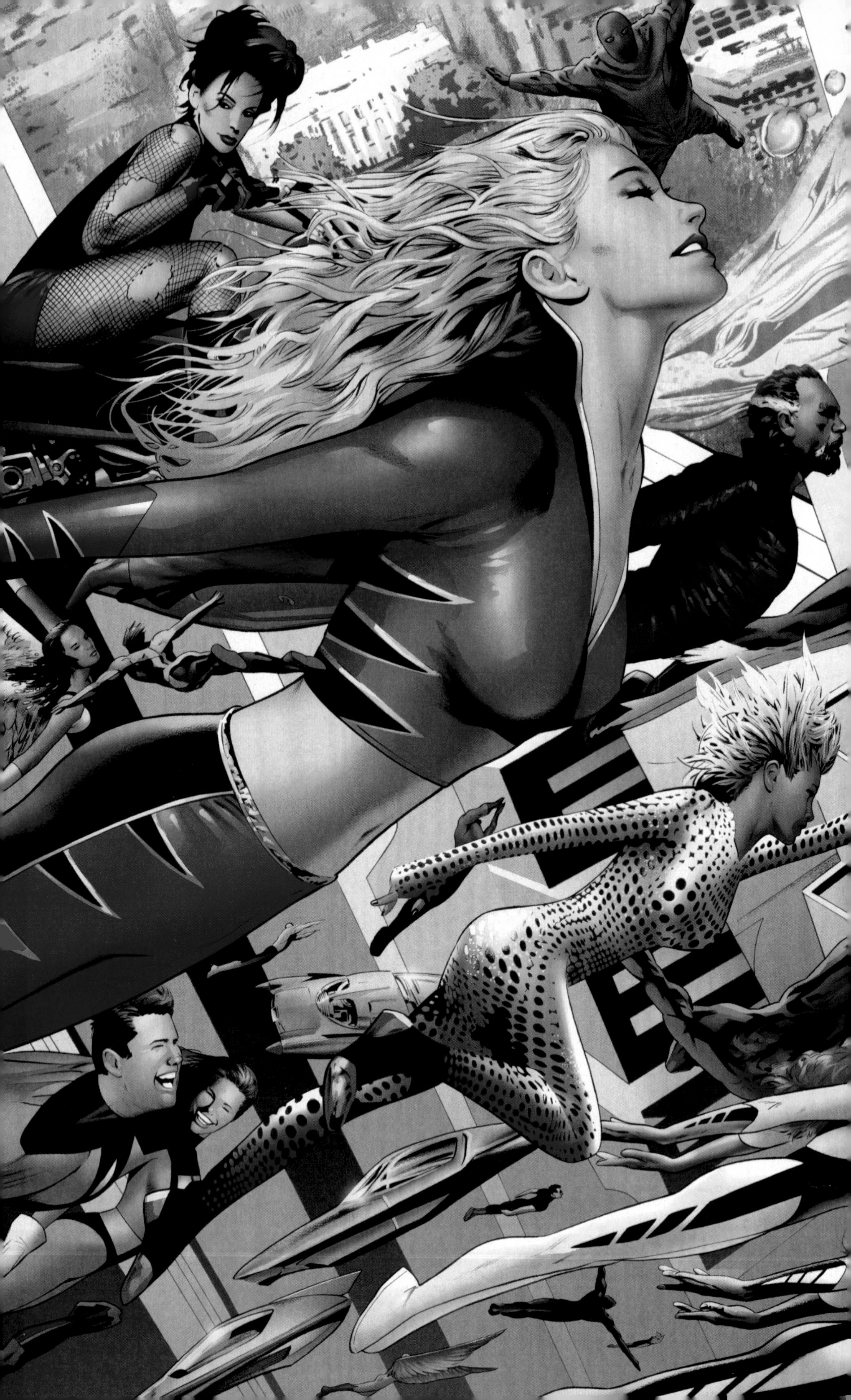

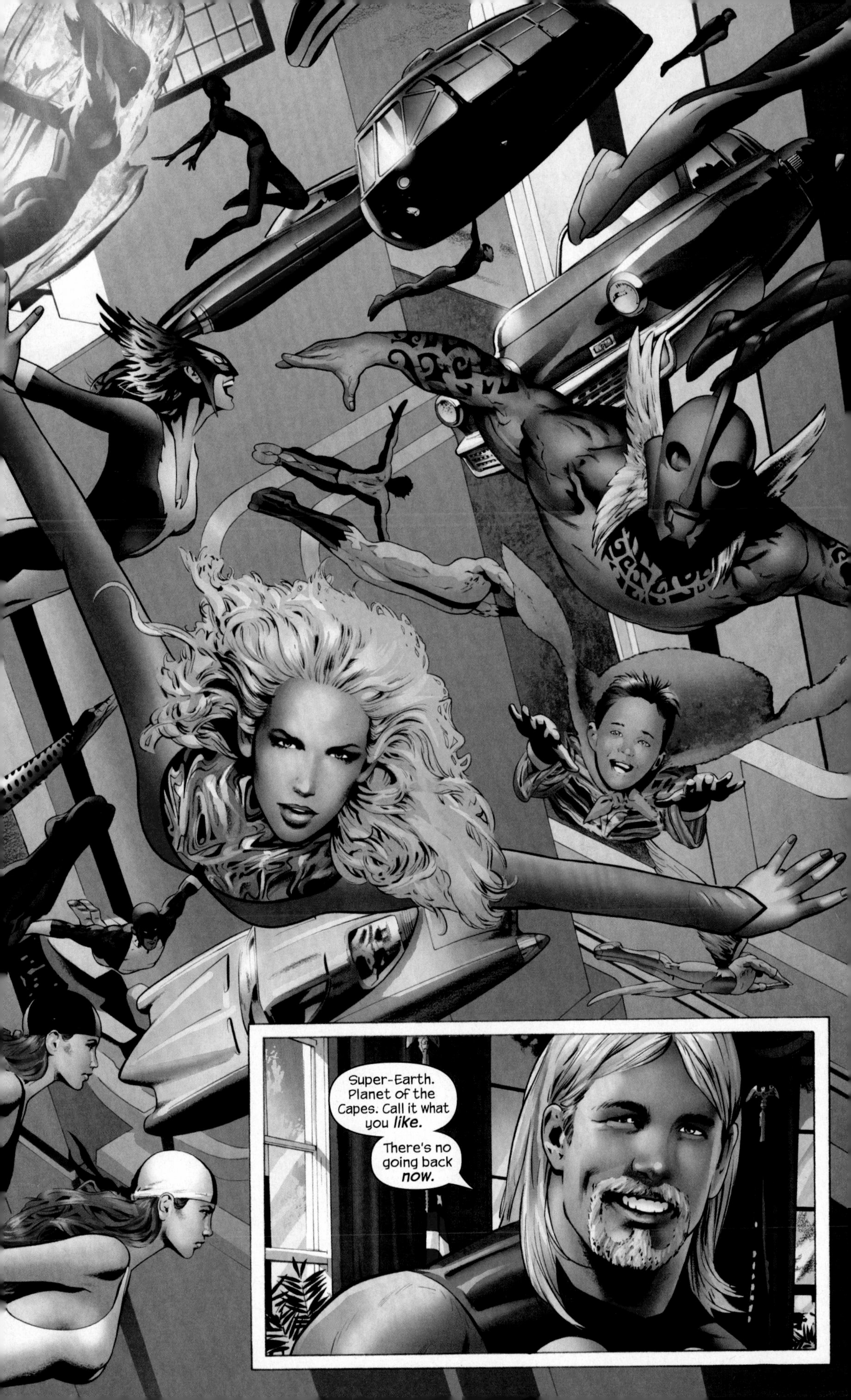

Super-Earth. Planet of the Capes. Call it what you *like.*
There's no going back *now.*

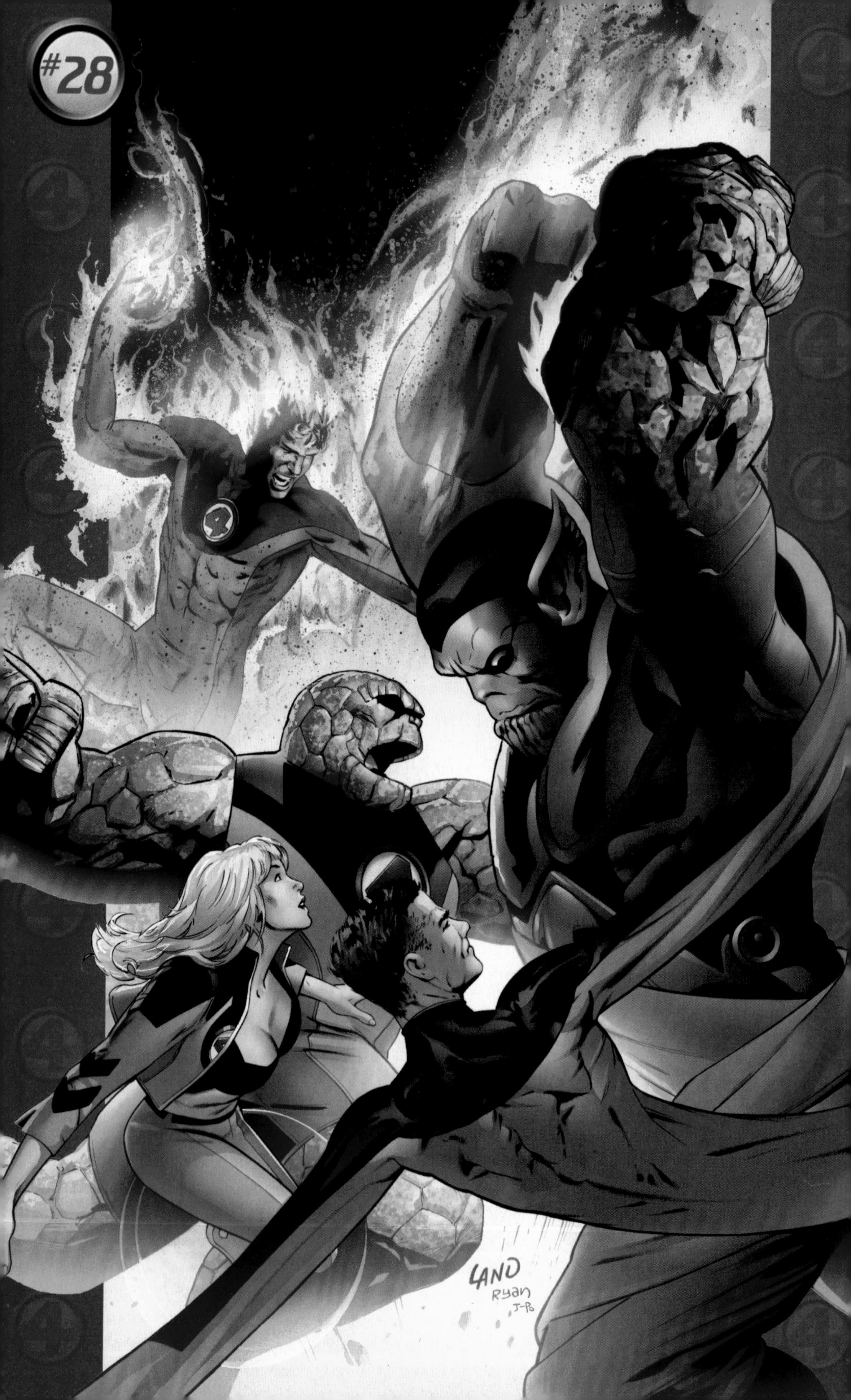
#28
LAND
Ryan
J-Po

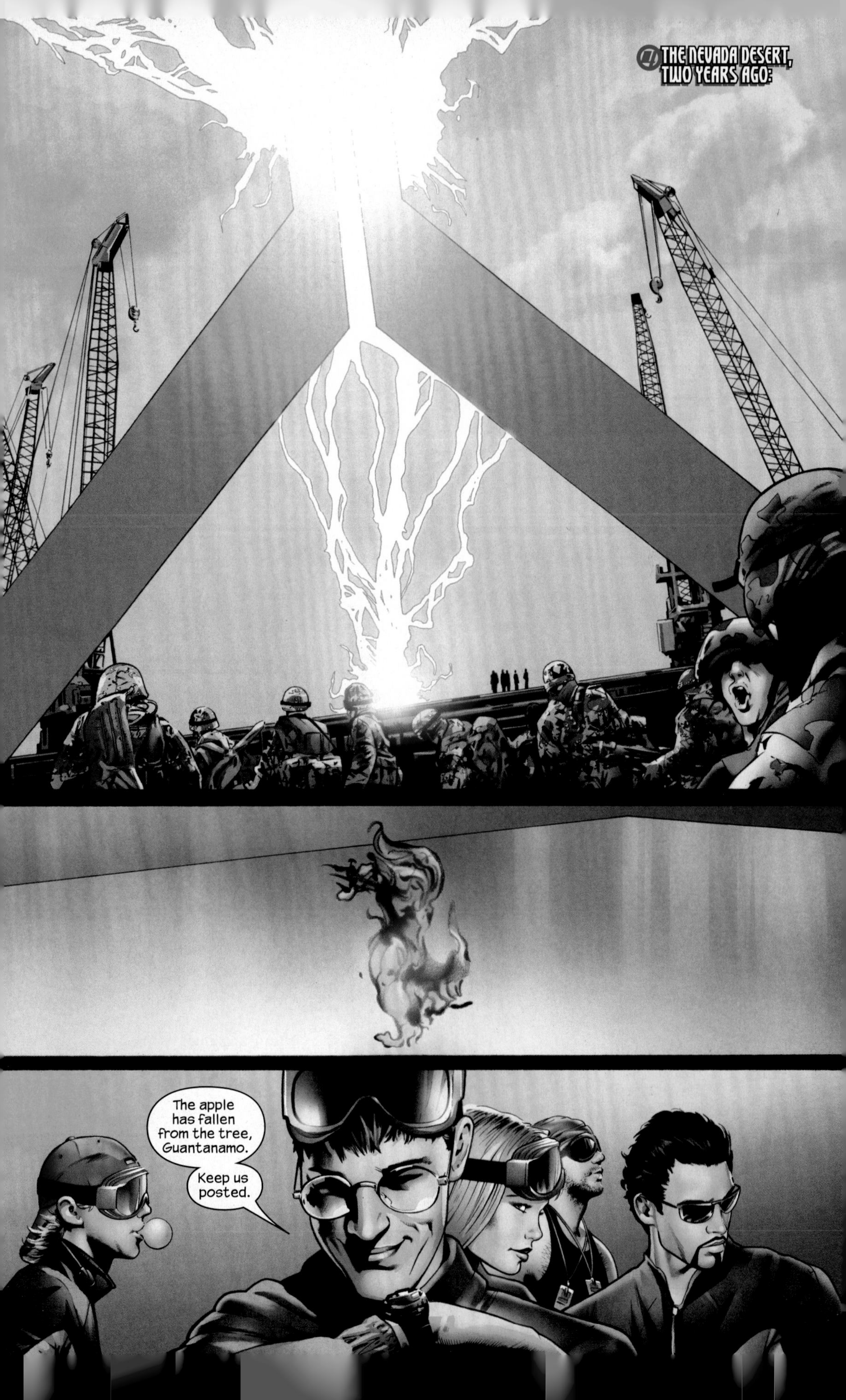
THE NEVADA DESERT, TWO YEARS AGO:
The apple has fallen from the tree, Guantanamo.
Keep us posted.

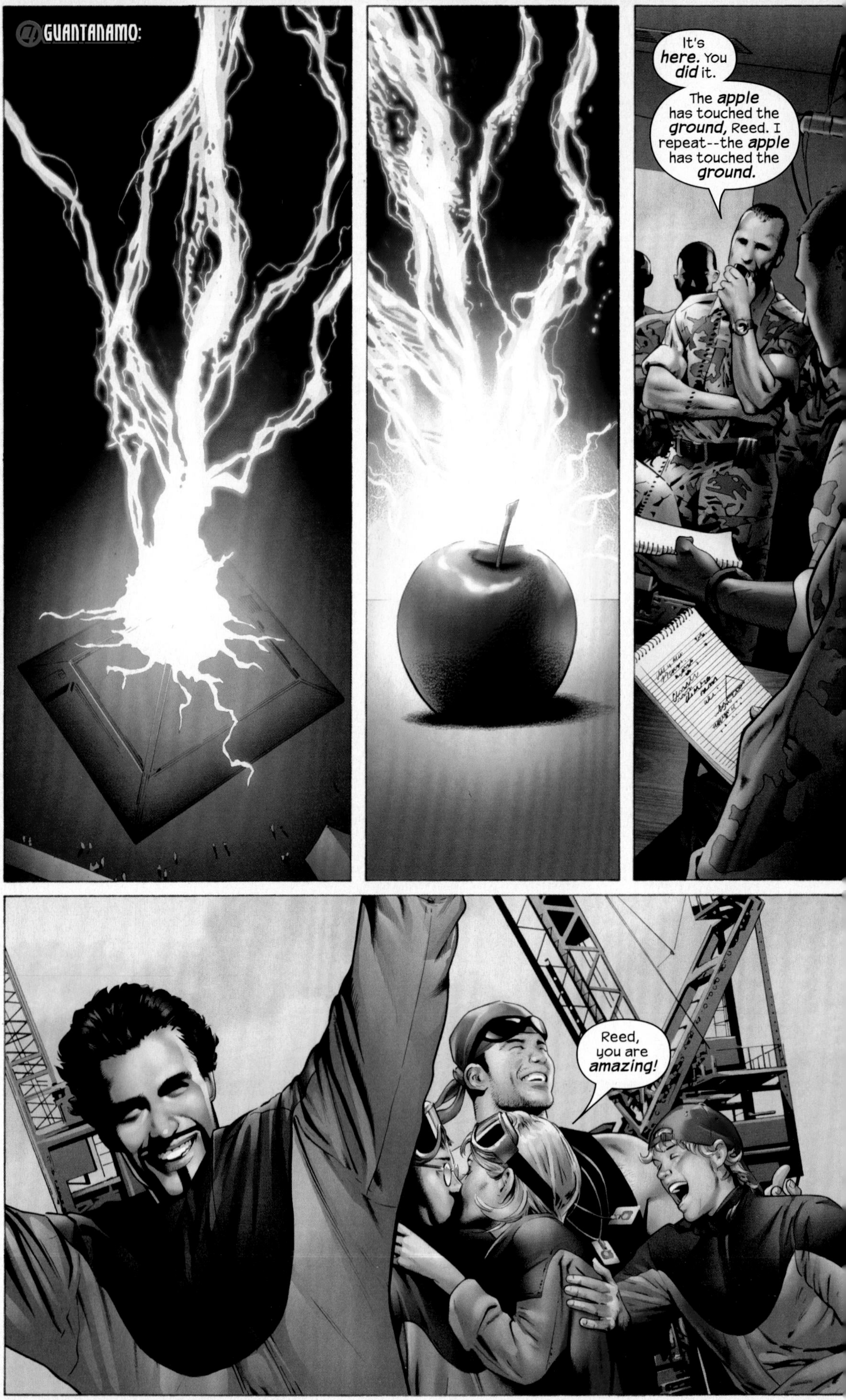
GUANTANAMO:
It's here. You did it.
The apple has touched the ground, Reed. I repeat--the apple has touched the ground.
Reed, you are amazing!

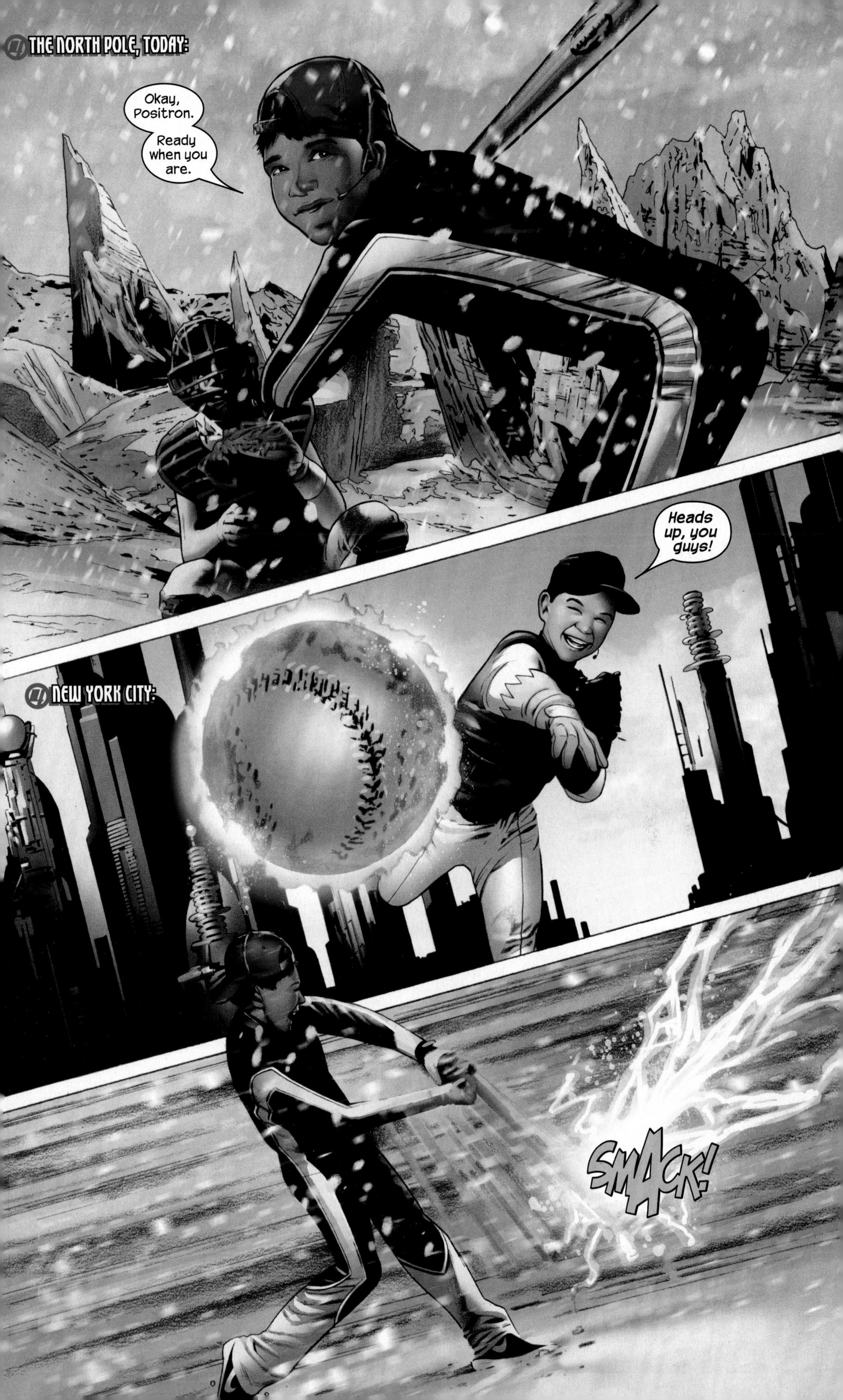
THE NORTH POLE, TODAY:
Okay, Positron.
Ready when you are.
Heads up, you guys!
NEW YORK CITY:
SMACK!

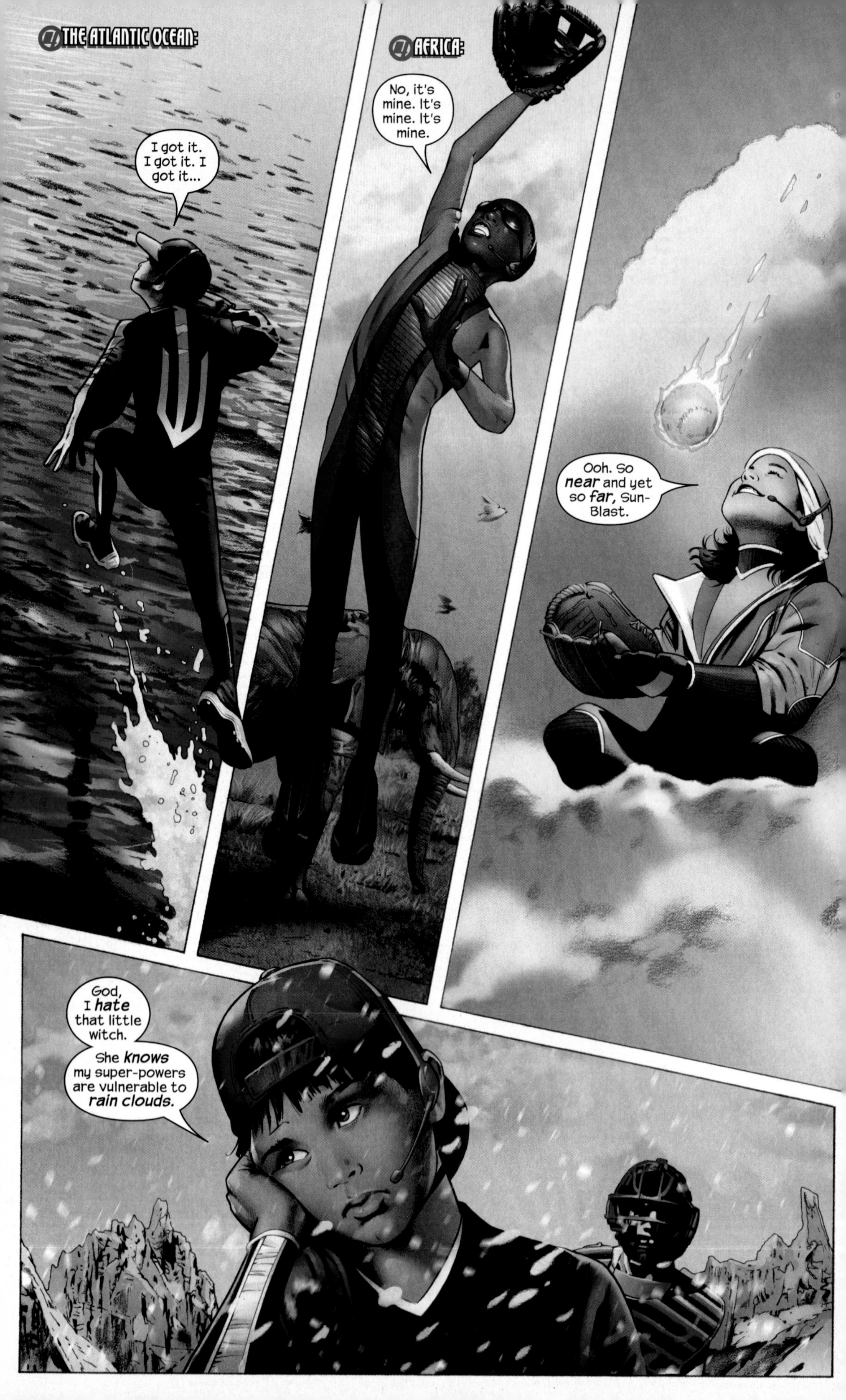
THE ATLANTIC OCEAN:
I got it. I got it. I got it...
AFRICA:
No, it's mine. It's mine. It's mine.
Ooh. So near and yet so far, Sun-Blast.
God, I hate that little witch.
She knows my super-powers are vulnerable to rain clouds.

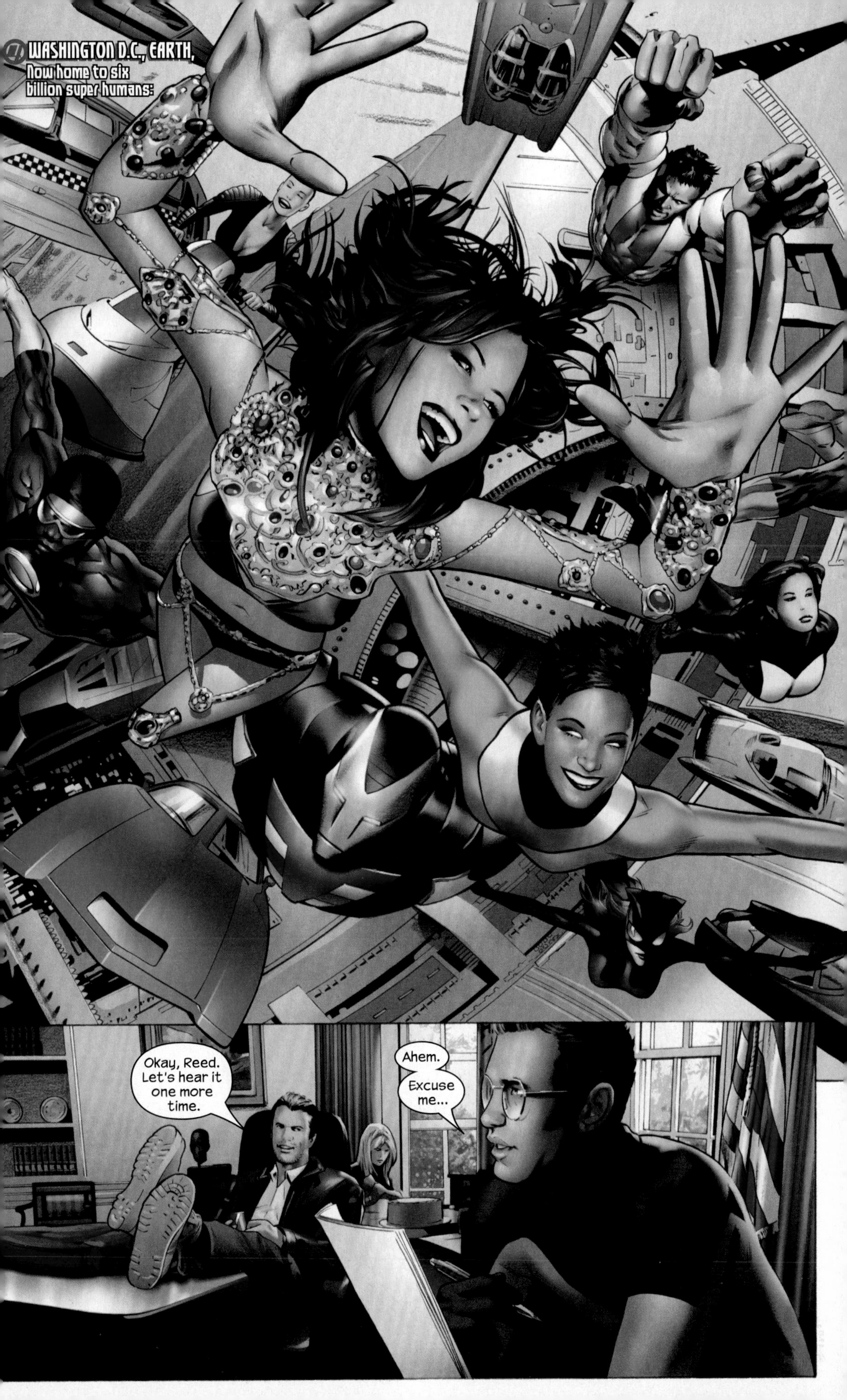
WASHINGTON D.C., EARTH,
Now home to six billion super humans:
Okay, Reed. Let's hear it one more time.
Ahem.
Excuse me...

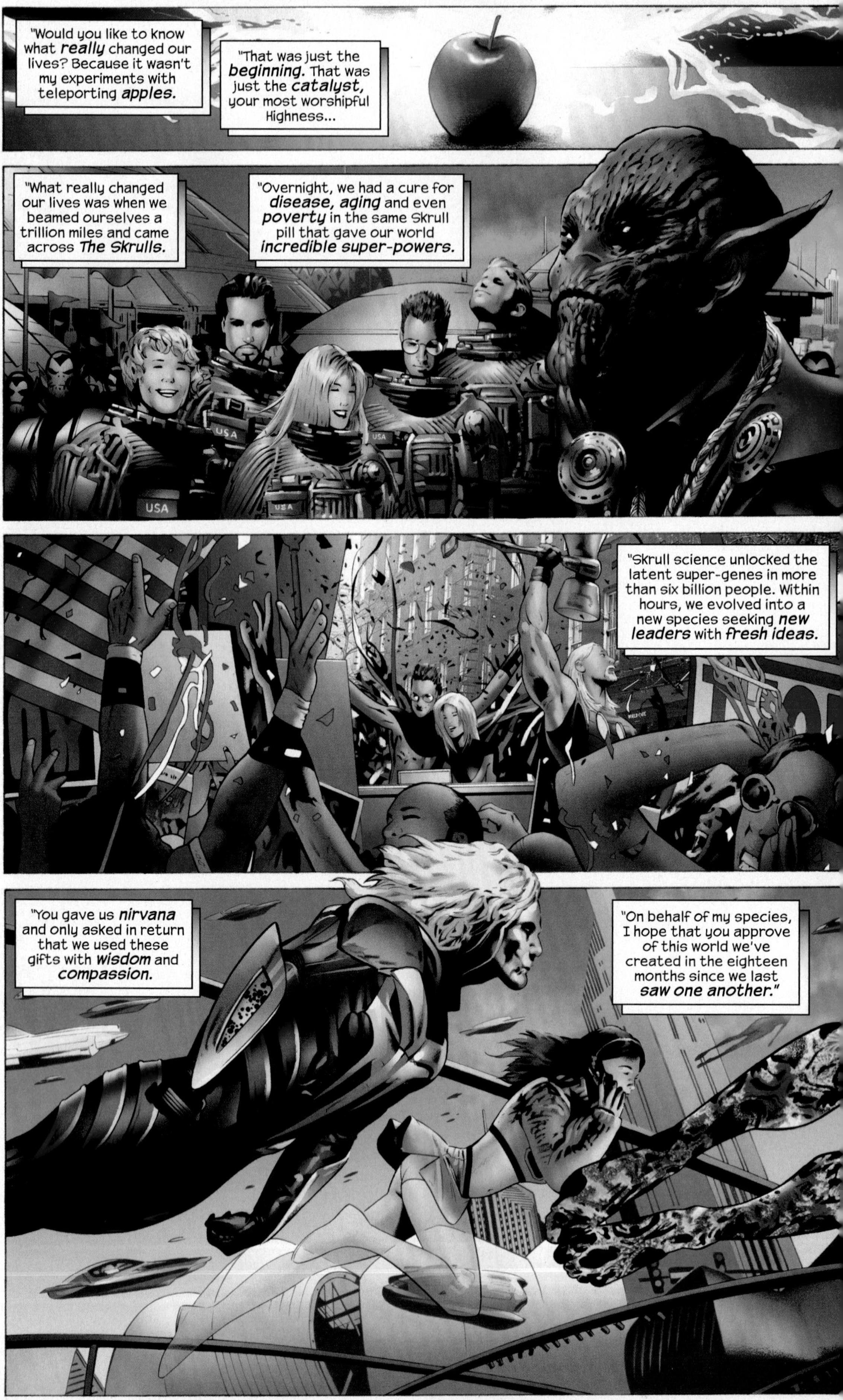
"Would you like to know what really changed our lives? Because it wasn't my experiments with teleporting apples.
"That was just the beginning. That was just the catalyst, your most worshipful Highness...
"What really changed our lives was when we beamed ourselves a trillion miles and came across The Skrulls.
"Overnight, we had a cure for disease, aging and even poverty in the same Skrull pill that gave our world incredible super-powers.
USA
USA
USA
USA
"Skrull science unlocked the latent super-genes in more than six billion people. Within hours, we evolved into a new species seeking new leaders with fresh ideas.
"You gave us nirvana and only asked in return that we used these gifts with wisdom and compassion.
"On behalf of my species, I hope that you approve of this world we've created in the eighteen months since we last saw one another."

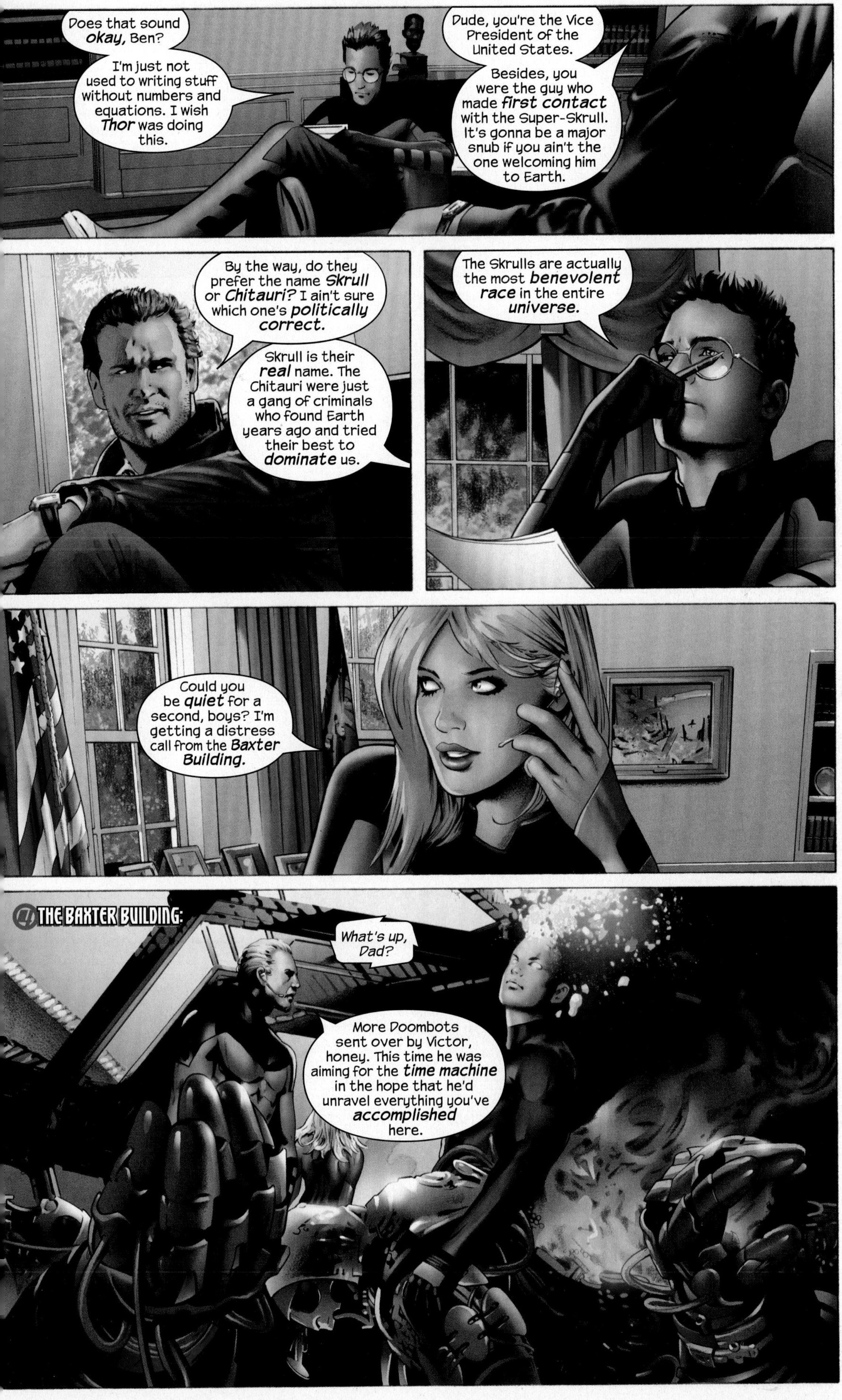
Does that sound okay, Ben?
I'm just not used to writing stuff without numbers and equations. I wish Thor was doing this.
Dude, you're the Vice President of the United States.
Besides, you were the guy who made first contact with the Super-Skrull. It's gonna be a major snub if you ain't the one welcoming him to Earth.
By the way, do they prefer the name Skrull or Chitauri? I ain't sure which one's politically correct.
Skrull is their real name. The Chitauri were just a gang of criminals who found Earth years ago and tried their best to dominate us.
The Skrulls are actually the most benevolent race in the entire universe.
Could you be quiet for a second, boys? I'm getting a distress call from the Baxter Building.
THE BAXTER BUILDING:
What's up, Dad?
More Doombots sent over by Victor, honey. This time he was aiming for the time machine in the hope that he'd unravel everything you've accomplished here.

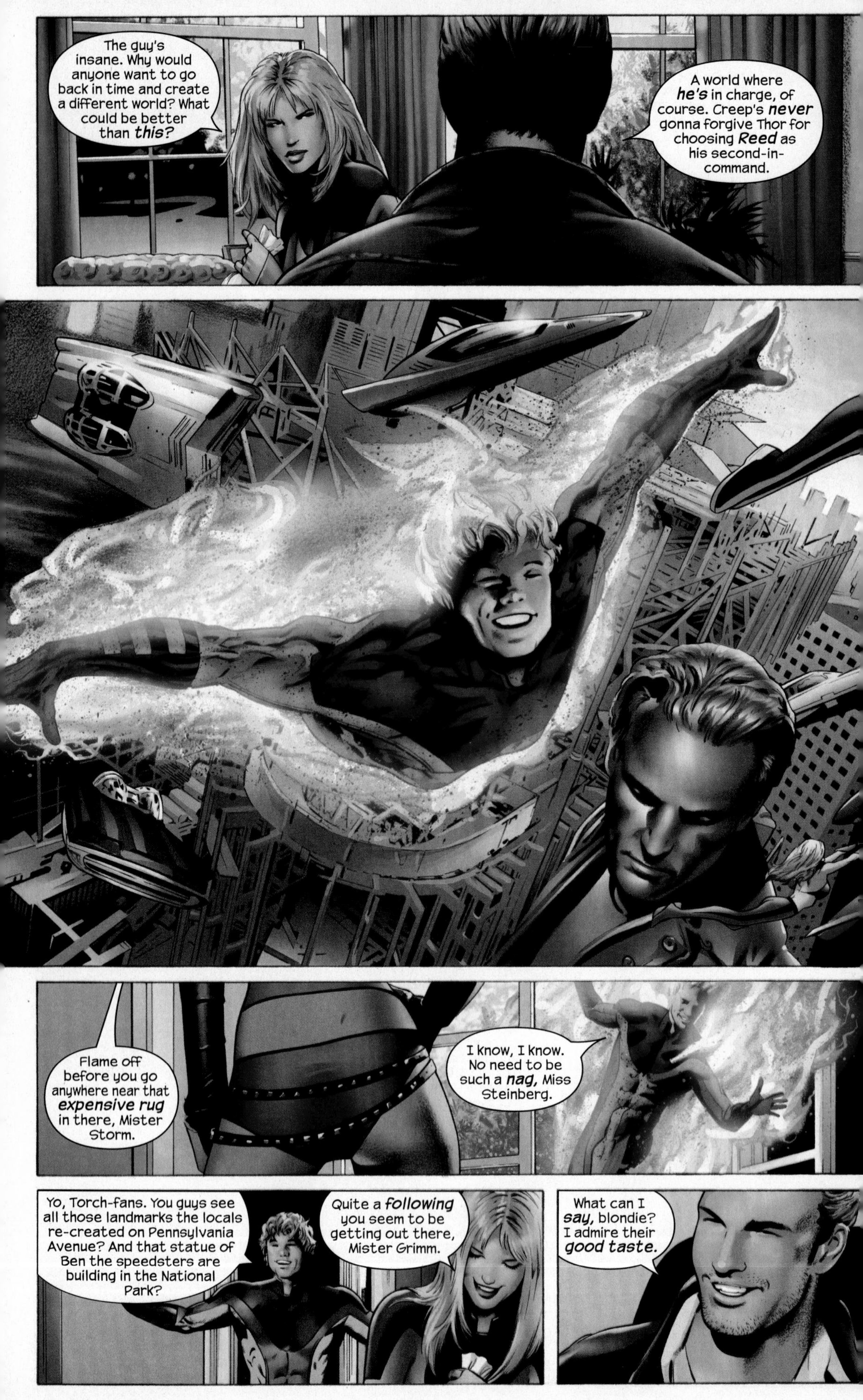
The guy's insane. Why would anyone want to go back in time and create a different world? What could be better than *this?*
A world where ***he's*** in charge, of course. Creep's ***never*** gonna forgive Thor for choosing ***Reed*** as his second-in-command.
Flame off before you go anywhere near that ***expensive rug*** in there, Mister Storm.
I know, I know. No need to be such a ***nag,*** Miss Steinberg.
Yo, Torch-fans. You guys see all those landmarks the locals re-created on Pennsylvania Avenue? And that statue of Ben the speedsters are building in the National Park?
Quite a ***following*** you seem to be getting out there, Mister Grimm.
What can I ***say,*** blondie? I admire their ***good taste.***

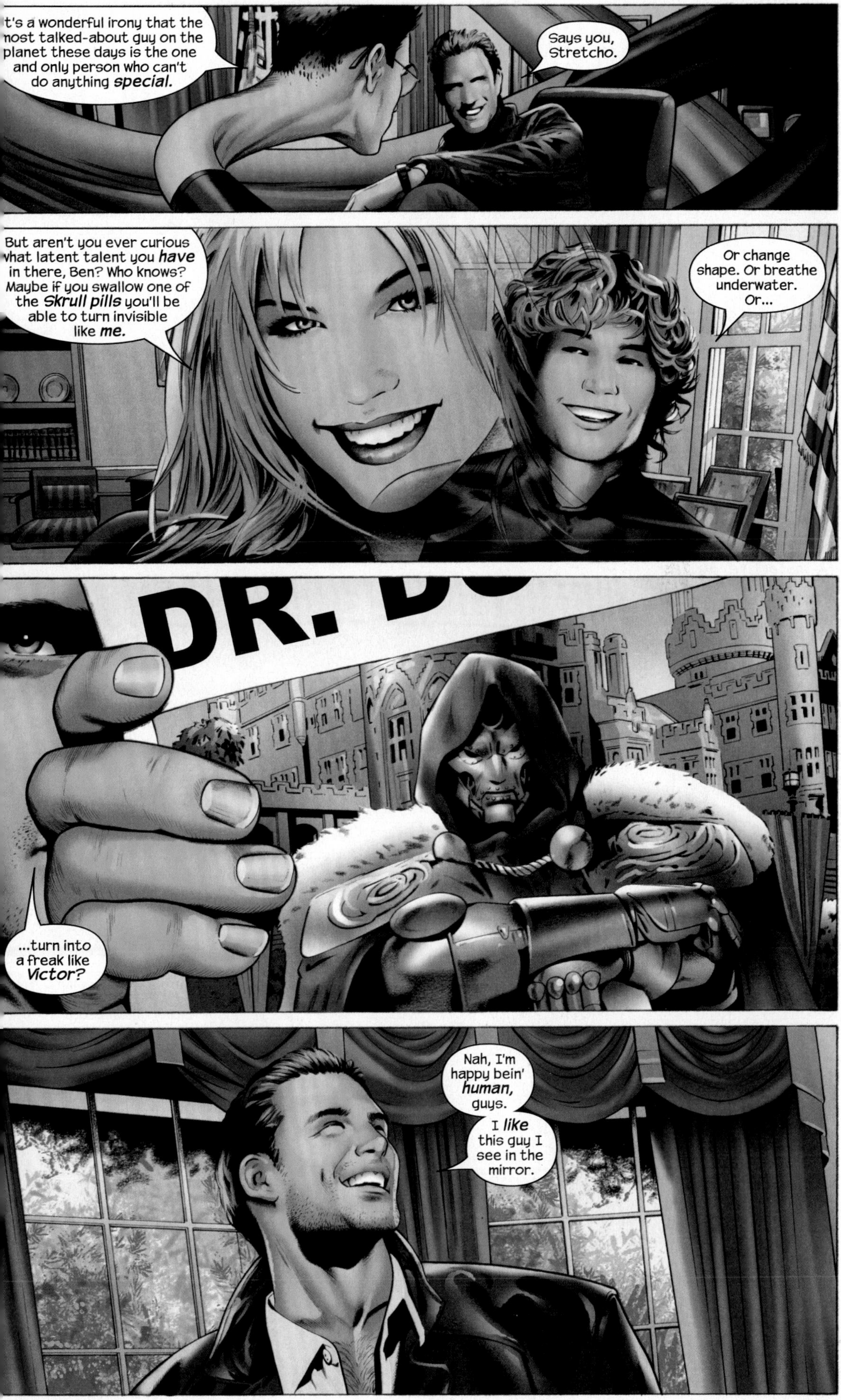
t's a wonderful irony that the nost talked-about guy on the planet these days is the one and only person who can't do anything *special.*
Says you, Stretcho.
But aren't you ever curious vhat latent talent you *have* in there, Ben? Who knows? Maybe if you swallow one of the *Skrull pills* you'll be able to turn invisible like *me.*
Or change shape. Or breathe underwater. Or...
DR.
...turn into a freak like *Victor?*
Nah, I'm happy bein' *human,* guys.
I *like* this guy I see in the mirror.

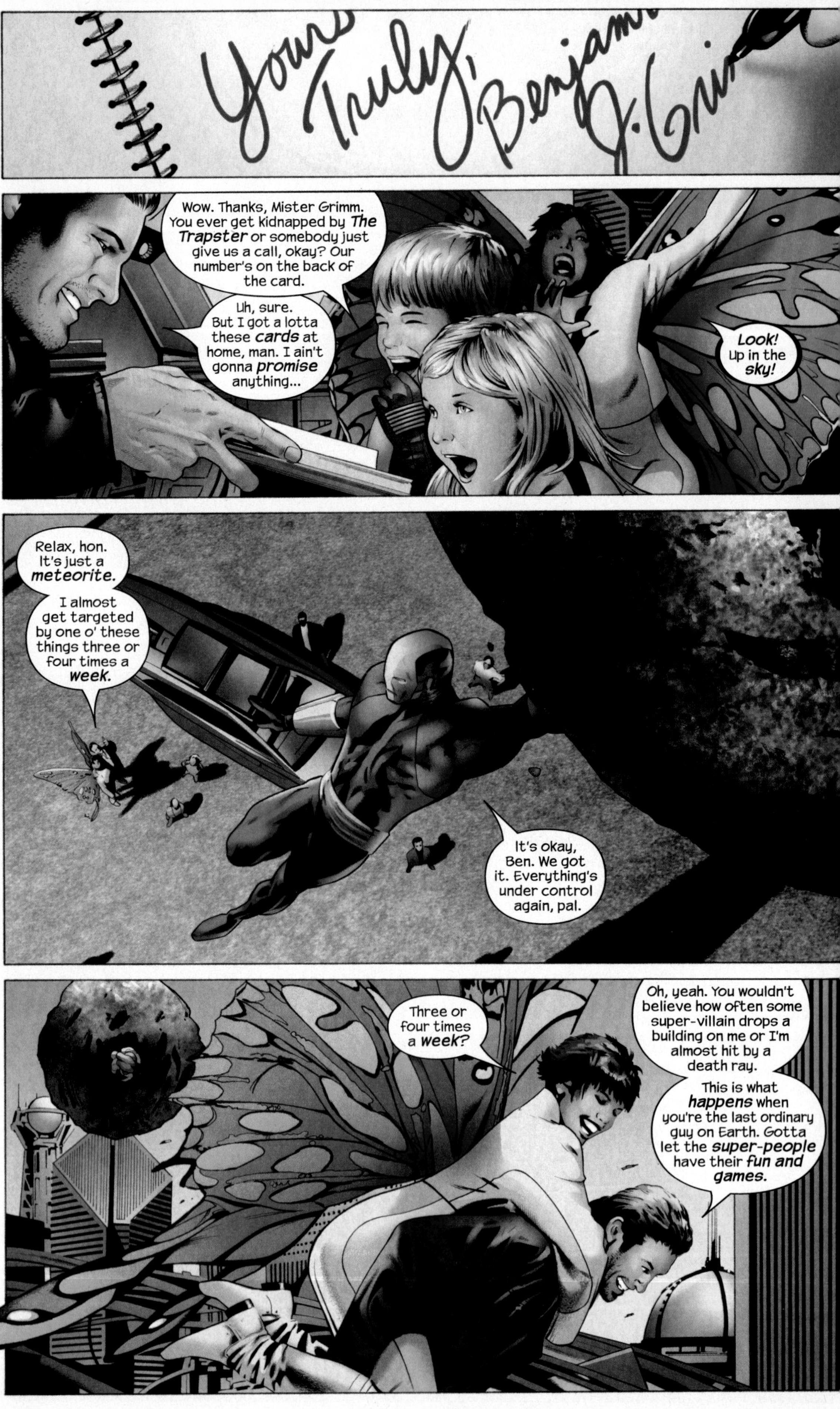
Yours Truly, Benjamin J. Grimm
Wow. Thanks, Mister Grimm. You ever get kidnapped by The Trapster or somebody just give us a call, okay? Our number's on the back of the card.
Uh, sure. But I got a lotta these cards at home, man. I ain't gonna promise anything...
Look! Up in the sky!
Relax, hon. It's just a meteorite.
I almost get targeted by one o' these things three or four times a week.
It's okay, Ben. We got it. Everything's under control again, pal.
Three or four times a week?
Oh, yeah. You wouldn't believe how often some super-villain drops a building on me or I'm almost hit by a death ray.
This is what happens when you're the last ordinary guy on Earth. Gotta let the super-people have their fun and games.

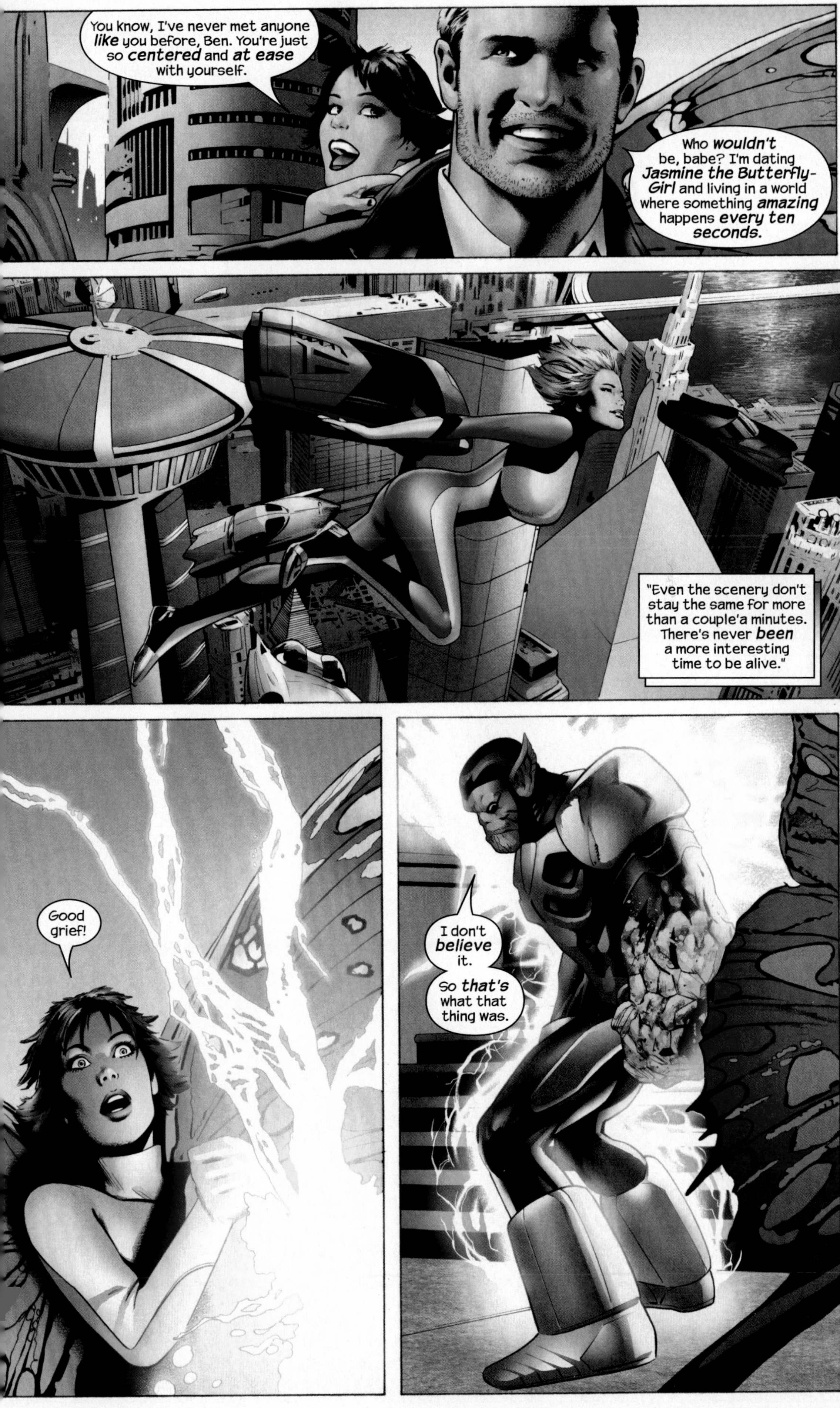
You know, I've never met anyone like you before, Ben. You're just so centered and at ease with yourself.
Who wouldn't be, babe? I'm dating Jasmine the Butterfly-Girl and living in a world where something amazing happens every ten seconds.
"Even the scenery don't stay the same for more than a couple'a minutes. There's never been a more interesting time to be alive."
Good grief!
I don't believe it.
So that's what that thing was.

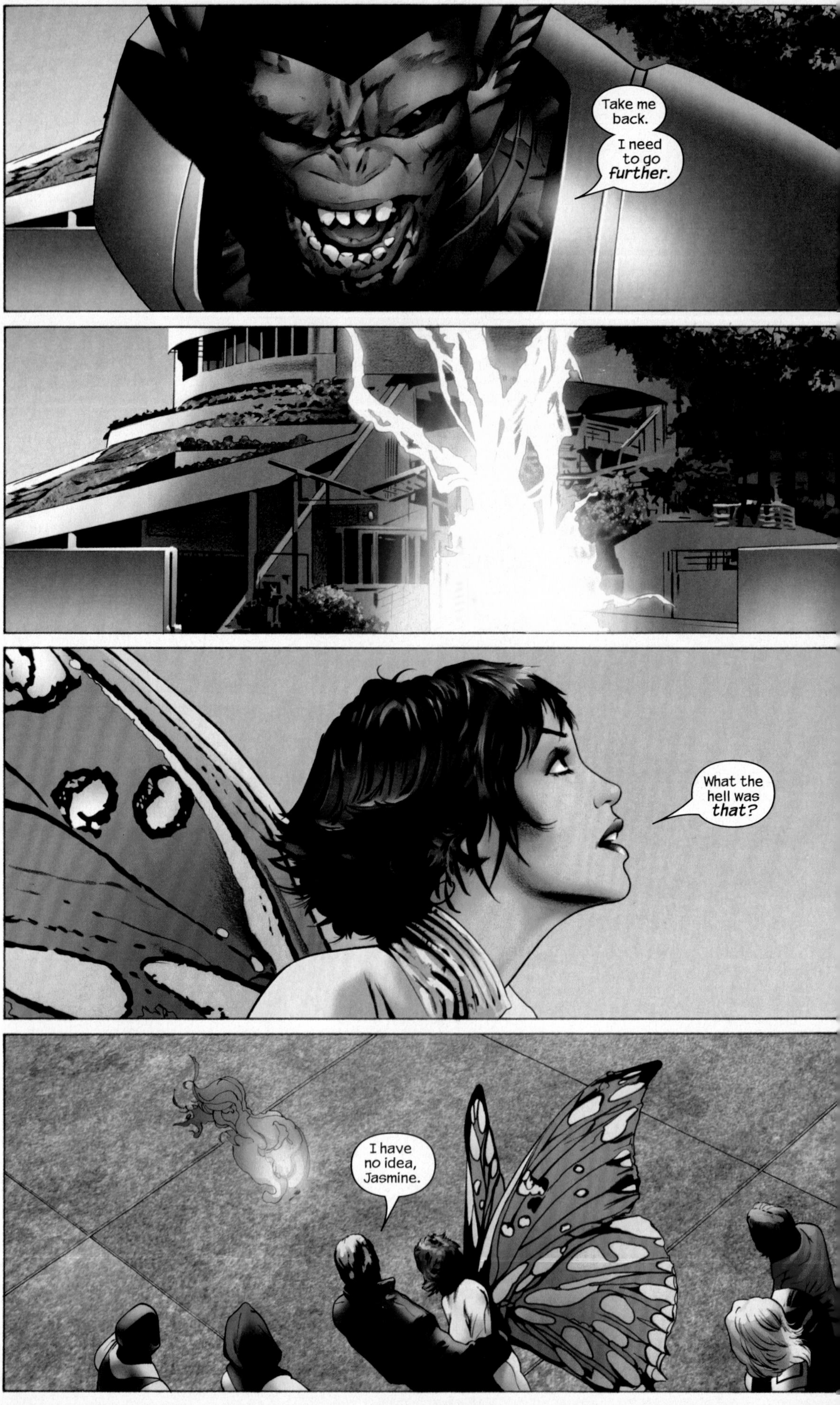
Take me back.
I need to go *further*.
What the hell was *that*?
I have no idea, Jasmine.

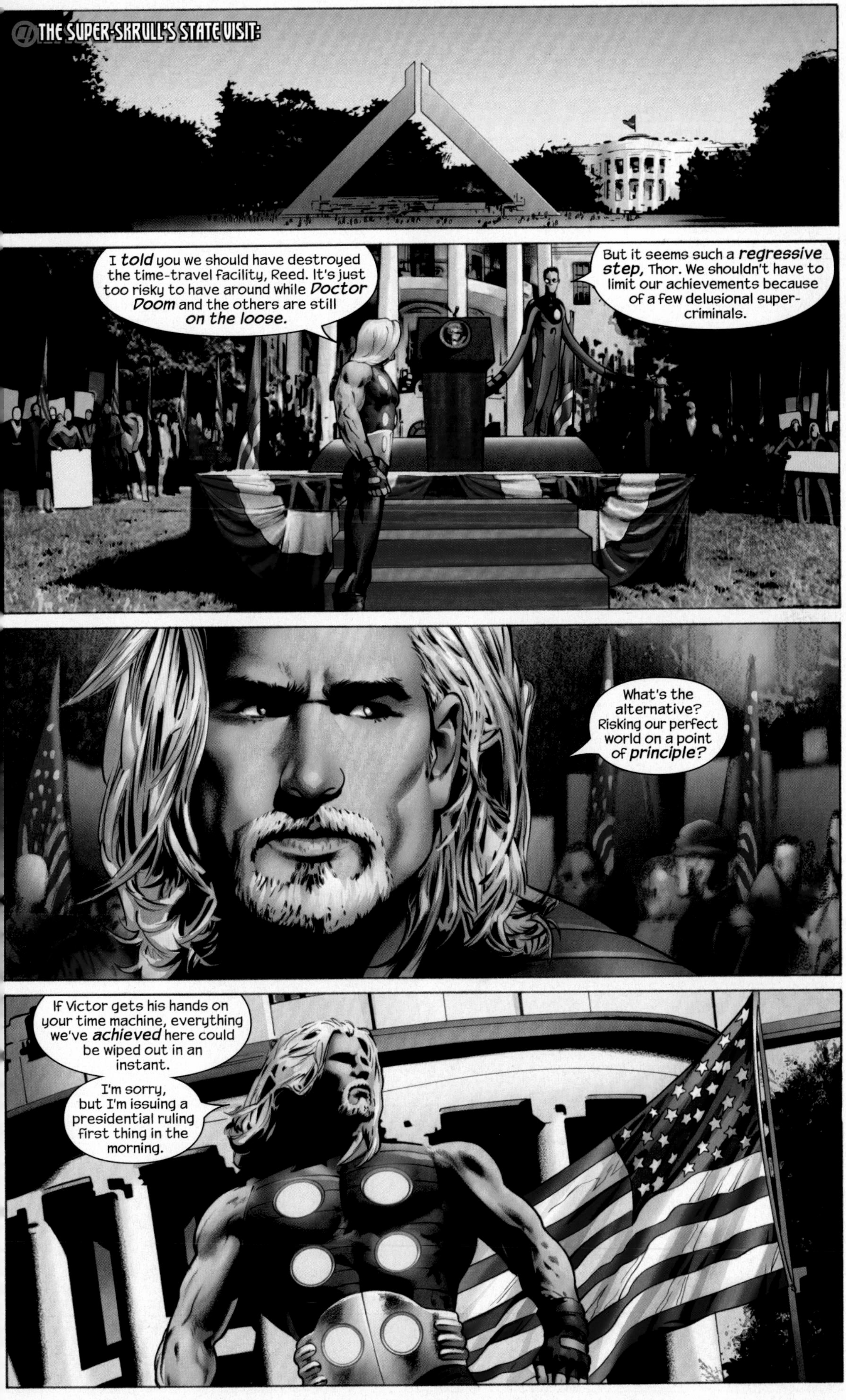
THE SUPER-SKRULL'S STATE VISIT:
I told you we should have destroyed the time-travel facility, Reed. It's just too risky to have around while Doctor Doom and the others are still on the loose.
But it seems such a regressive step, Thor. We shouldn't have to limit our achievements because of a few delusional super-criminals.
What's the alternative? Risking our perfect world on a point of principle?
If Victor gets his hands on your time machine, everything we've achieved here could be wiped out in an instant.
I'm sorry, but I'm issuing a presidential ruling first thing in the morning.

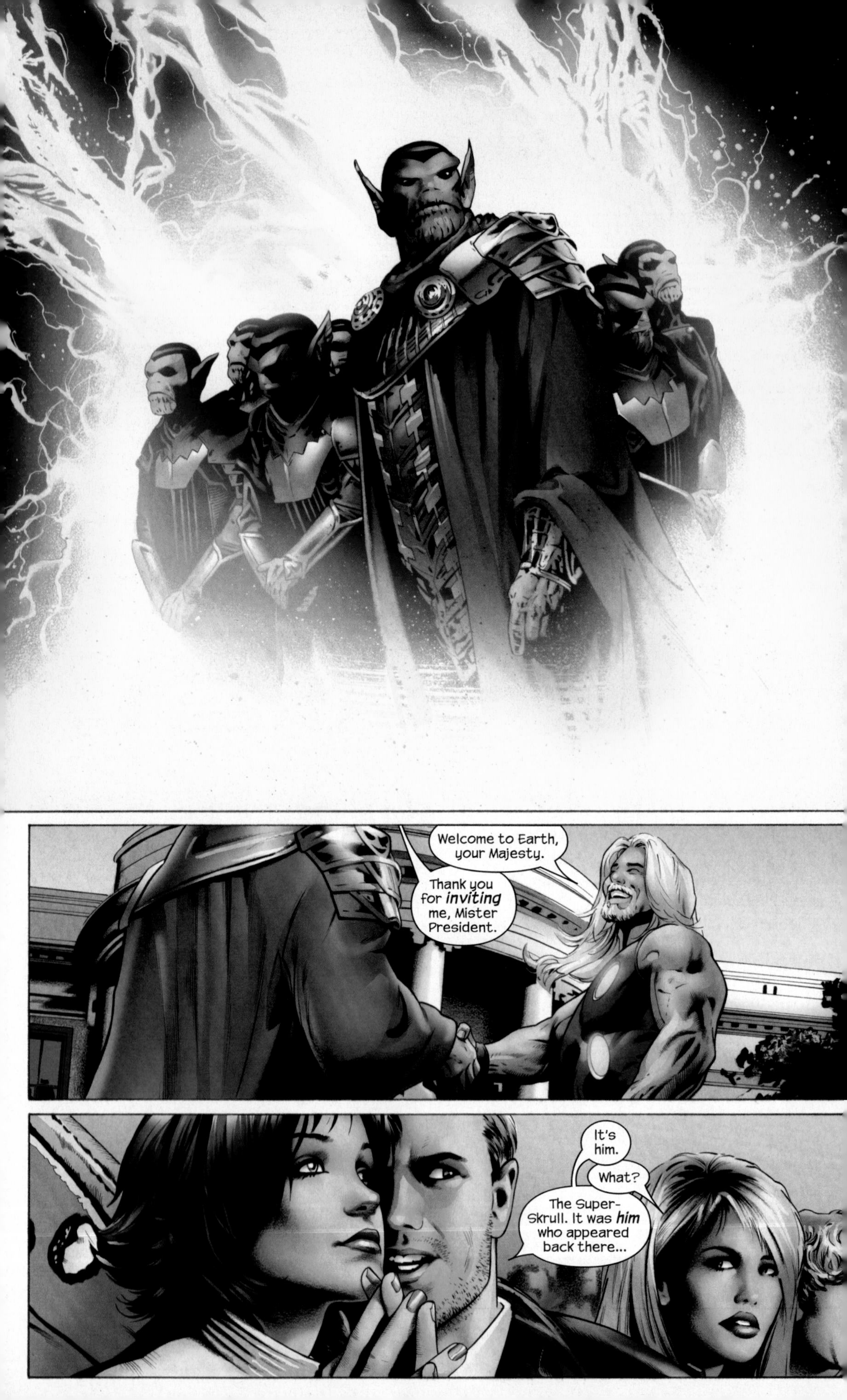
Welcome to Earth, your Majesty.
Thank you for *inviting* me, Mister President.
It's him.
What?
The Super-Skrull. It was *him* who appeared back there...

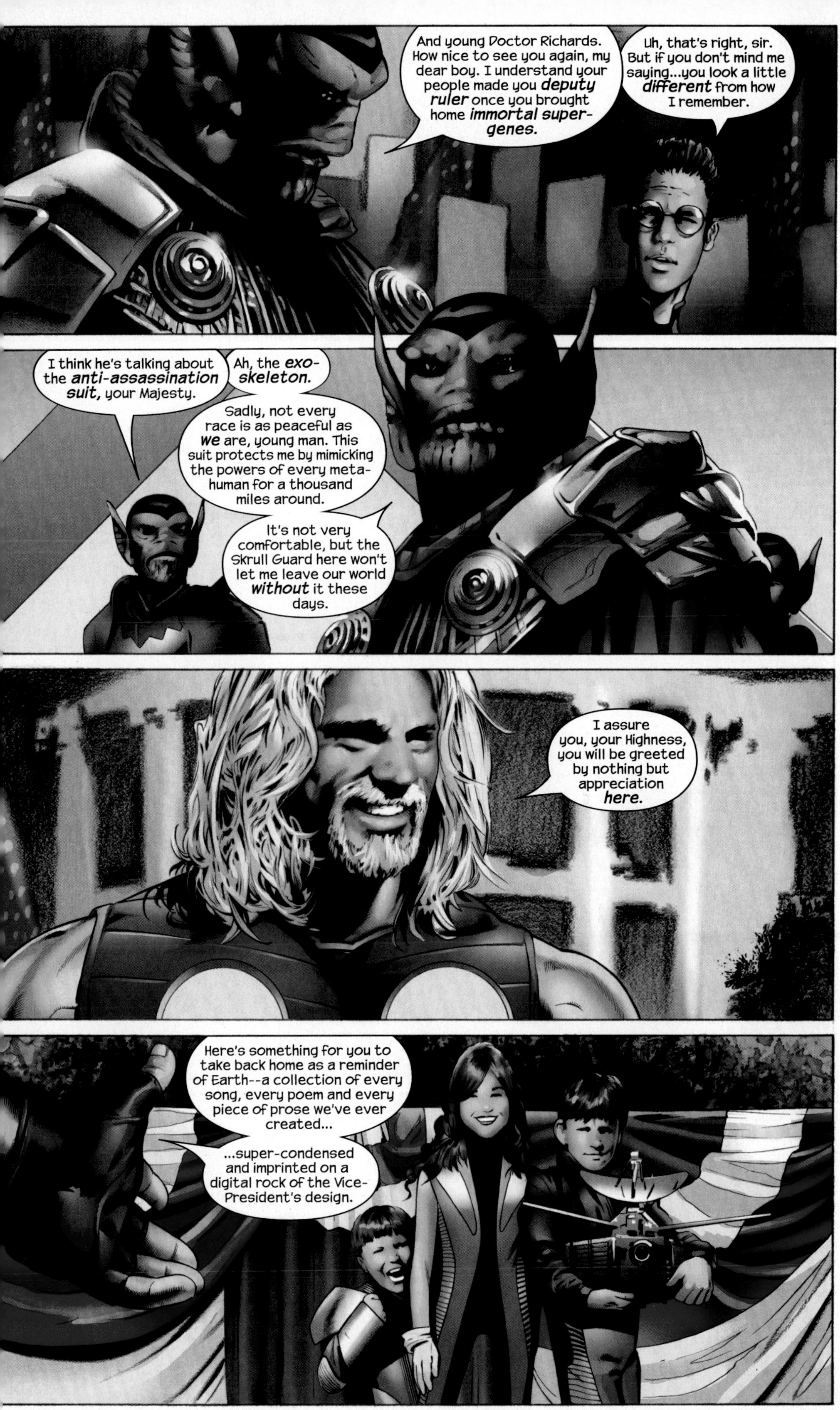
And young Doctor Richards. How nice to see you again, my dear boy. I understand your people made you *deputy ruler* once you brought home *immortal super-genes.*
Uh, that's right, sir. But if you don't mind me saying...you look a little *different* from how I remember.
I think he's talking about the *anti-assassination suit,* your Majesty.
Ah, the *exo-skeleton.*
Sadly, not every race is as peaceful as *we* are, young man. This suit protects me by mimicking the powers of every meta-human for a thousand miles around.
It's not very comfortable, but the Skrull Guard here won't let me leave our world *without* it these days.
I assure you, your Highness, you will be greeted by nothing but appreciation *here.*
Here's something for you to take back home as a reminder of Earth--a collection of every song, every poem and every piece of prose we've ever created...
...super-condensed and imprinted on a digital rock of the Vice-President's design.

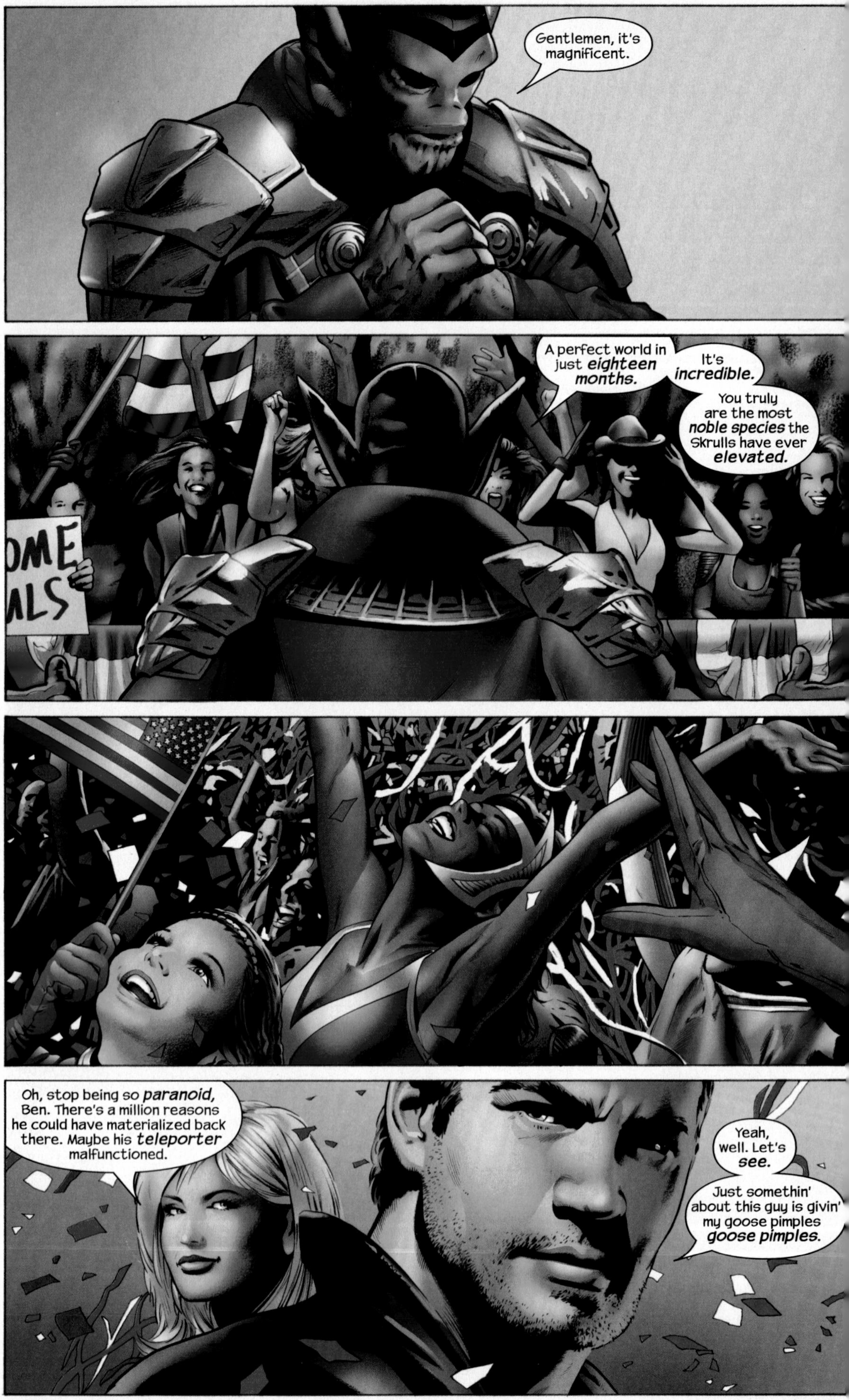
Gentlemen, it's magnificent.
A perfect world in just *eighteen months.*
It's *incredible.*
You truly are the most *noble species* the Skrulls have ever *elevated.*
Oh, stop being so *paranoid,* Ben. There's a million reasons he could have materialized back there. Maybe his *teleporter* malfunctioned.
Yeah, well. Let's *see.*
Just somethin' about this guy is givin' my goose pimples *goose pimples.*

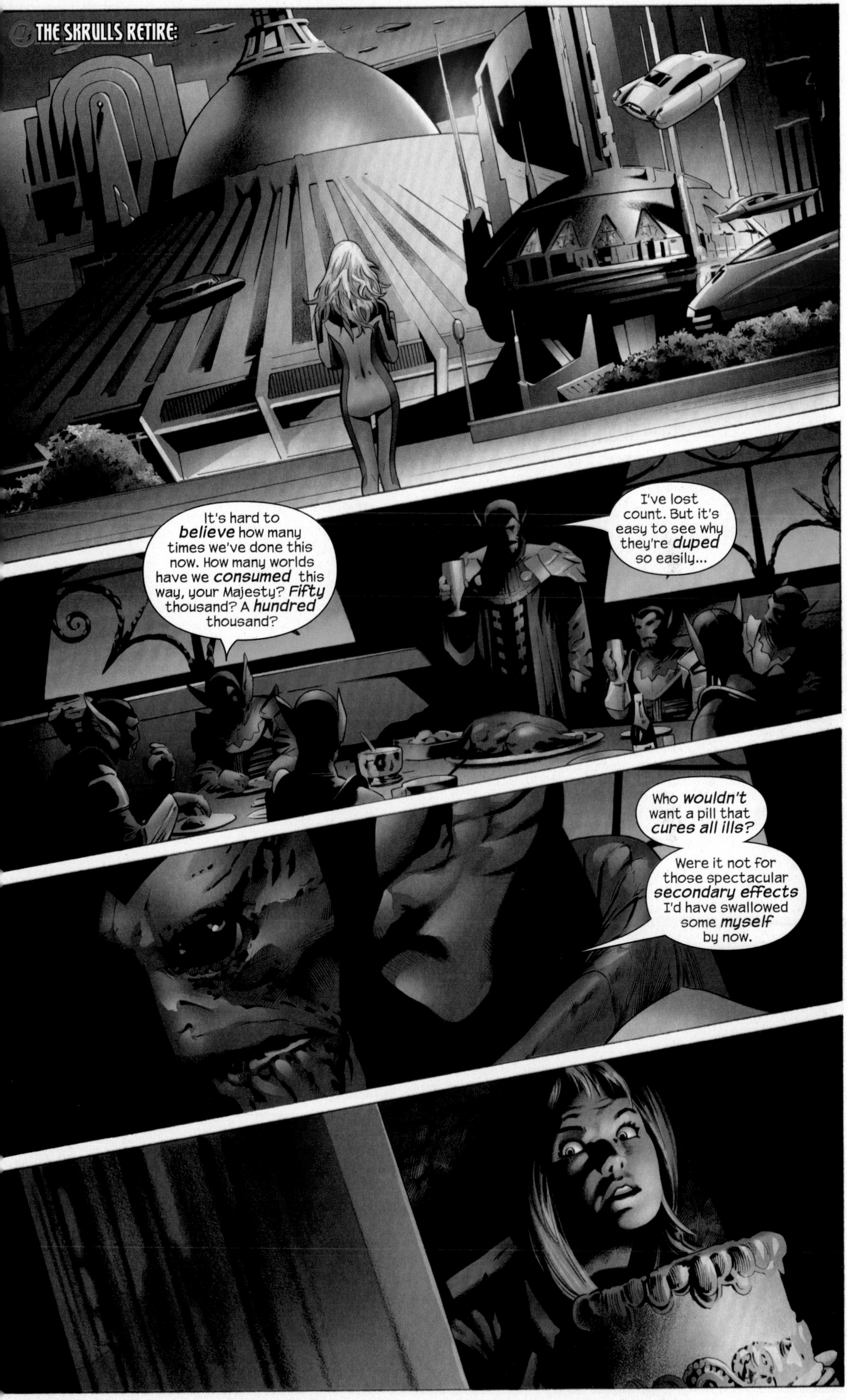
THE SKRULLS RETIRE:
It's hard to believe how many times we've done this now. How many worlds have we consumed this way, your Majesty? Fifty thousand? A hundred thousand?
I've lost count. But it's easy to see why they're duped so easily...
Who wouldn't want a pill that cures all ills?
Were it not for those spectacular secondary effects I'd have swallowed some myself by now.

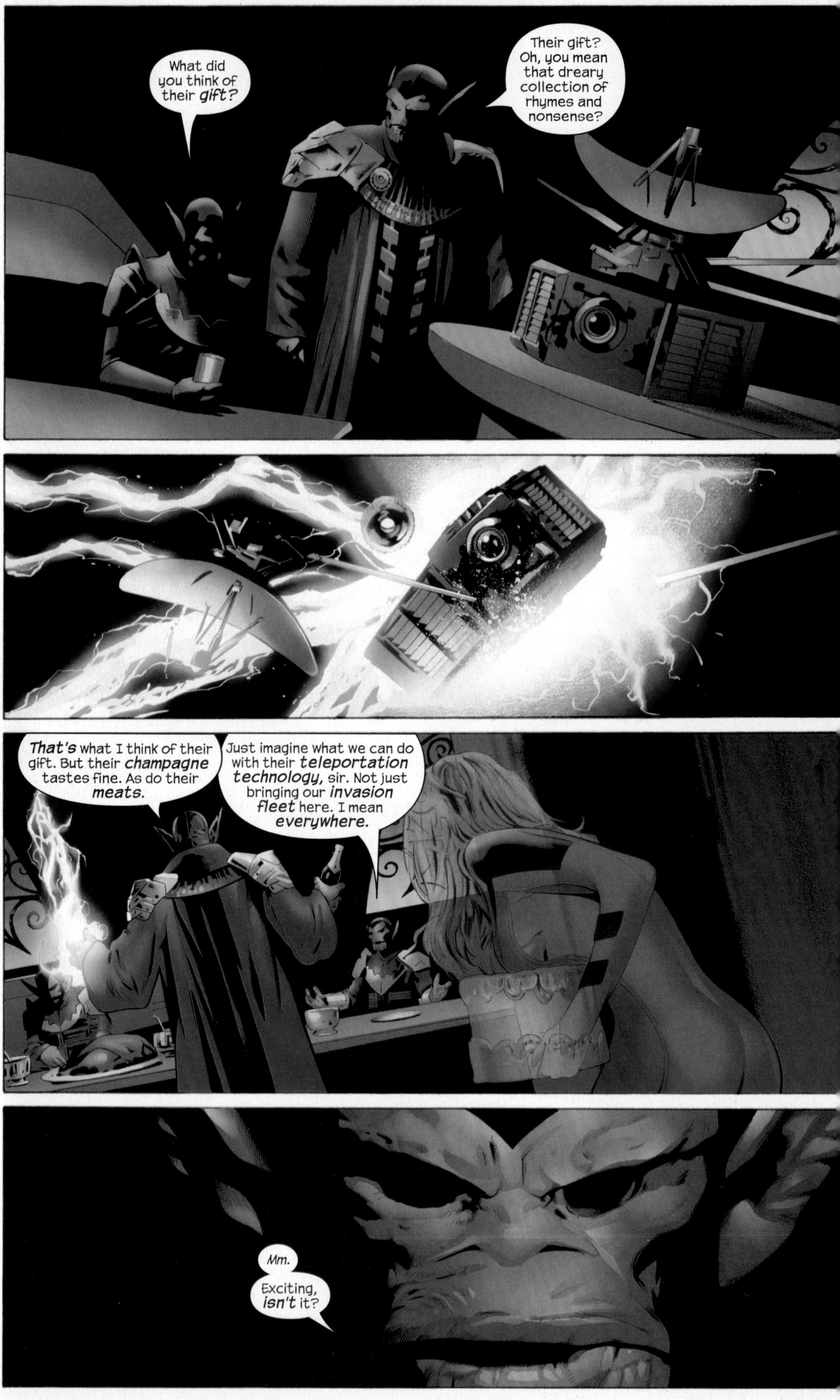
What did you think of their *gift?*
Their gift? Oh, you mean that dreary collection of rhymes and nonsense?
That's what I think of their gift. But their *champagne* tastes fine. As do their *meats.*
Just imagine what we can do with their *teleportation technology,* sir. Not just bringing our *invasion fleet* here. I mean *everywhere.*
Mm.
Exciting, *isn't* it?

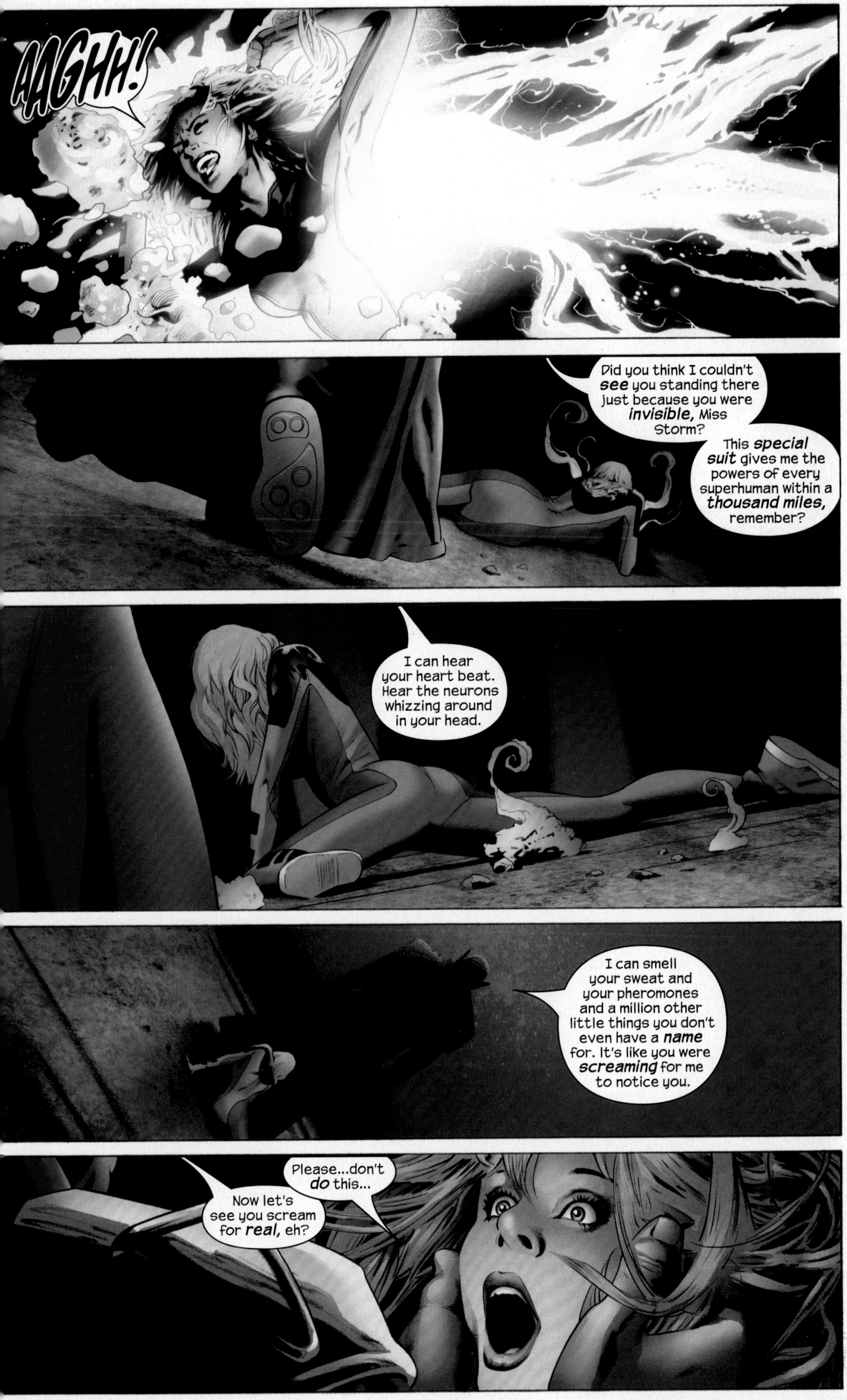
AAGHH!
Did you think I couldn't see you standing there just because you were invisible, Miss Storm?
This special suit gives me the powers of every superhuman within a thousand miles, remember?
I can hear your heart beat. Hear the neurons whizzing around in your head.
I can smell your sweat and your pheromones and a million other little things you don't even have a name for. It's like you were screaming for me to notice you.
Now let's see you scream for real, eh?
Please...don't do this...

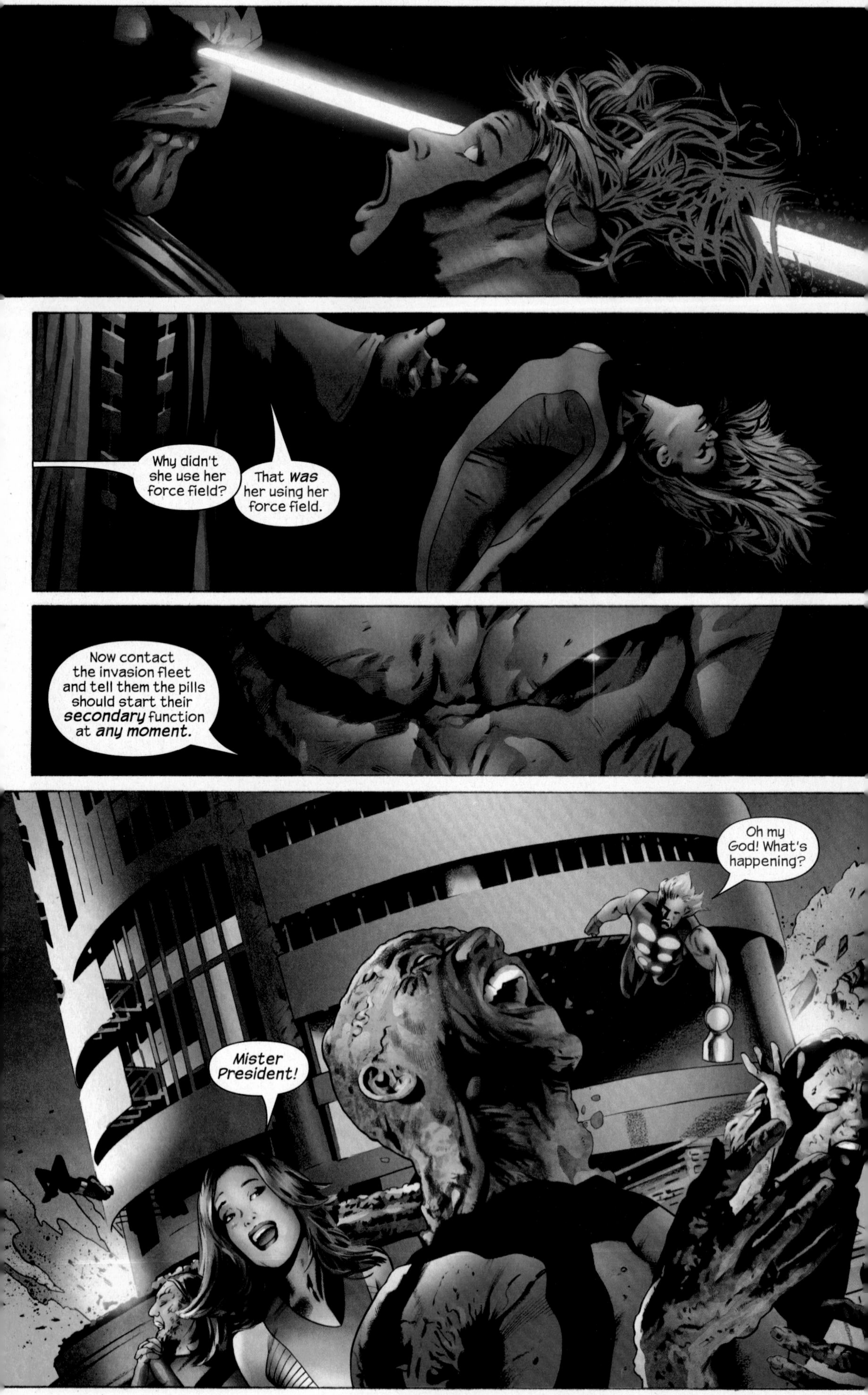
Why didn't she use her force field?
That *was* her using her force field.
Now contact the invasion fleet and tell them the pills should start their *secondary* function at *any moment.*
Oh my God! What's happening?
Mister President!

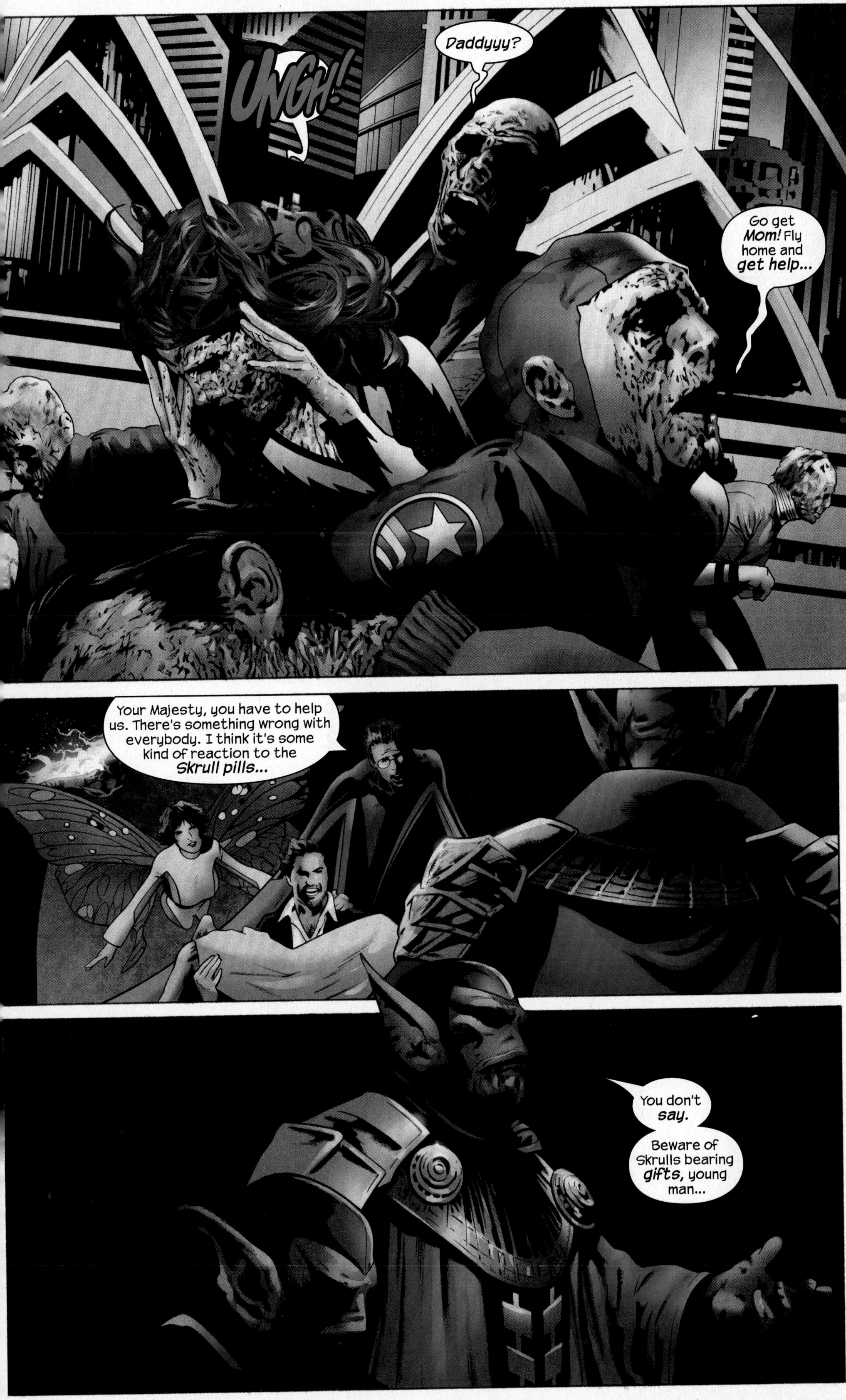
UNGH!
Daddyyy?
Go get Mom! Fly home and get help...
Your Majesty, you have to help us. There's something wrong with everybody. I think it's some kind of reaction to the Skrull pills...
You don't say.
Beware of Skrulls bearing gifts, young man...

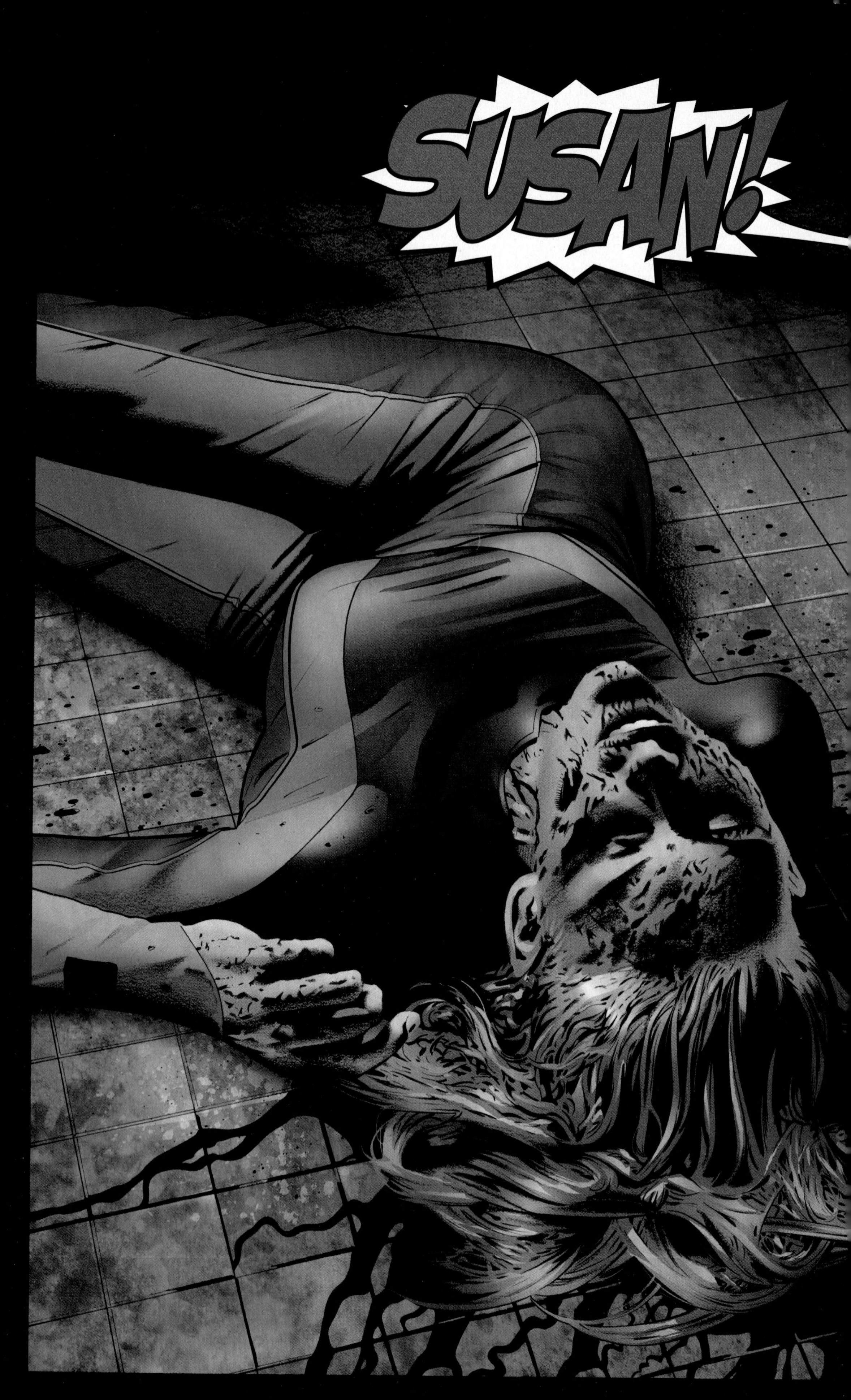
SUSAN!

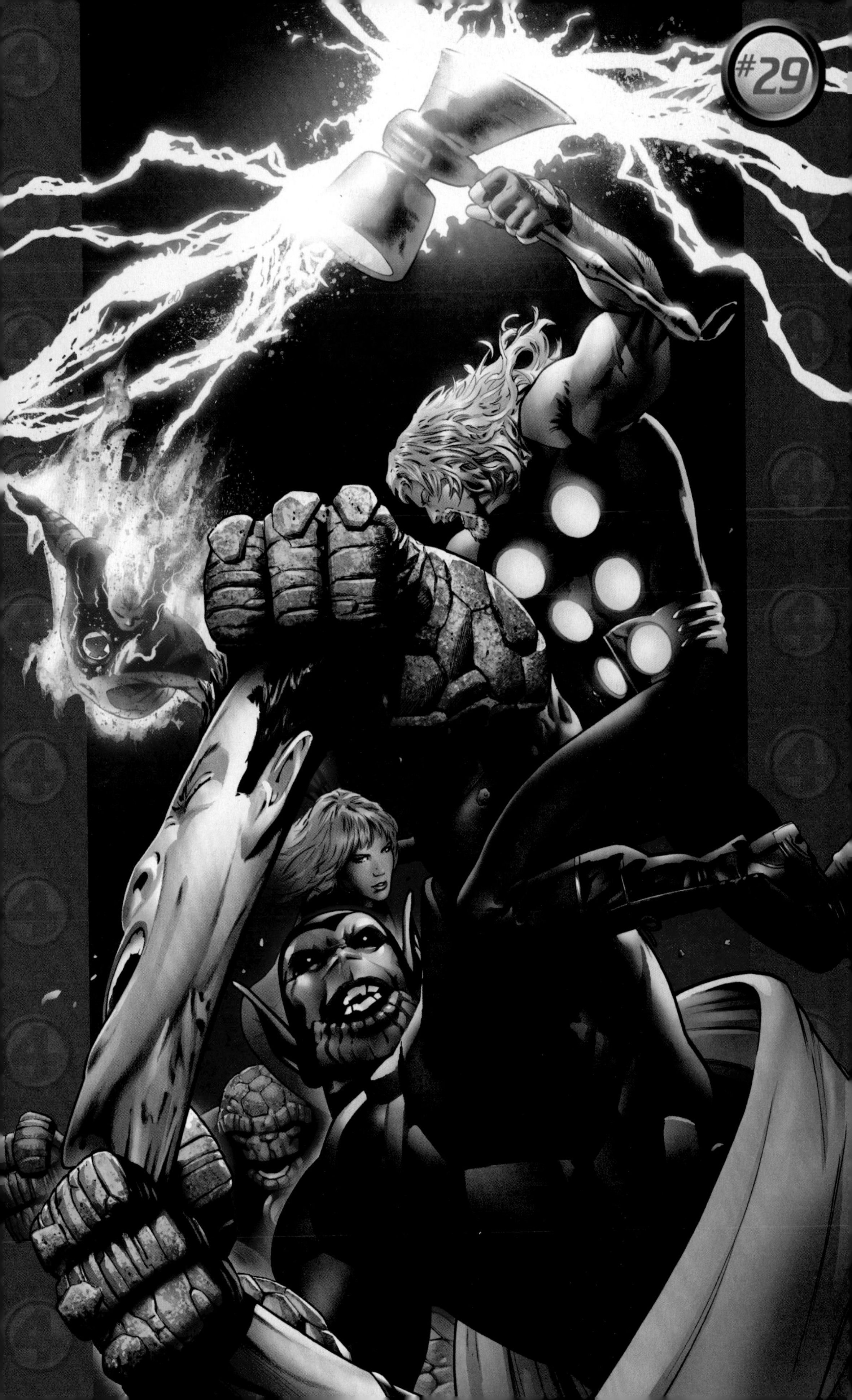
#29

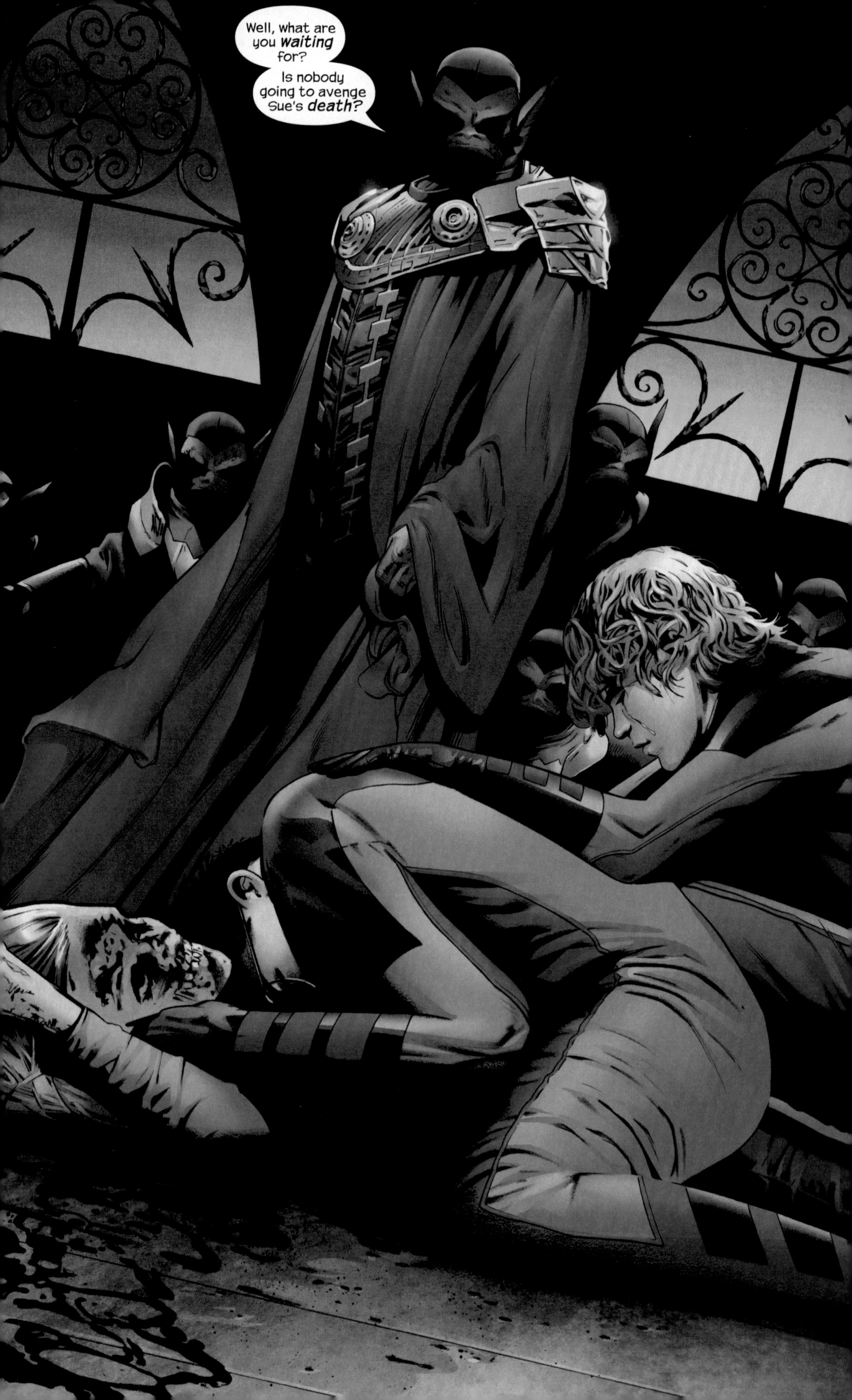
Well, what are you *waiting* for?
Is nobody going to avenge Sue's *death?*

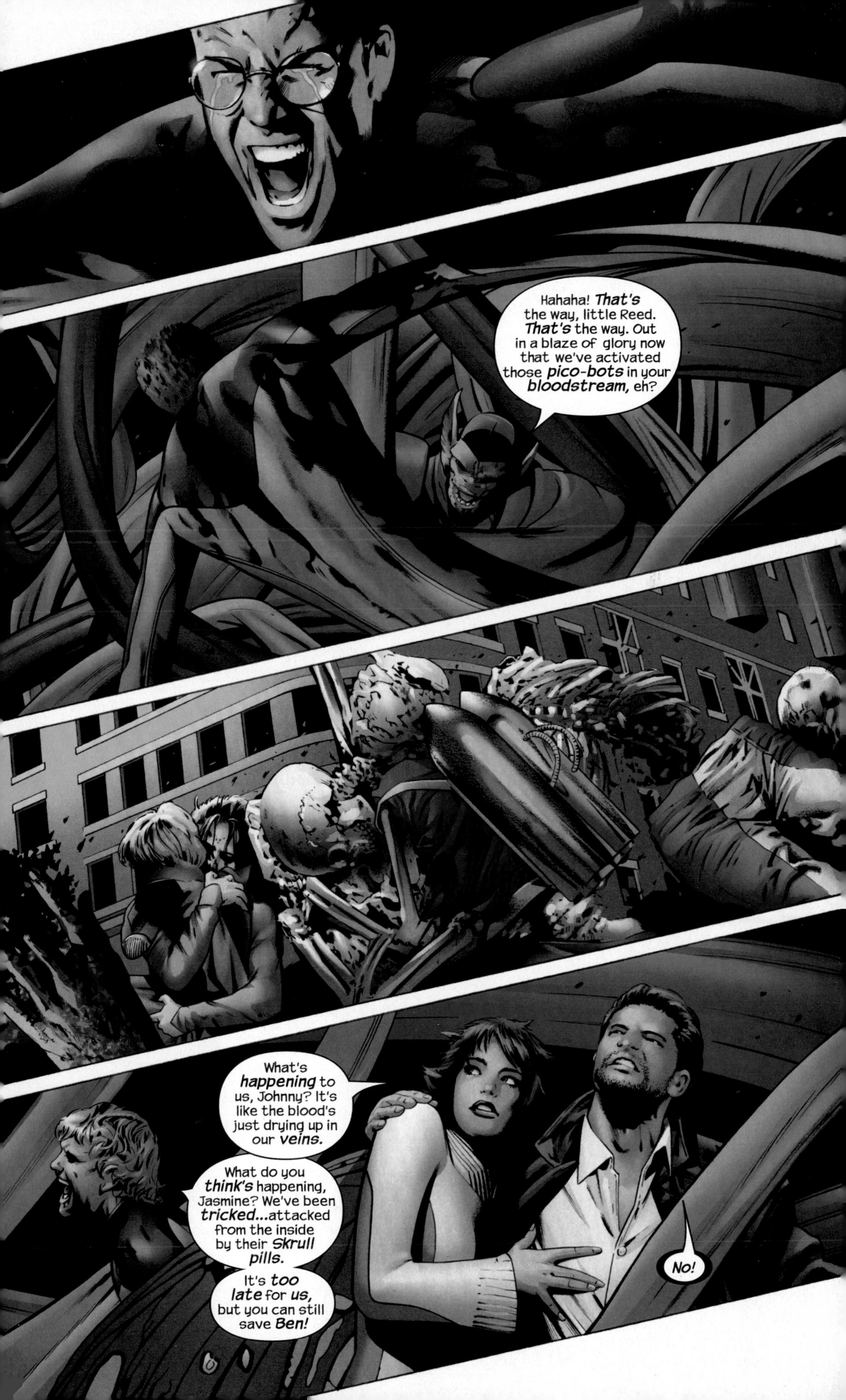
Hahaha! *That's* the way, little Reed. *That's* the way. Out in a blaze of glory now that we've activated those *pico-bots* in your *bloodstream,* eh?
What's *happening* to us, Johnny? It's like the blood's just drying up in our *veins.*
What do you *think's* happening, Jasmine? We've been *tricked*...attacked from the inside by their *Skrull pills.*
It's *too late* for *us,* but you can still save *Ben!*
No!

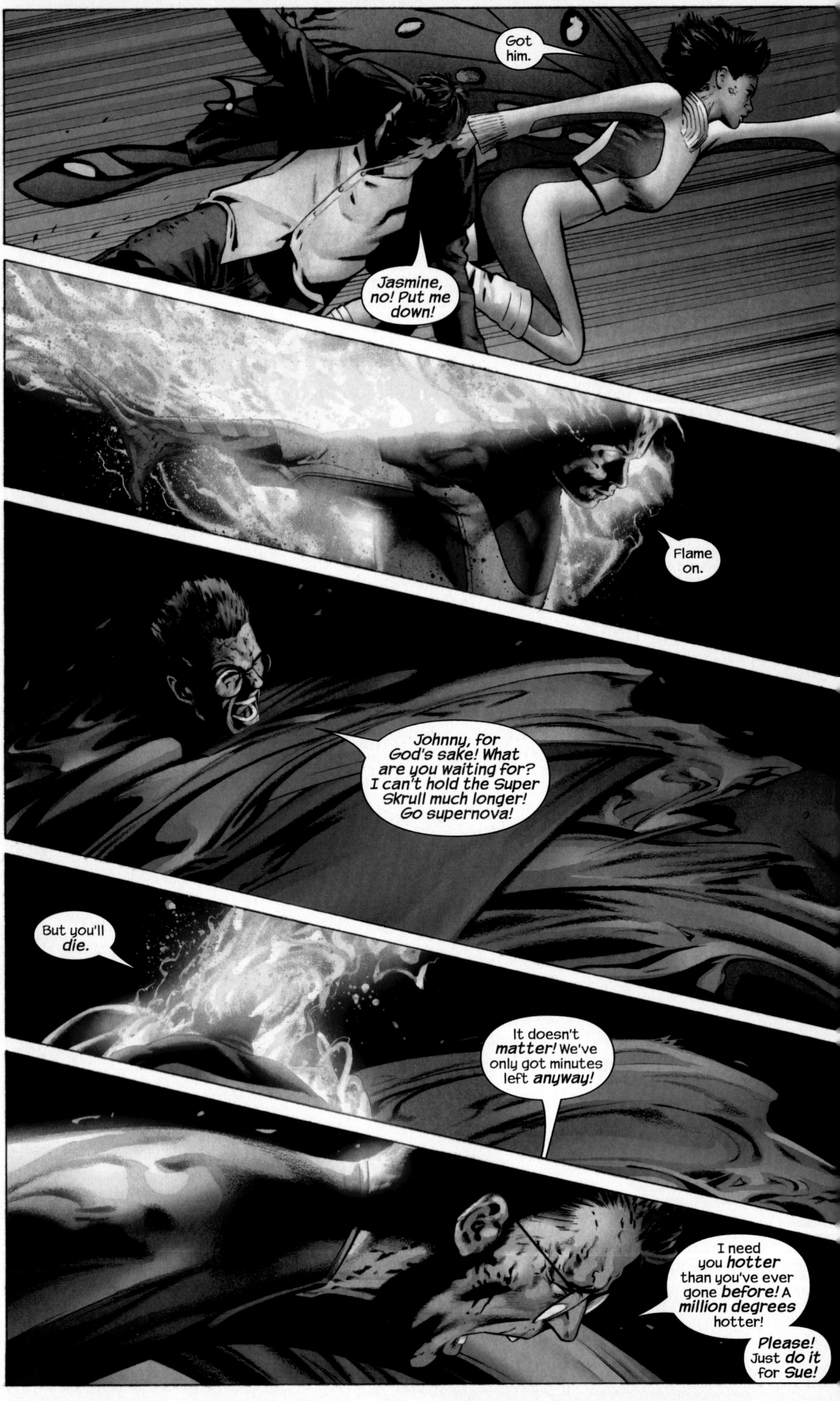
Got him.
Jasmine, no! Put me down!
Flame on.
Johnny, for God's sake! What are you waiting for? I can't hold the Super Skrull much longer! Go supernova!
But you'll *die.*
It doesn't *matter!* We've only got minutes left *anyway!*
I need you *hotter* than you've ever gone *before!* A *million degrees* hotter!
Please! Just *do it* for *Sue!*

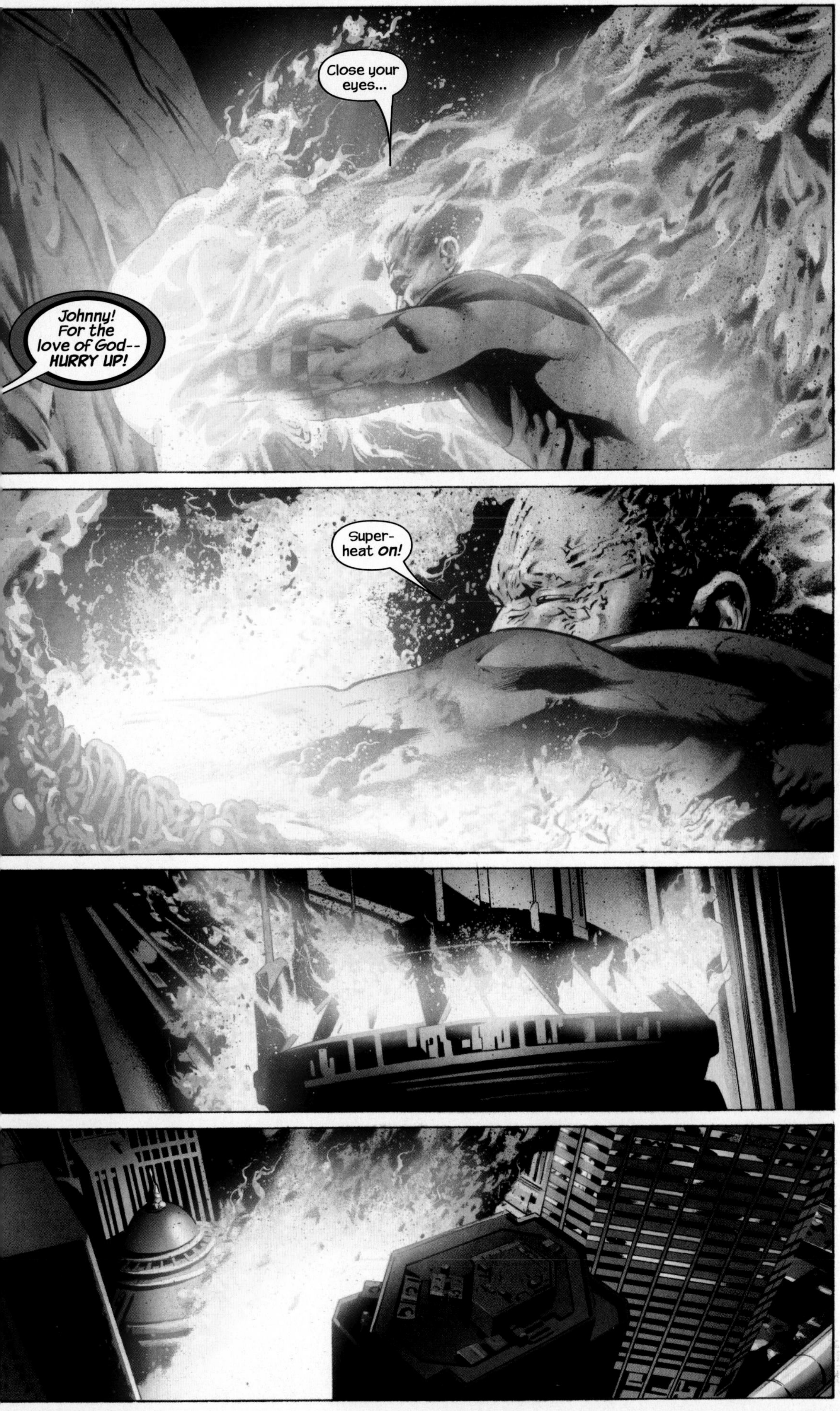
Close your eyes...
Johnny! For the love of God-- HURRY UP!
Super-heat ON!

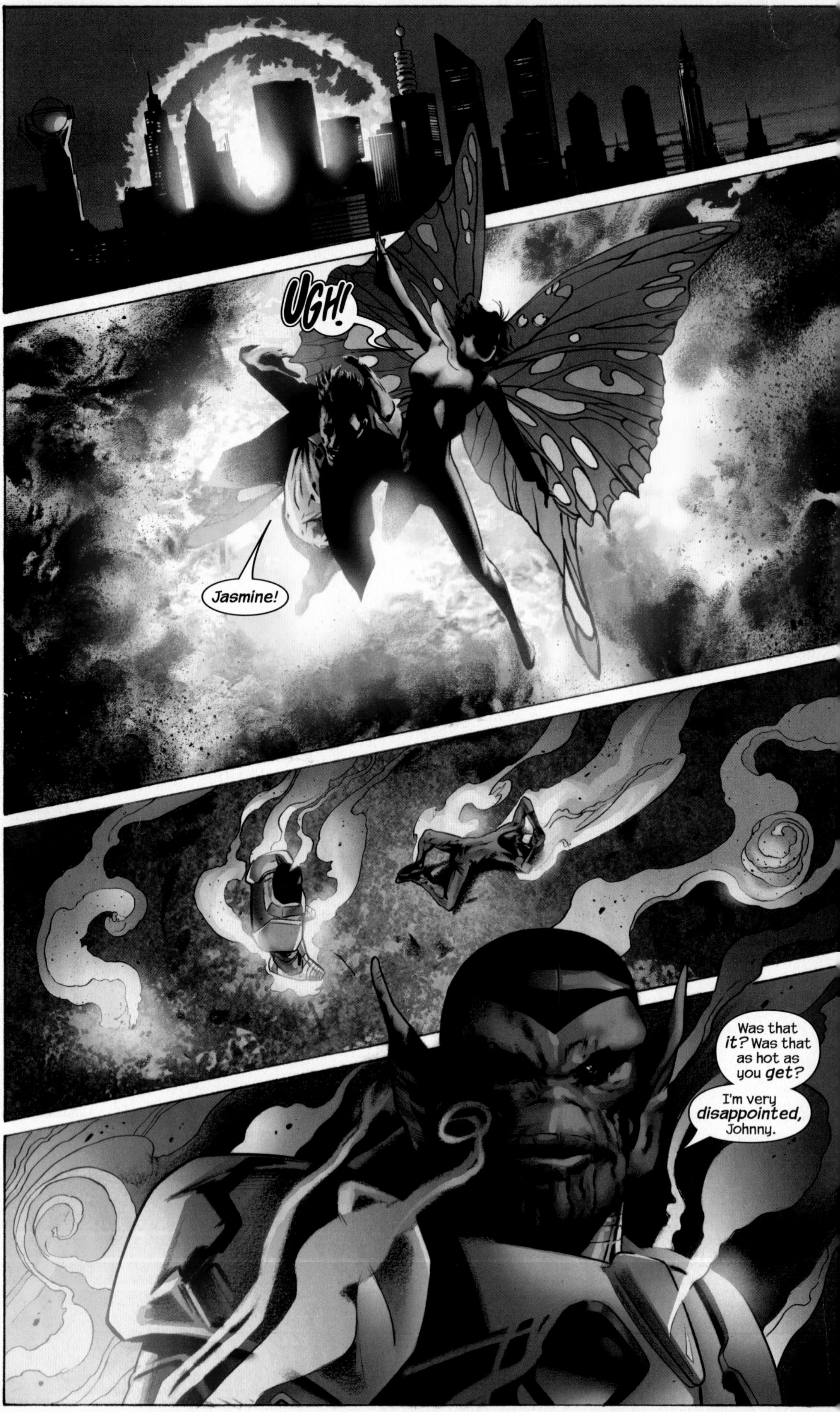
UGH!
Jasmine!
Was that it? Was that as hot as you get?
I'm very disappointed, Johnny.

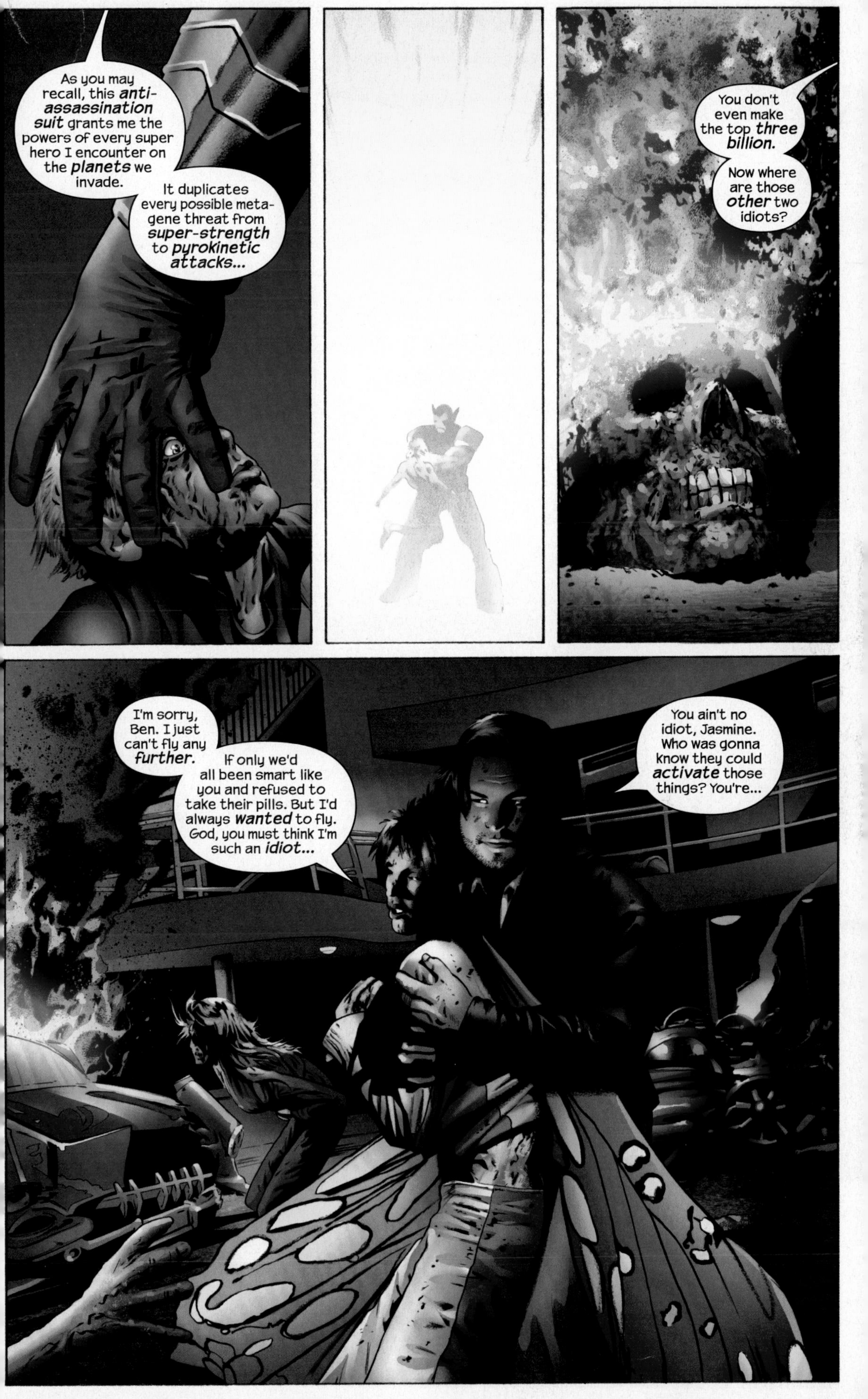
As you may recall, this anti-assassination suit grants me the powers of every super hero I encounter on the planets we invade.
It duplicates every possible meta-gene threat from super-strength to pyrokinetic attacks...
You don't even make the top three billion.
Now where are those other two idiots?
I'm sorry, Ben. I just can't fly any further.
If only we'd all been smart like you and refused to take their pills. But I'd always wanted to fly. God, you must think I'm such an idiot...
You ain't no idiot, Jasmine. Who was gonna know they could activate those things? You're...

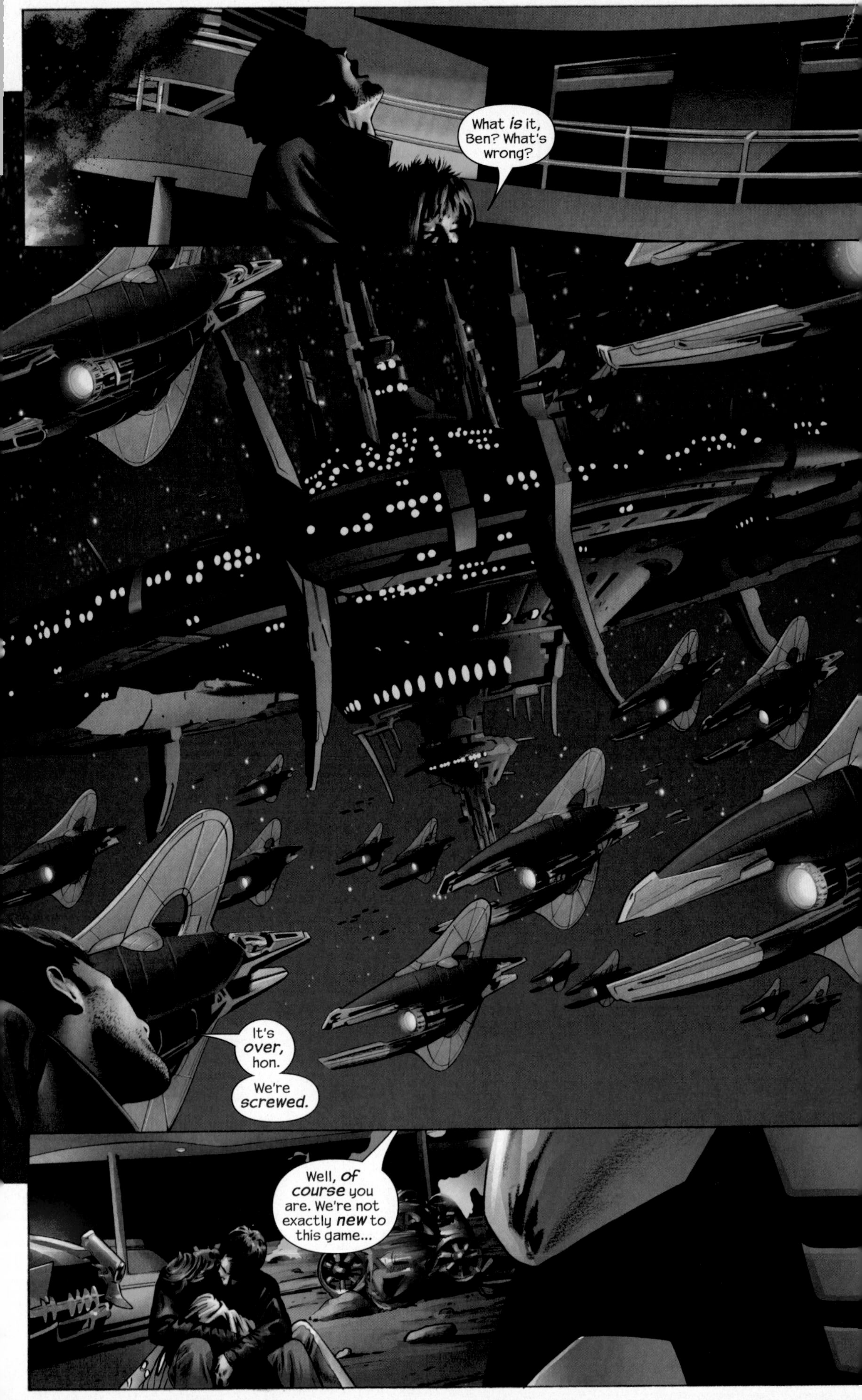

What *is* it, Ben? What's wrong?
It's *over,* hon.
We're *screwed.*
Well, *of course* you are. We're not exactly *new* to this game...

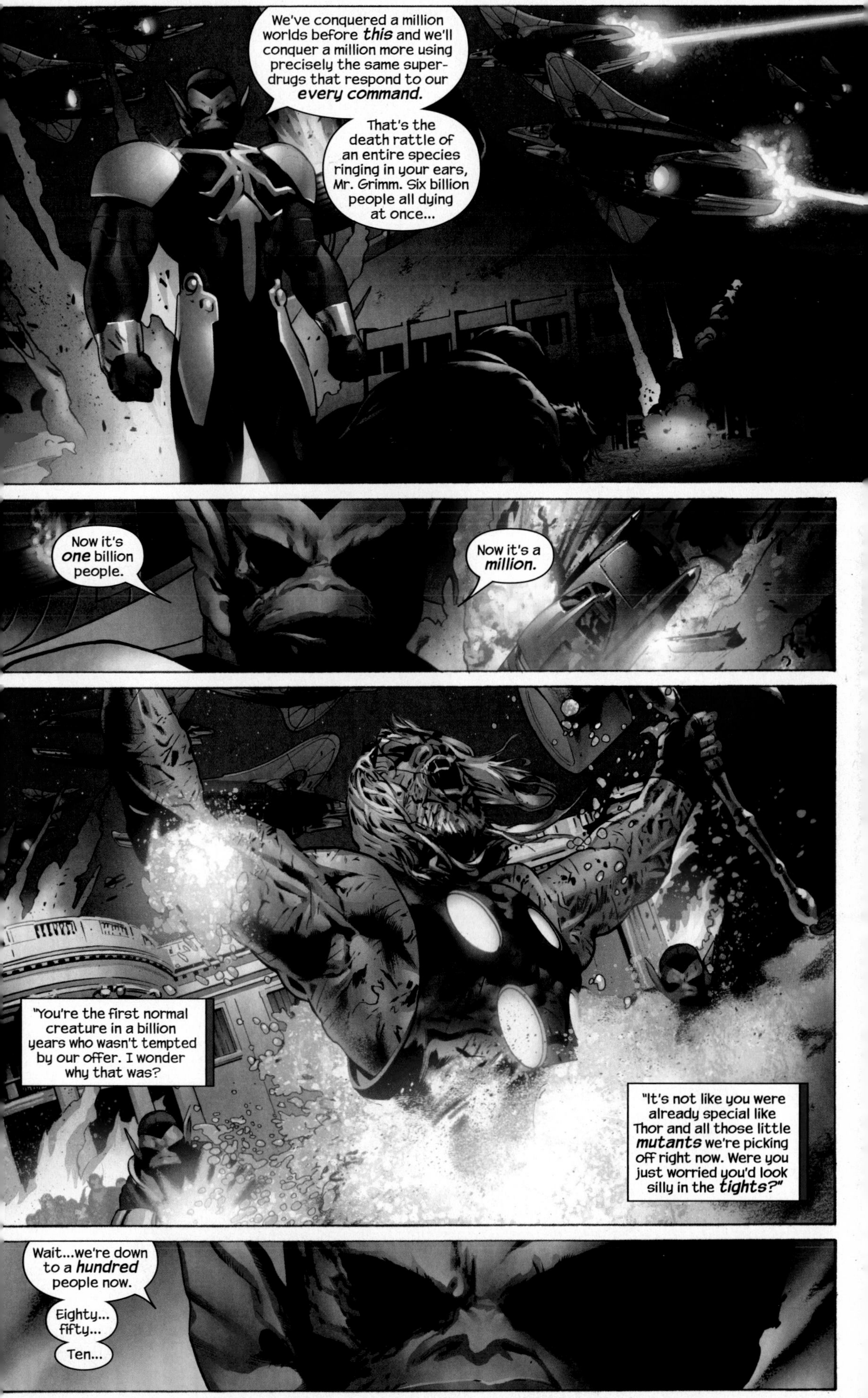
We've conquered a million worlds before this and we'll conquer a million more using precisely the same super-drugs that respond to our every command.
That's the death rattle of an entire species ringing in your ears, Mr. Grimm. Six billion people all dying at once...
Now it's one billion people.
Now it's a million.
"You're the first normal creature in a billion years who wasn't tempted by our offer. I wonder why that was?
"It's not like you were already special like Thor and all those little mutants we're picking off right now. Were you just worried you'd look silly in the tights?"
Wait...we're down to a hundred people now.
Eighty... fifty...
Ten...

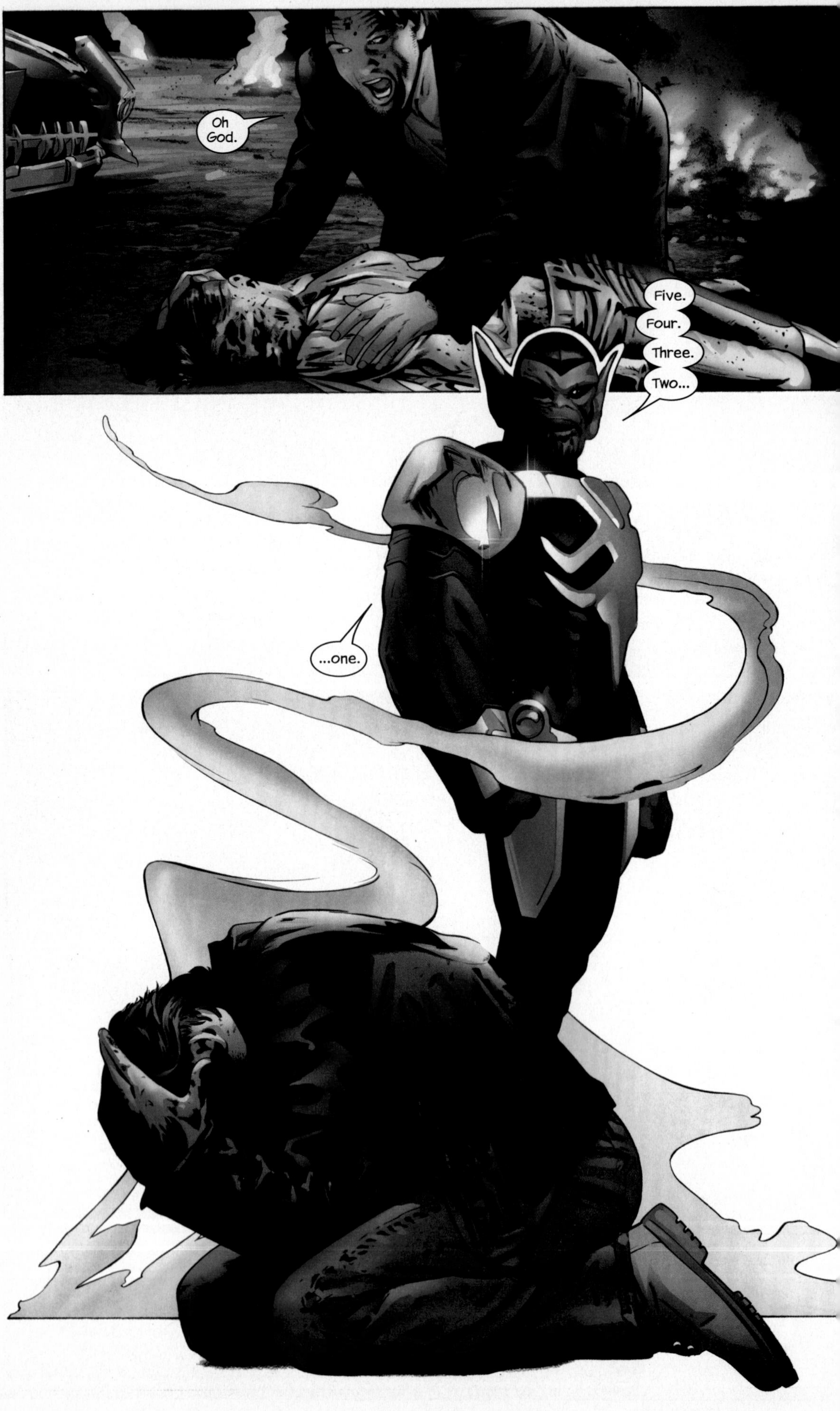

Oh God.
Five.
Four.
Three.
Two...
...one.

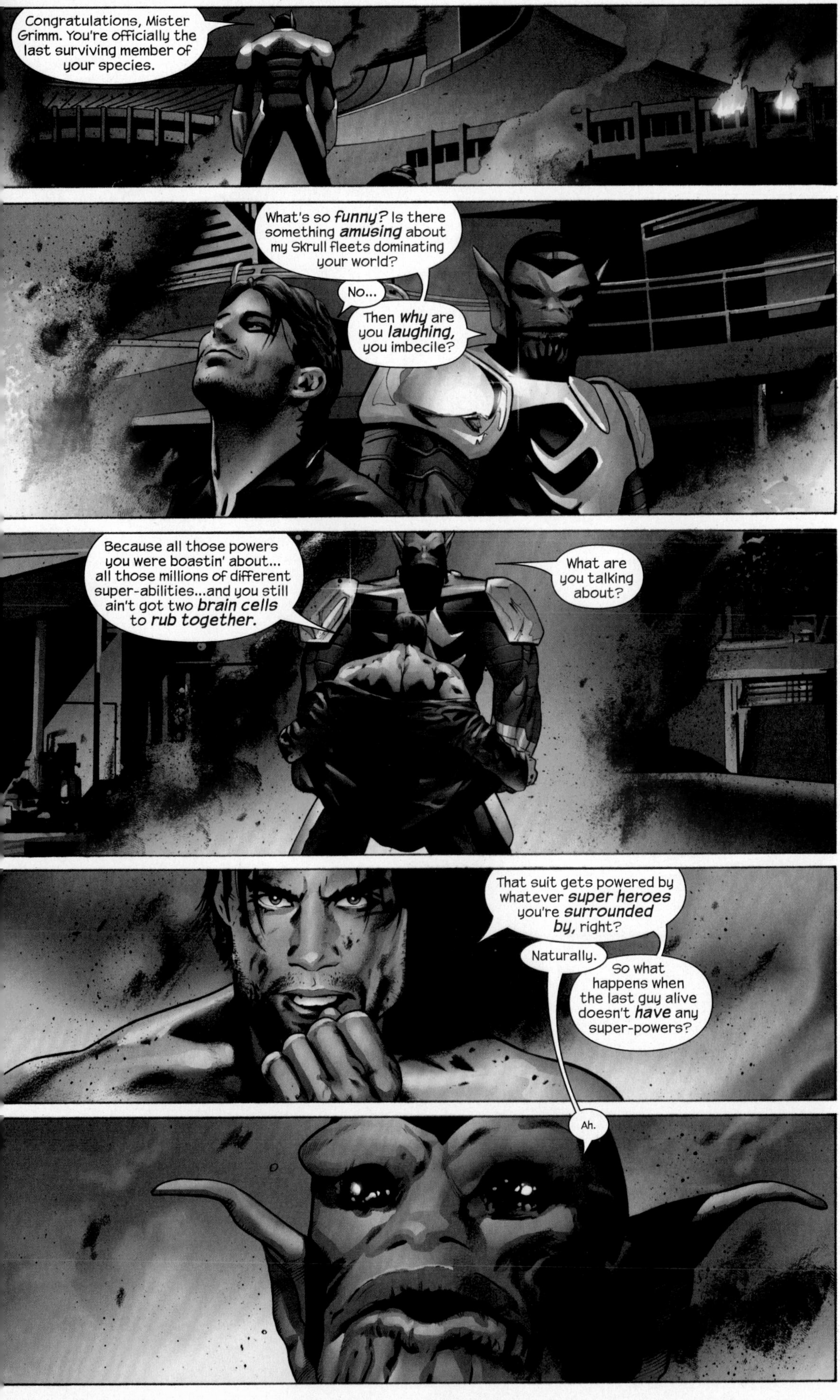
Congratulations, Mister Grimm. You're officially the last surviving member of your species.
What's so funny? Is there something amusing about my Skrull fleets dominating your world?
No...
Then why are you laughing, you imbecile?
Because all those powers you were boastin' about... all those millions of different super-abilities...and you still ain't got two brain cells to rub together.
What are you talking about?
That suit gets powered by whatever super heroes you're surrounded by, right?
Naturally.
So what happens when the last guy alive doesn't have any super-powers?
Ah.

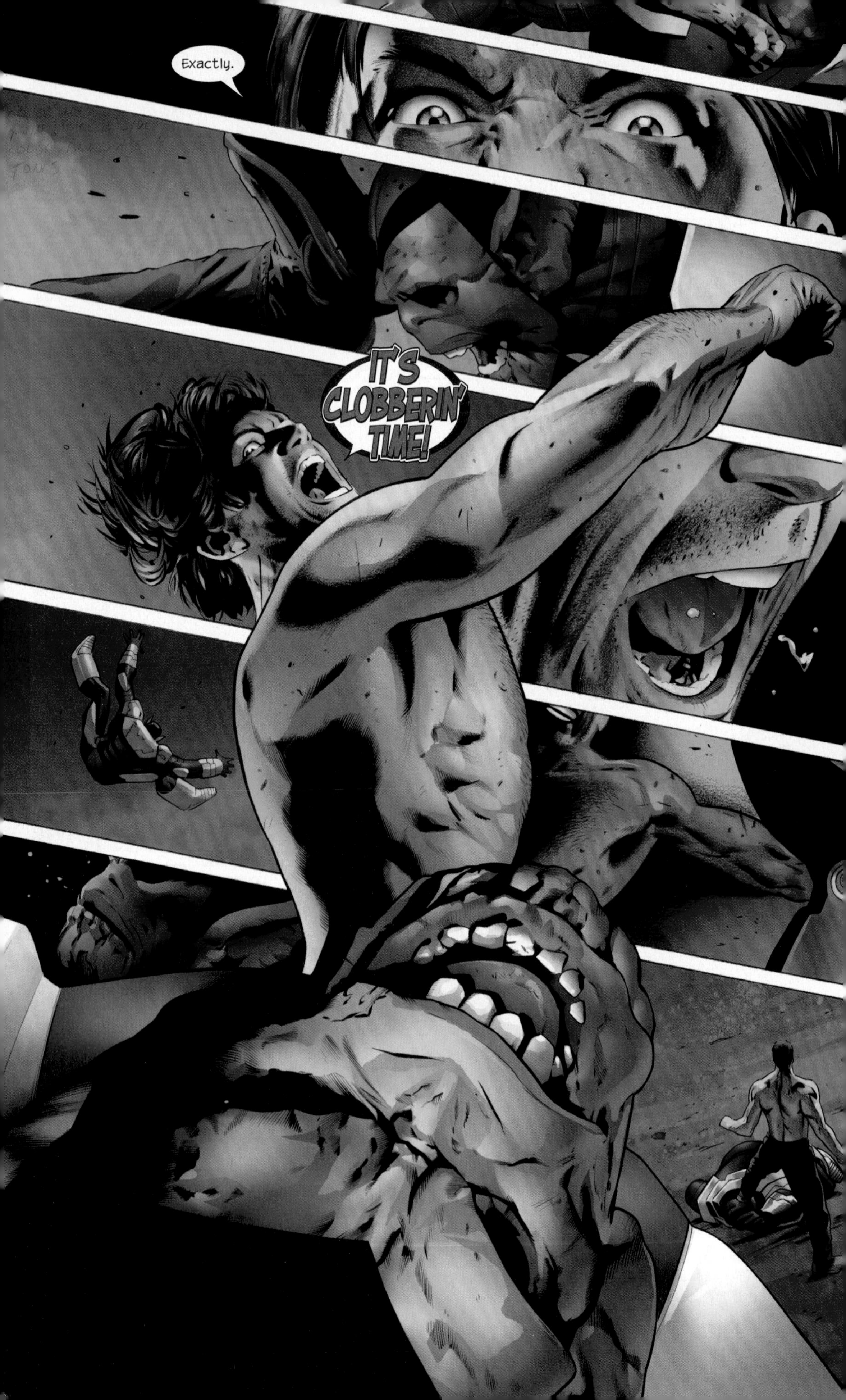
Exactly.
IT'S CLOBBERIN' TIME!

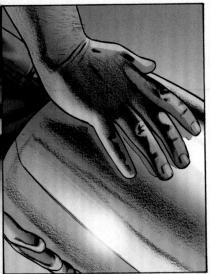

P-please...you can't just *leave* me like this. I'm the oldest living Skrull...almost a *billion years* old.

I won't survive *ten minutes* in Earth's atmosphere without my *anti-assassination suit.*

Ten minutes time and this'll *all be over,* toots.

I do this right and I can stop it even happening in the *first* place.

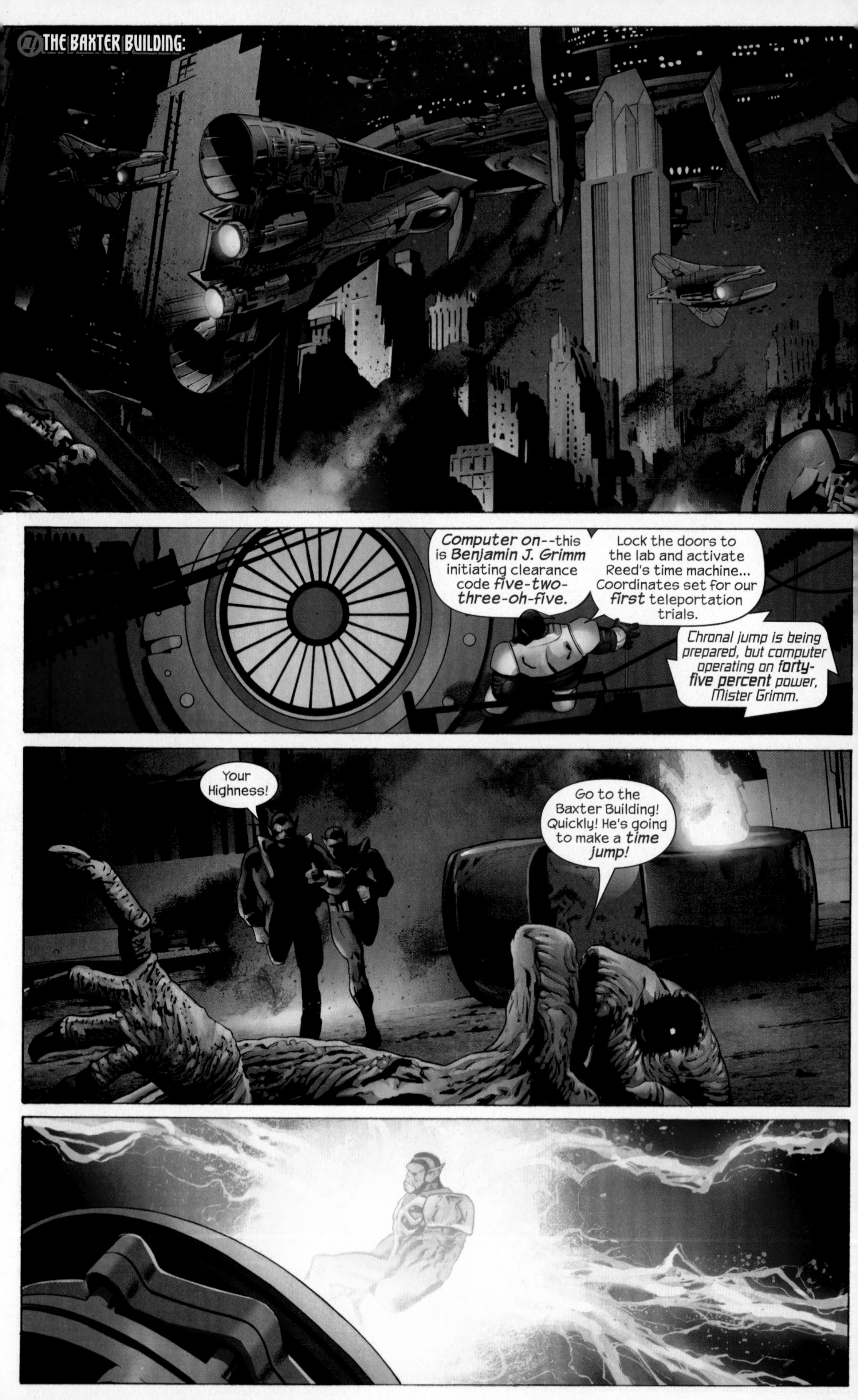
THE BAXTER BUILDING:
Computer on--this is Benjamin J. Grimm initiating clearance code five-two-three-oh-five.
Lock the doors to the lab and activate Reed's time machine... Coordinates set for our first teleportation trials.
Chronal jump is being prepared, but computer operating on forty-five percent power, Mister Grimm.
Your Highness!
Go to the Baxter Building! Quickly! He's going to make a time jump!

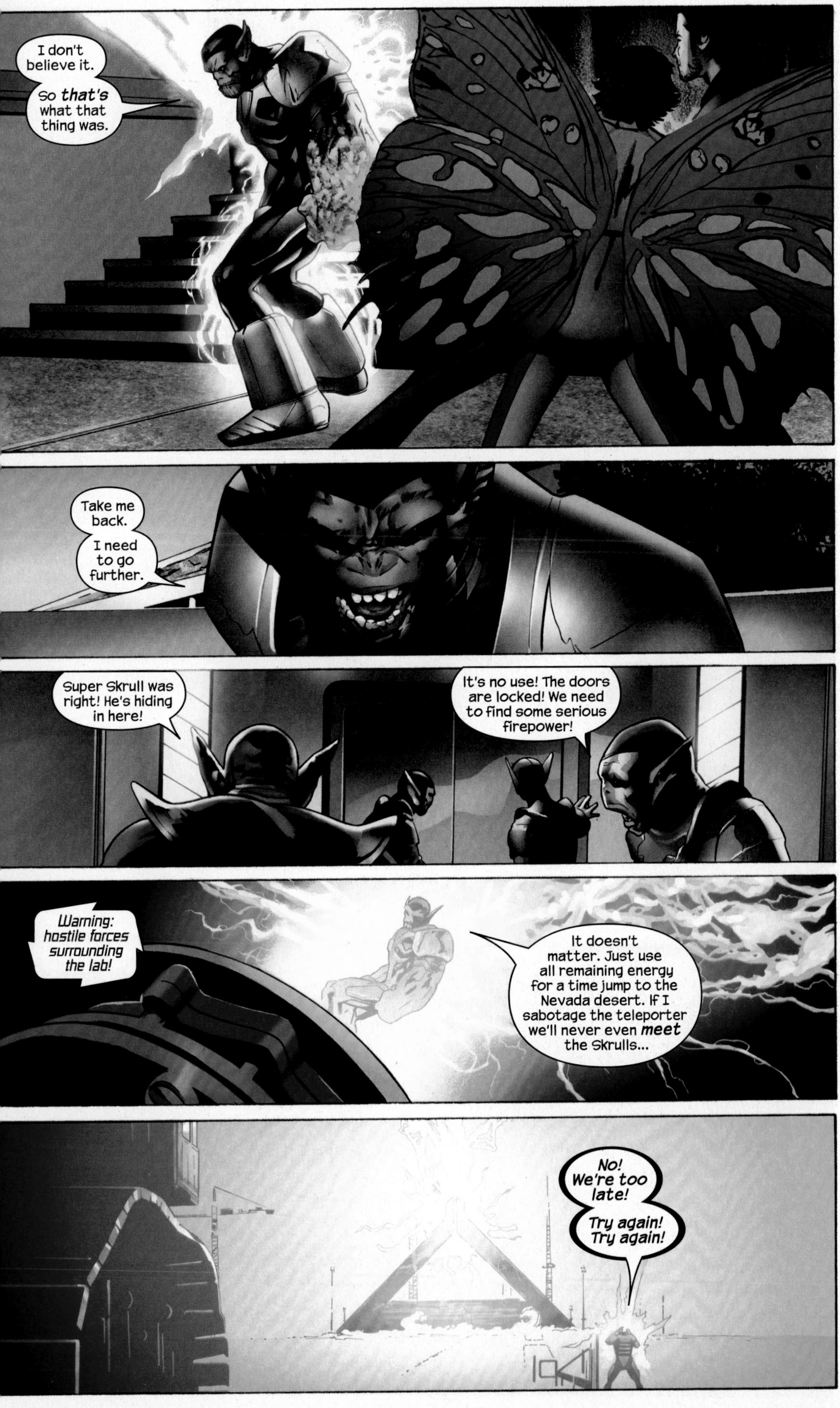
I don't believe it.
So *that's* what that thing was.
Take me back.
I need to go further.
Super Skrull was right! He's hiding in here!
It's no use! The doors are locked! We need to find some serious firepower!
Warning: hostile forces surrounding the lab!
It doesn't matter. Just use all remaining energy for a time jump to the Nevada desert. If I sabotage the teleporter we'll never even *meet* the Skrulls...
No! We're too late!
Try again! Try again!

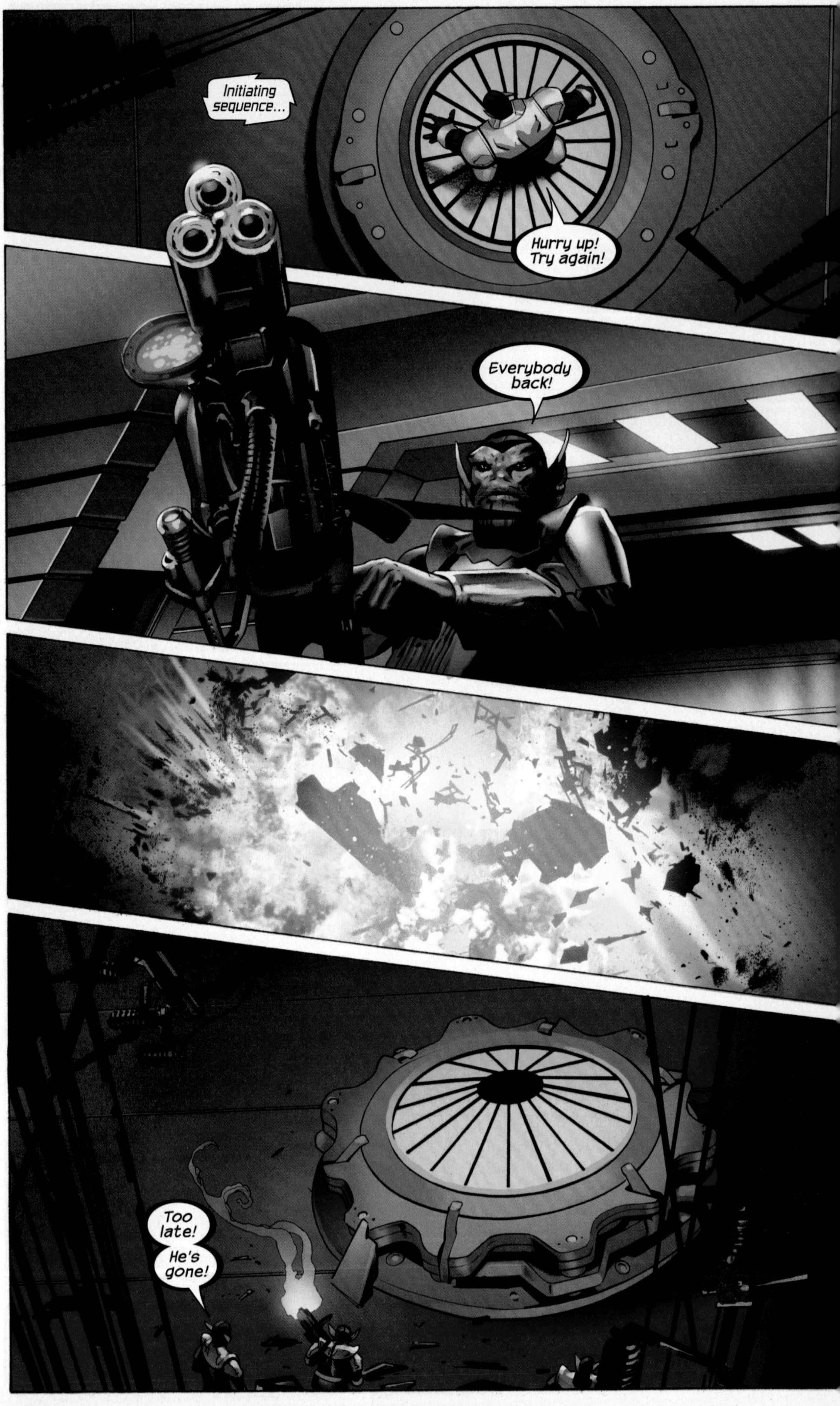

Initiating sequence...
Hurry up! Try again!
Everybody back!
Too late!
He's gone!

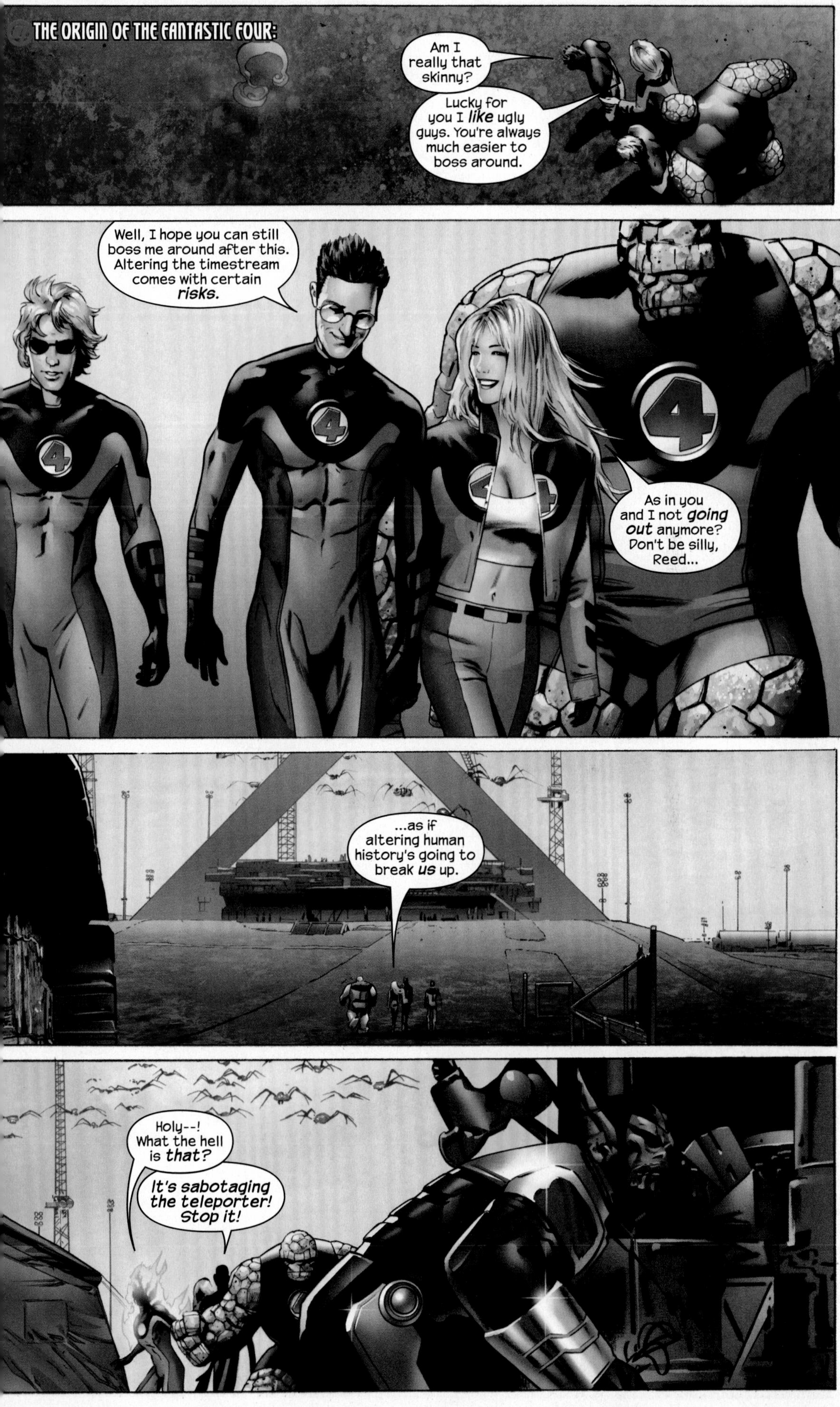
THE ORIGIN OF THE FANTASTIC FOUR:
Am I really that skinny?
Lucky for you I *like* ugly guys. You're always much easier to boss around.
Well, I hope you can still boss me around after this. Altering the timestream comes with certain *risks.*
As in you and I not *going out* anymore? Don't be silly, Reed...
...as if altering human history's going to break *us* up.
Holy--! What the hell is *that?*
It's sabotaging the teleporter! Stop it!

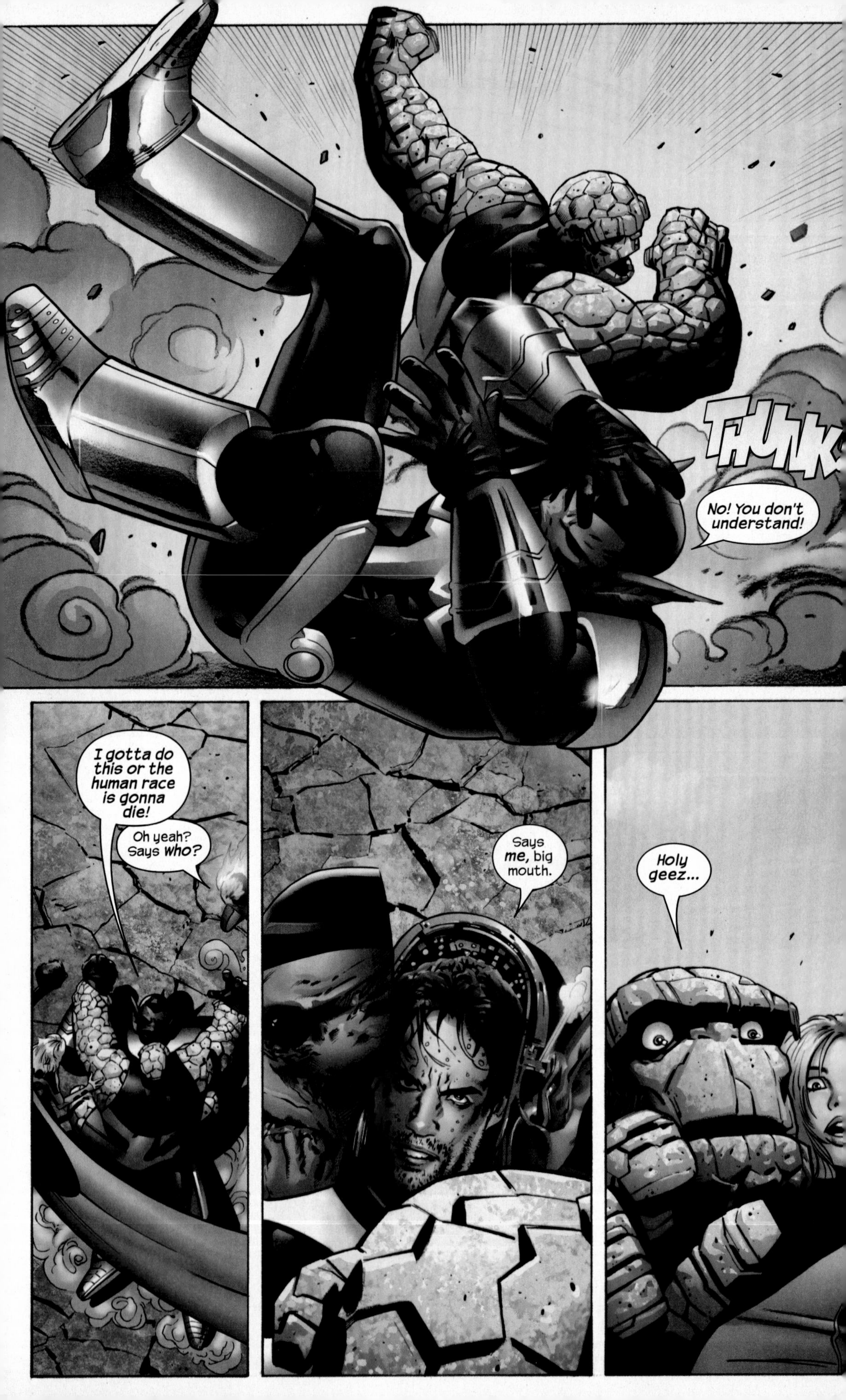
THUNK
No! You don't understand!
I gotta do this or the human race is gonna die!
Oh yeah? Says who?
Says me, big mouth.
Holy geez...

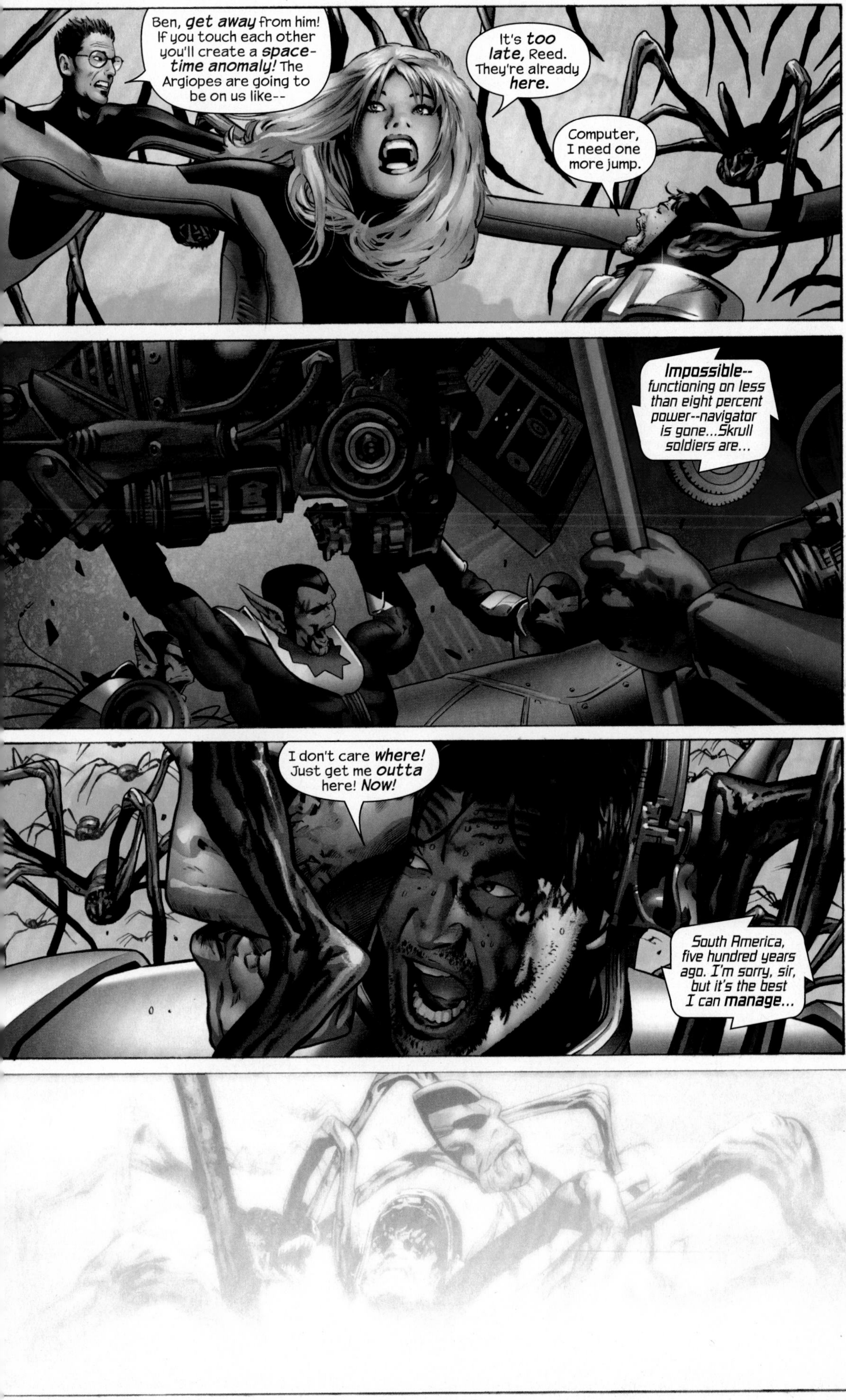
Ben, get away from him! If you touch each other you'll create a space-time anomaly! The Argiopes are going to be on us like--
It's too late, Reed. They're already here.
Computer, I need one more jump.
Impossible--functioning on less than eight percent power--navigator is gone...Skrull soldiers are...
I don't care where! Just get me outta here! Now!
South America, five hundred years ago. I'm sorry, sir, but it's the best I can manage...

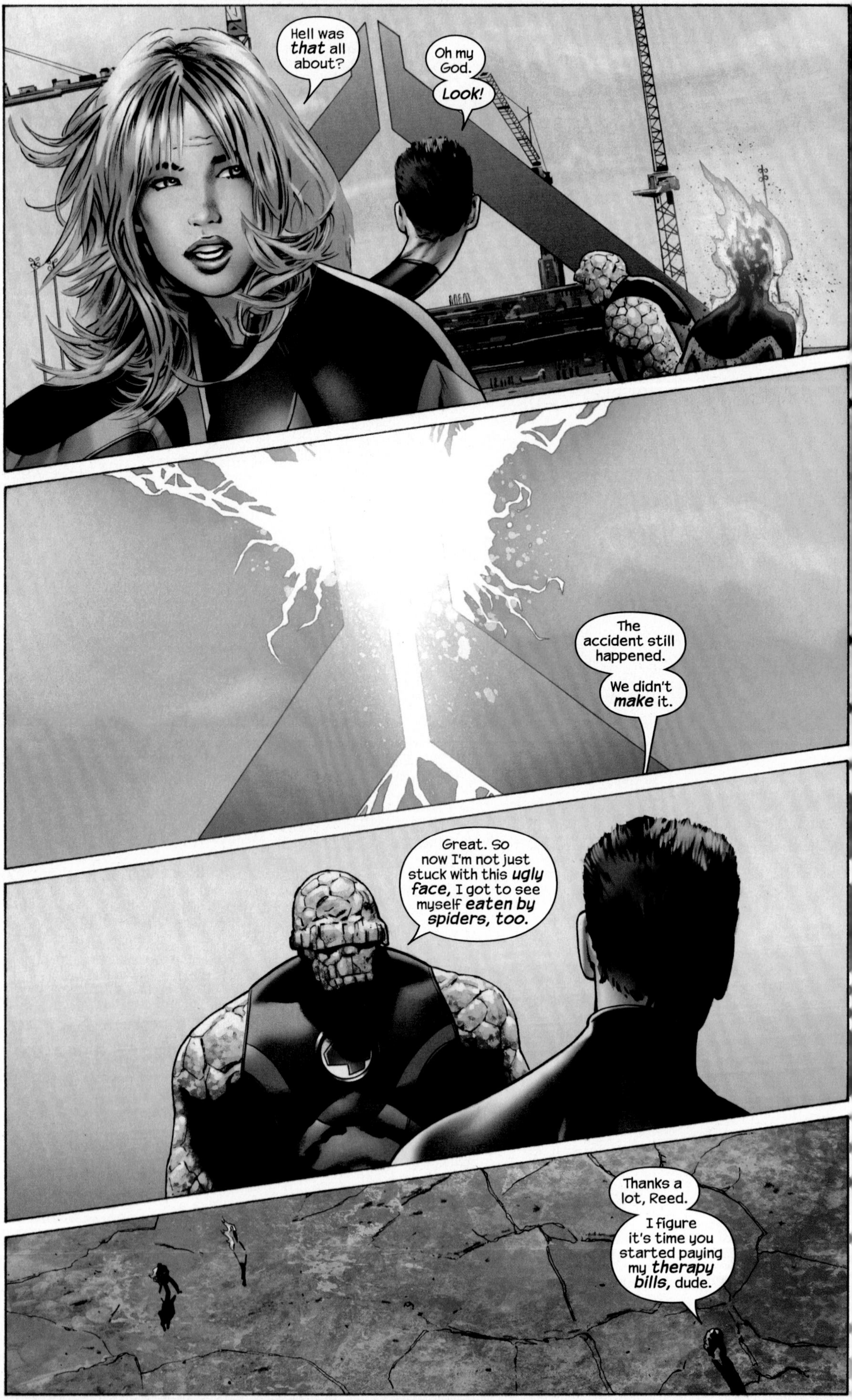
Hell was *that* all about?
Oh my God.
Look!
The accident still happened.
We didn't *make* it.
Great. So now I'm not just stuck with this *ugly face,* I got to see myself *eaten by spiders, too.*
Thanks a lot, Reed.
I figure it's time you started paying my *therapy bills,* dude.

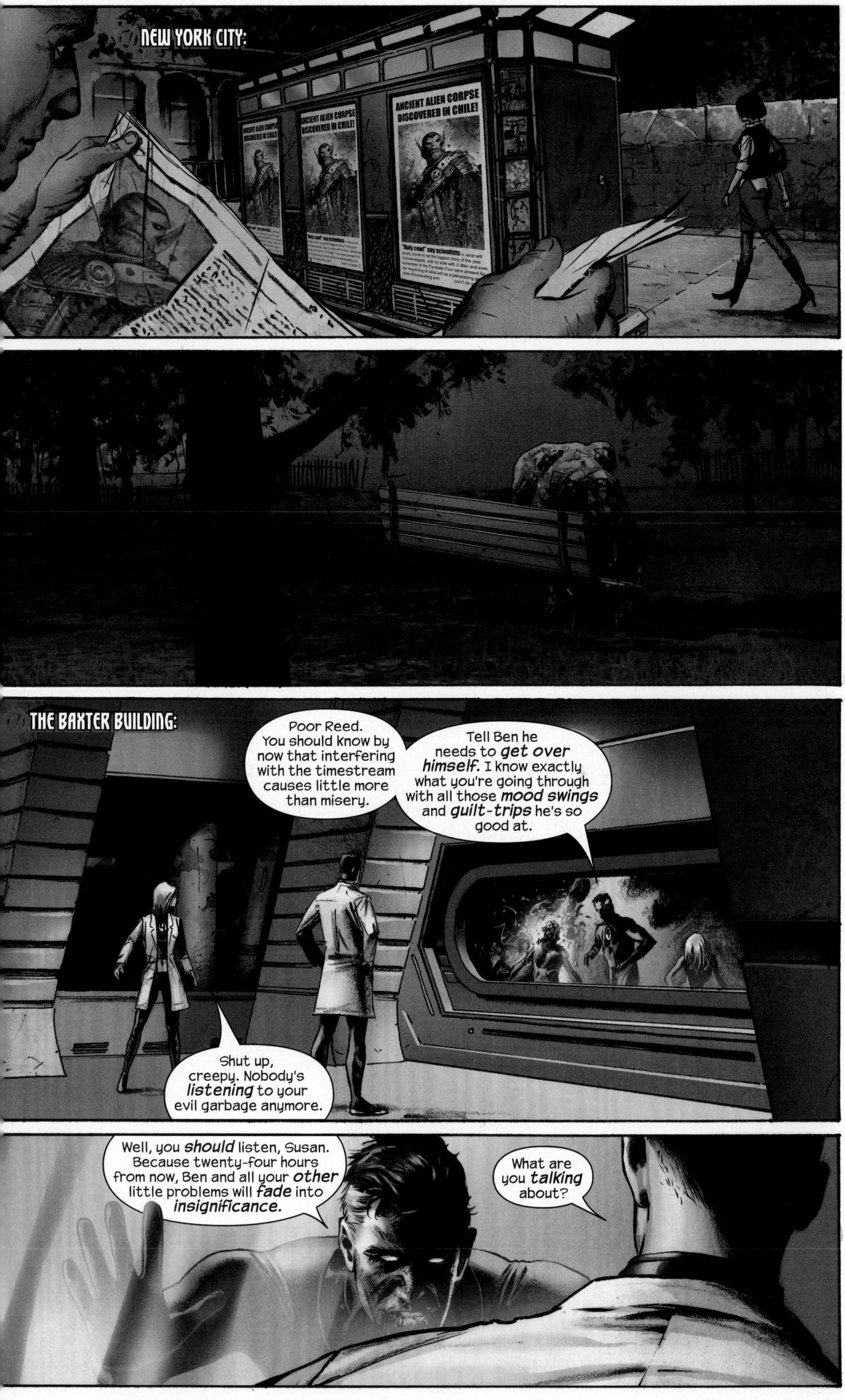
NEW YORK CITY:
ANCIENT ALIEN CORPSE DISCOVERED IN CHILE!
THE BAXTER BUILDING:
Poor Reed. You should know by now that interfering with the timestream causes little more than misery.
Tell Ben he needs to get over himself. I know exactly what you're going through with all those mood swings and guilt-trips he's so good at.
Shut up, creepy. Nobody's listening to your evil garbage anymore.
Well, you should listen, Susan. Because twenty-four hours from now, Ben and all your other little problems will fade into insignificance.
What are you talking about?

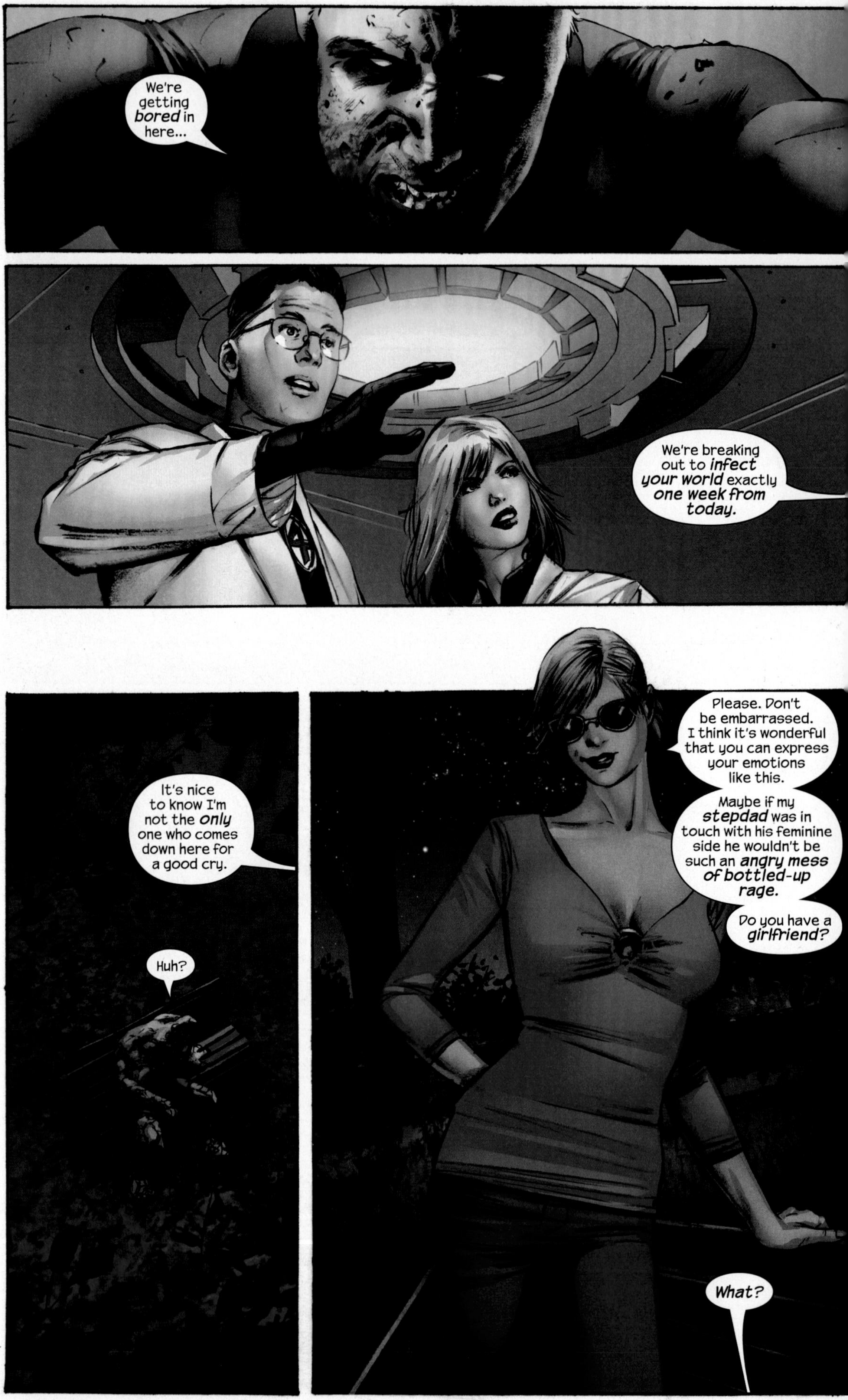
We're getting *bored* in here...
We're breaking out to *infect your world* exactly *one week from today.*
It's nice to know I'm not the *only* one who comes down here for a good cry.
Huh?
Please. Don't be embarrassed. I think it's wonderful that you can express your emotions like this.
Maybe if my *stepdad* was in touch with his feminine side he wouldn't be such an *angry mess of bottled-up rage.*
Do you have a *girlfriend?*
What?

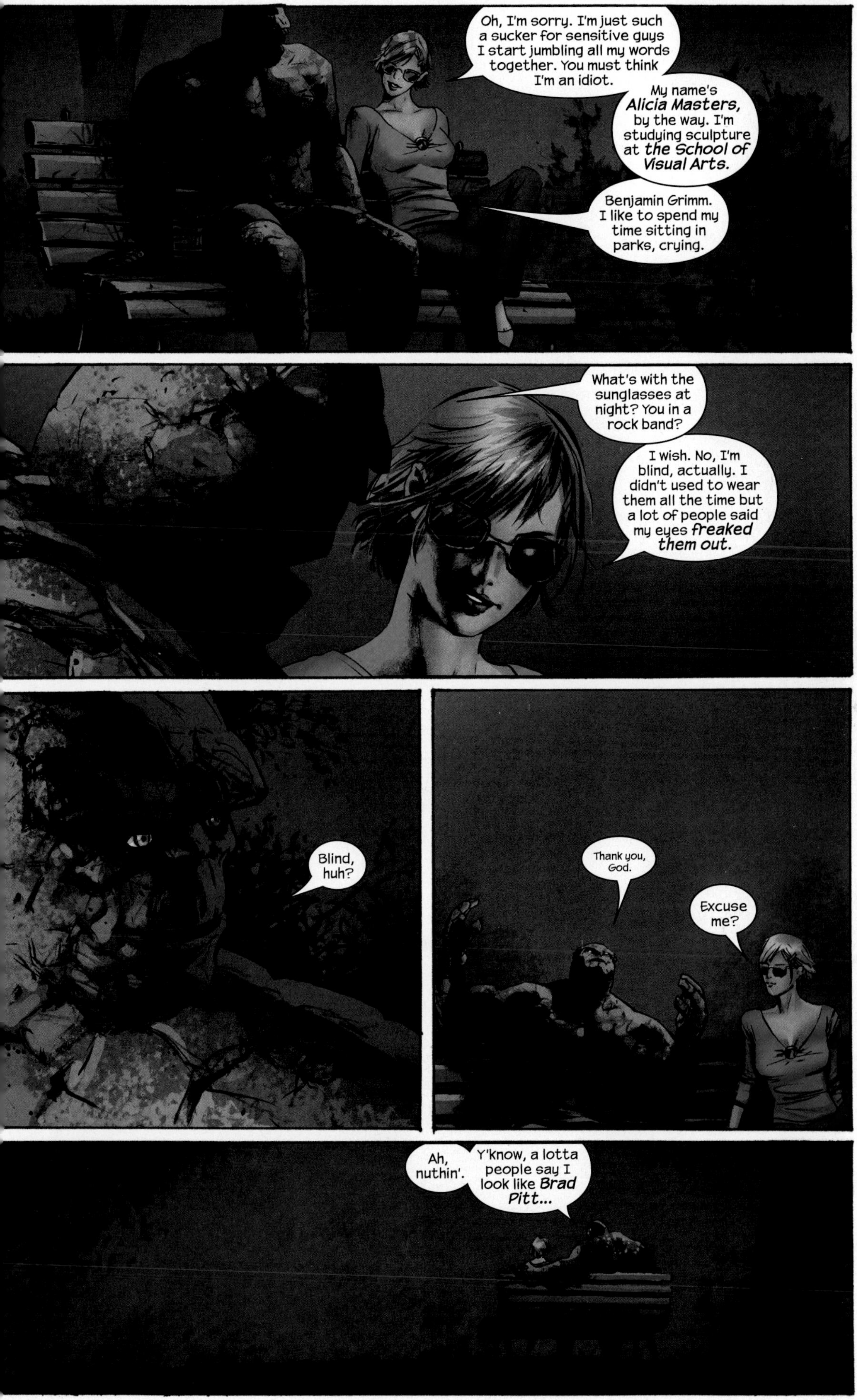
Oh, I'm sorry. I'm just such a sucker for sensitive guys I start jumbling all my words together. You must think I'm an idiot.
My name's *Alicia Masters,* by the way. I'm studying sculpture at *the School of Visual Arts.*
Benjamin Grimm. I like to spend my time sitting in parks, crying.
What's with the sunglasses at night? You in a rock band?
I wish. No, I'm blind, actually. I didn't used to wear them all the time but a lot of people said my eyes *freaked them out.*
Blind, huh?
Thank you, God.
Excuse me?
Ah, nuthin'.
Y'know, a lotta people say I look like *Brad Pitt...*

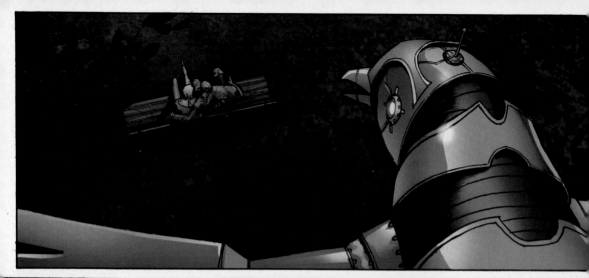

LATVERIA:

The Thing has found a mate? How amusing.

One more corpse for the pile, I suppose.

The plan begins tomorrow.

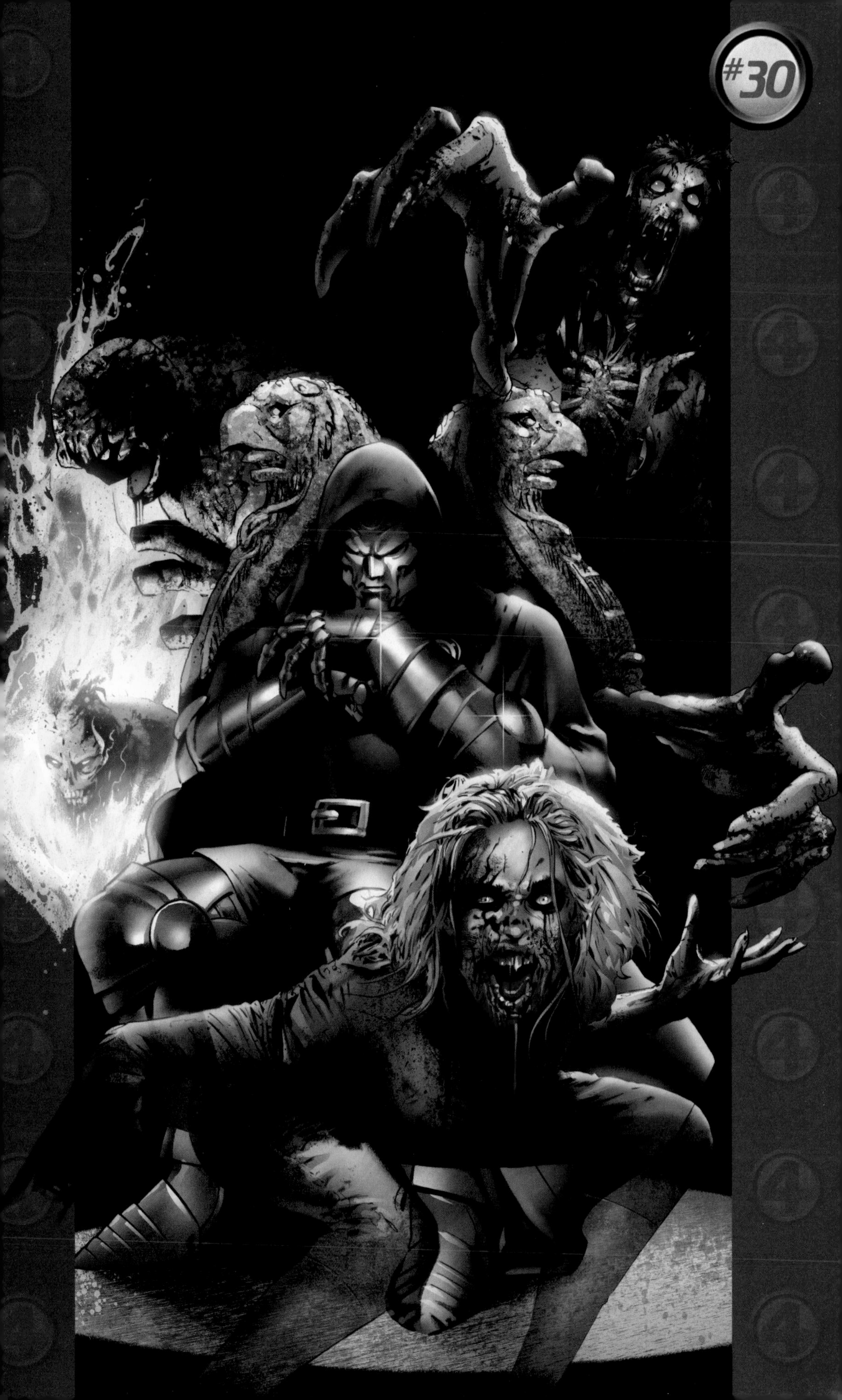
#30

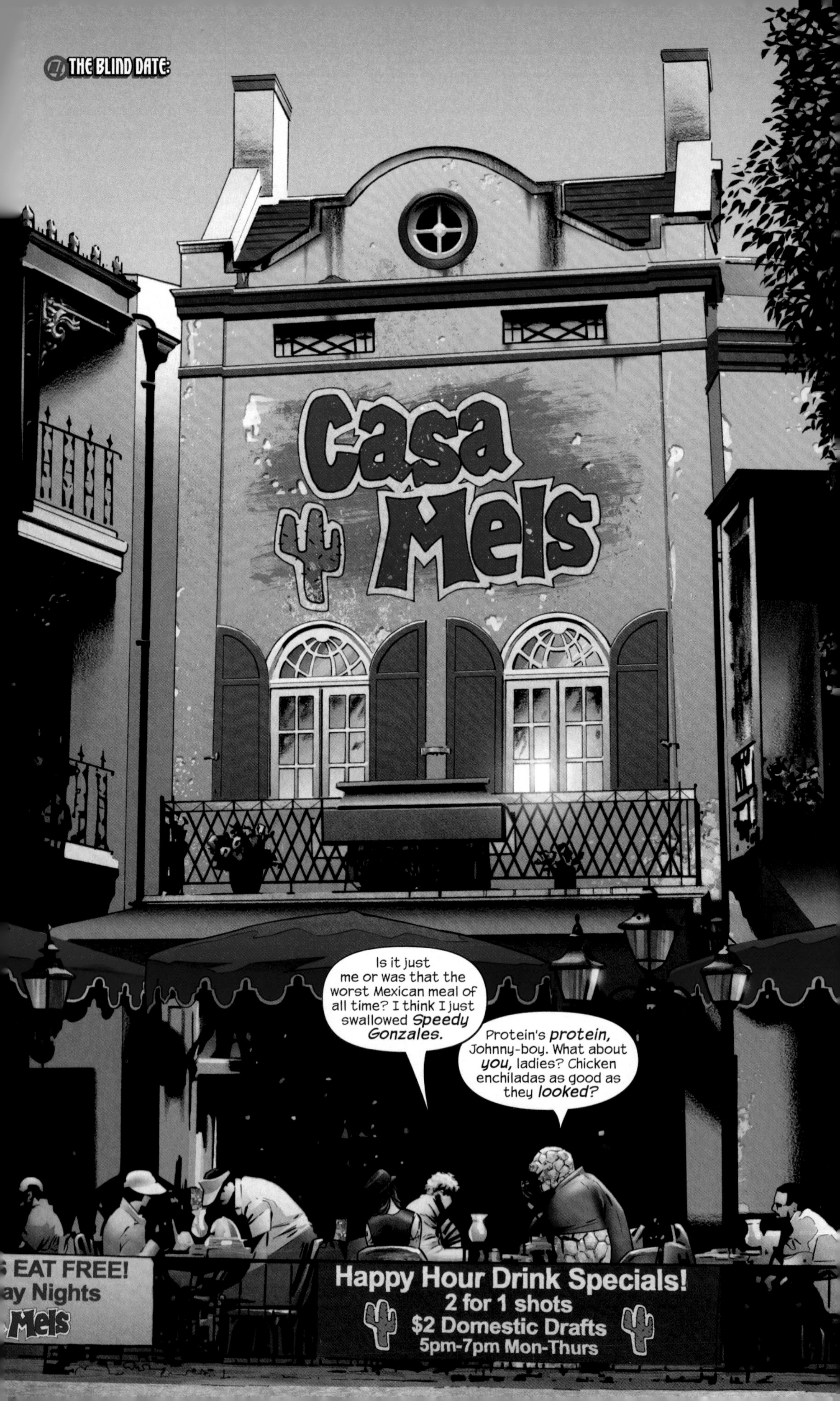
THE BLIND DATE:
Casa Mels
Is it just me or was that the worst Mexican meal of all time? I think I just swallowed *Speedy Gonzales.*
Protein's **protein,** Johnny-boy. What about **you,** ladies? Chicken enchiladas as good as they *looked?*
S EAT FREE!
ay Nights
Mels
Happy Hour Drink Specials!
2 for 1 shots
$2 Domestic Drafts
5pm-7pm Mon-Thurs

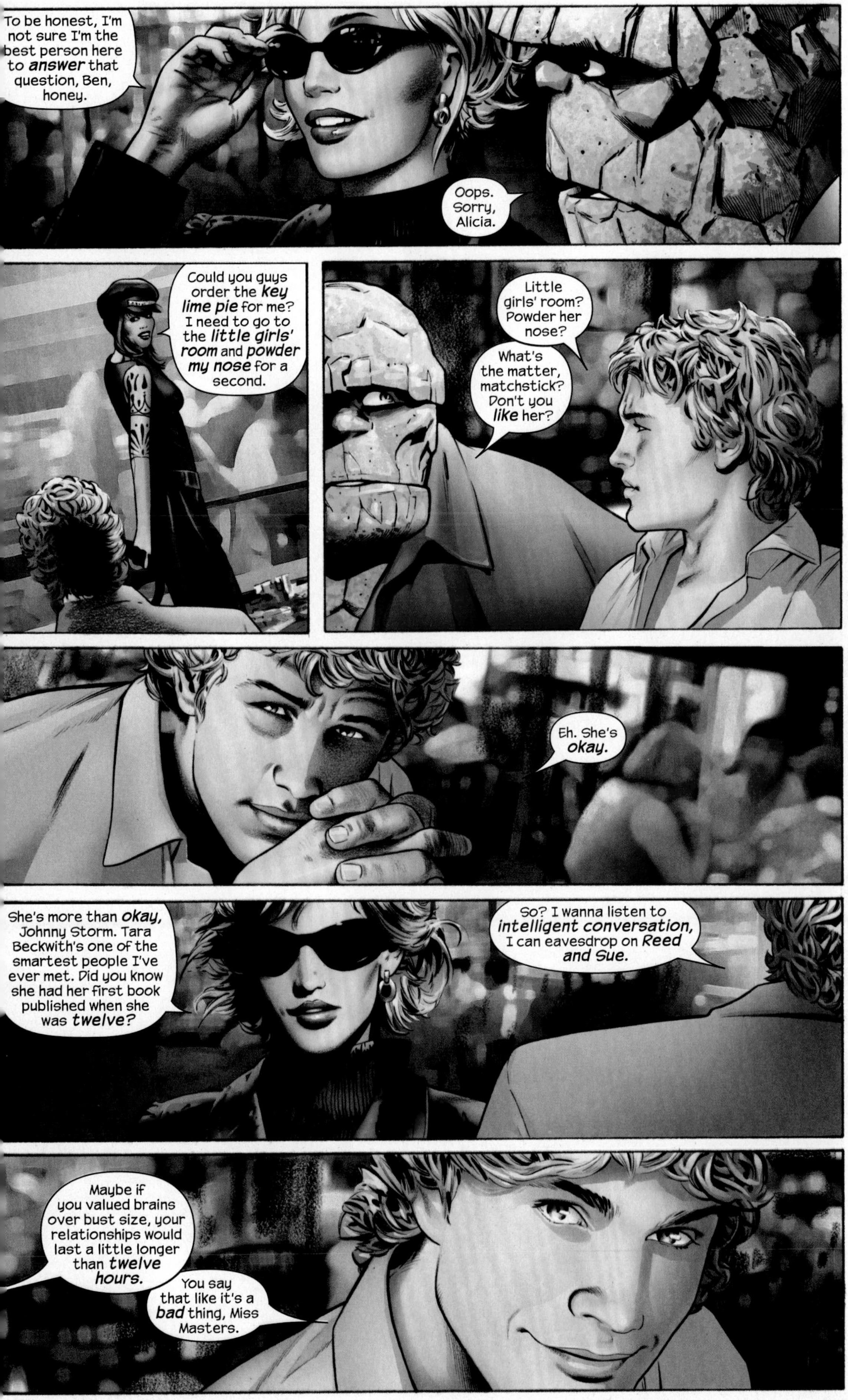
To be honest, I'm not sure I'm the best person here to answer that question, Ben, honey.
Oops. Sorry, Alicia.
Could you guys order the key lime pie for me? I need to go to the little girls' room and powder my nose for a second.
Little girls' room? Powder her nose?
What's the matter, matchstick? Don't you like her?
Eh. She's okay.
She's more than okay, Johnny Storm. Tara Beckwith's one of the smartest people I've ever met. Did you know she had her first book published when she was twelve?
So? I wanna listen to intelligent conversation, I can eavesdrop on Reed and Sue.
Maybe if you valued brains over bust size, your relationships would last a little longer than twelve hours.
You say that like it's a bad thing, Miss Masters.

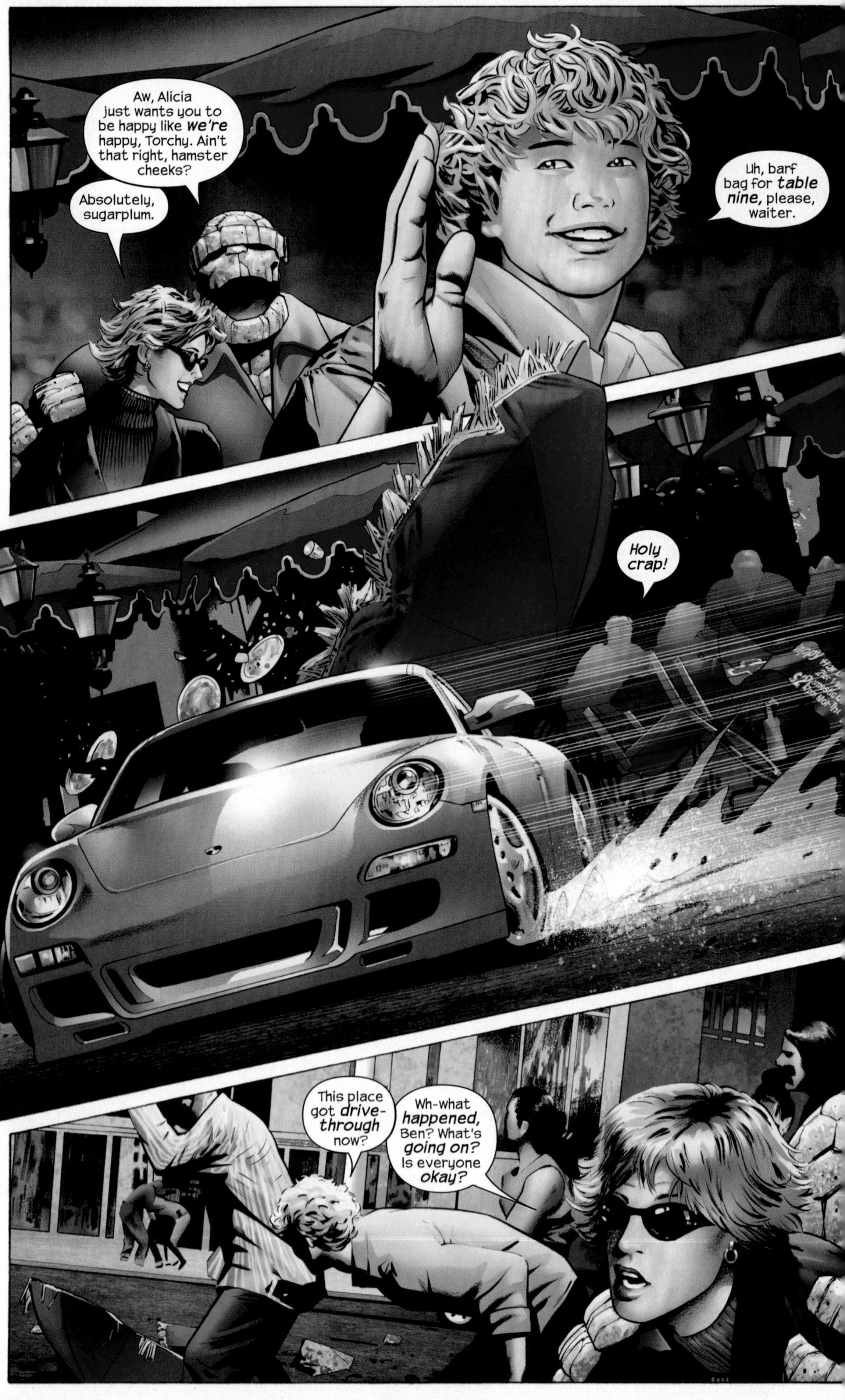

Aw, Alicia just wants you to be happy like we're happy, Torchy. Ain't that right, hamster cheeks?
Absolutely, sugarplum.
Uh, barf bag for table nine, please, waiter.
Holy crap!
This place got drive-through now?
Wh-what happened, Ben? What's going on? Is everyone okay?

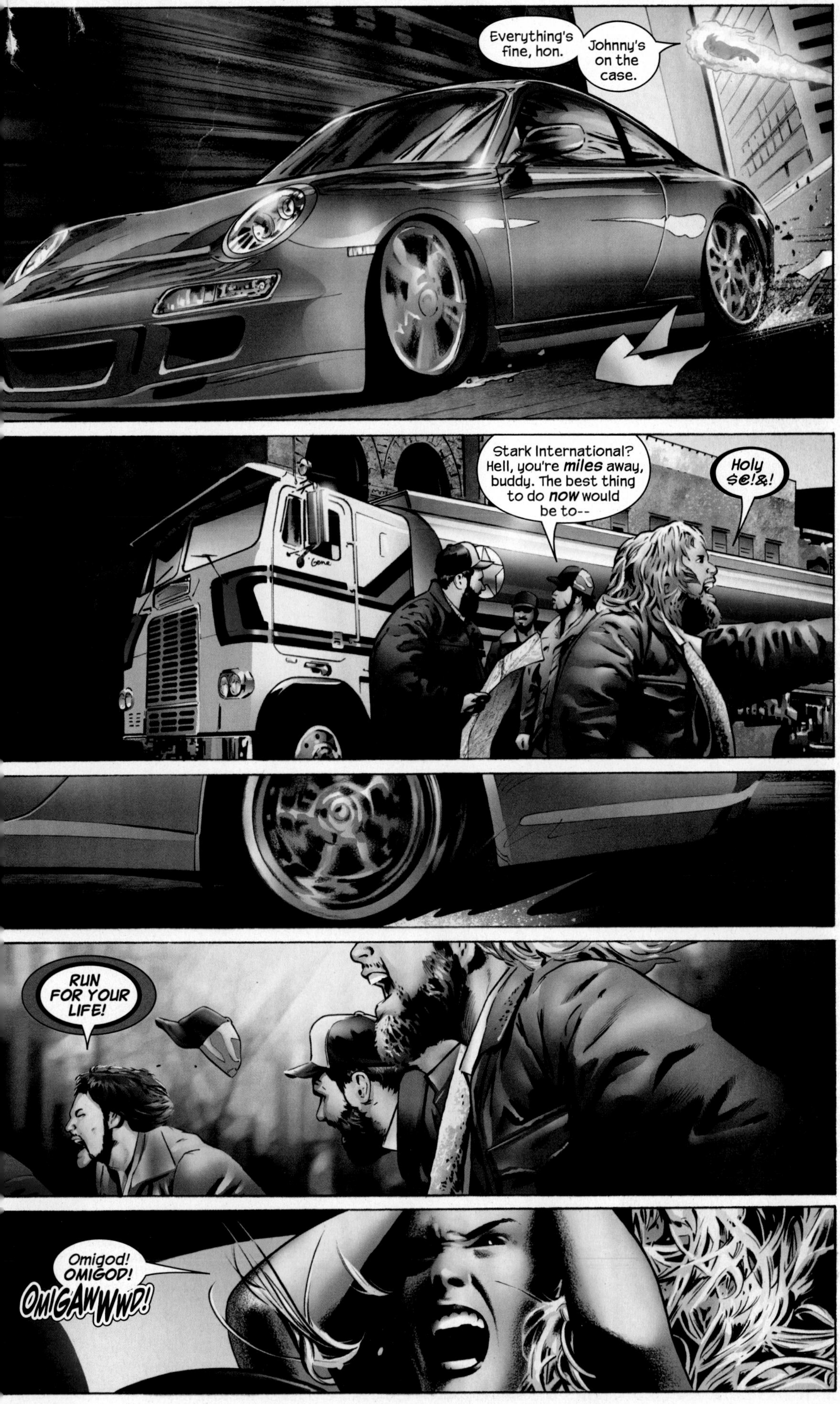

Everything's fine, hon.
Johnny's on the case.
Stark International? Hell, you're miles away, buddy. The best thing to do NOW would be to--
Holy $@!&!
RUN FOR YOUR LIFE!
Omigod! OMIGOD!
OMIGAWWWD!

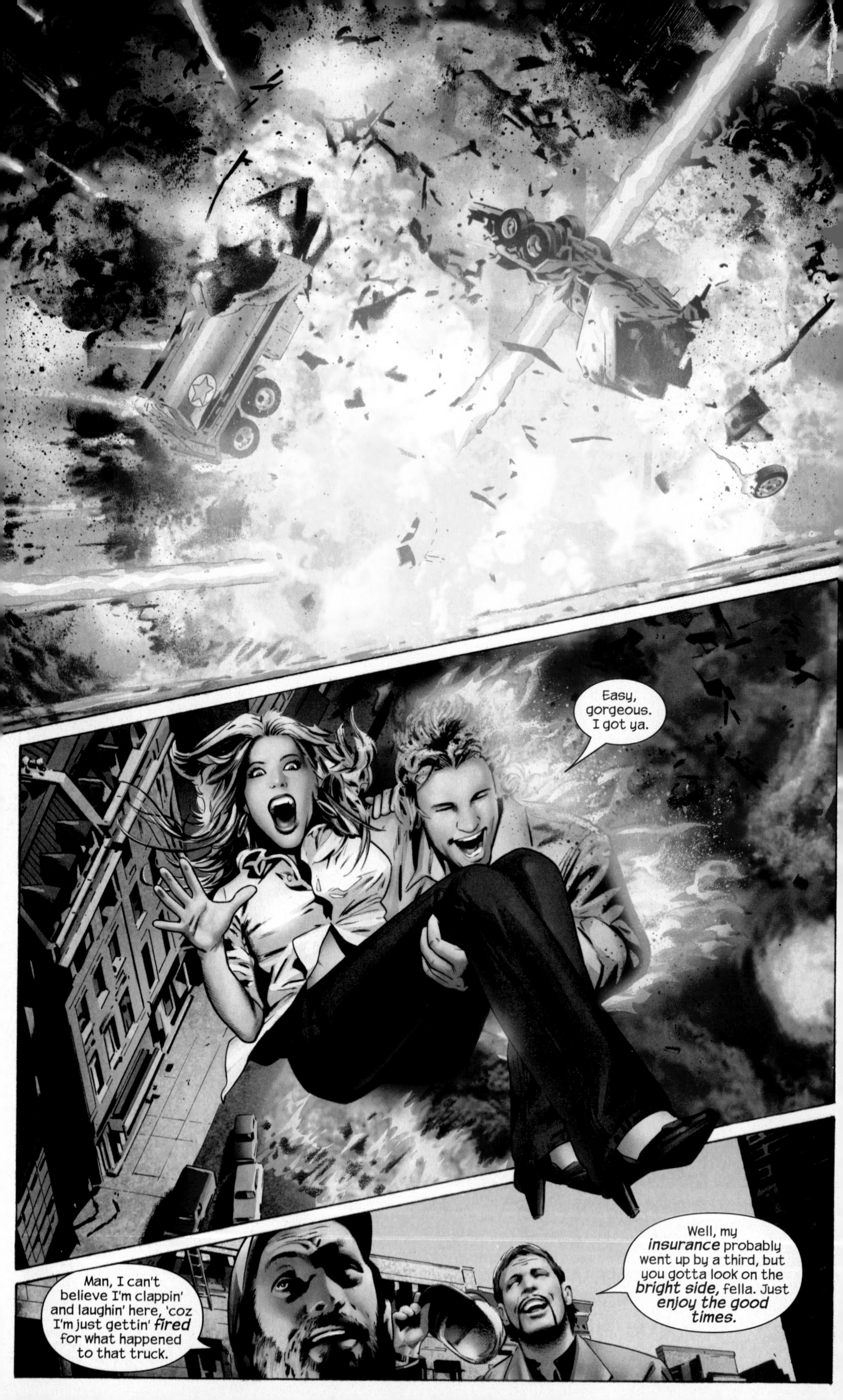
Easy, gorgeous. I got ya.
Man, I can't believe I'm clappin' and laughin' here, 'coz I'm just gettin' *fired* for what happened to that truck.
Well, my *insurance* probably went up by a third, but you gotta look on the *bright side,* fella. Just *enjoy the good times.*

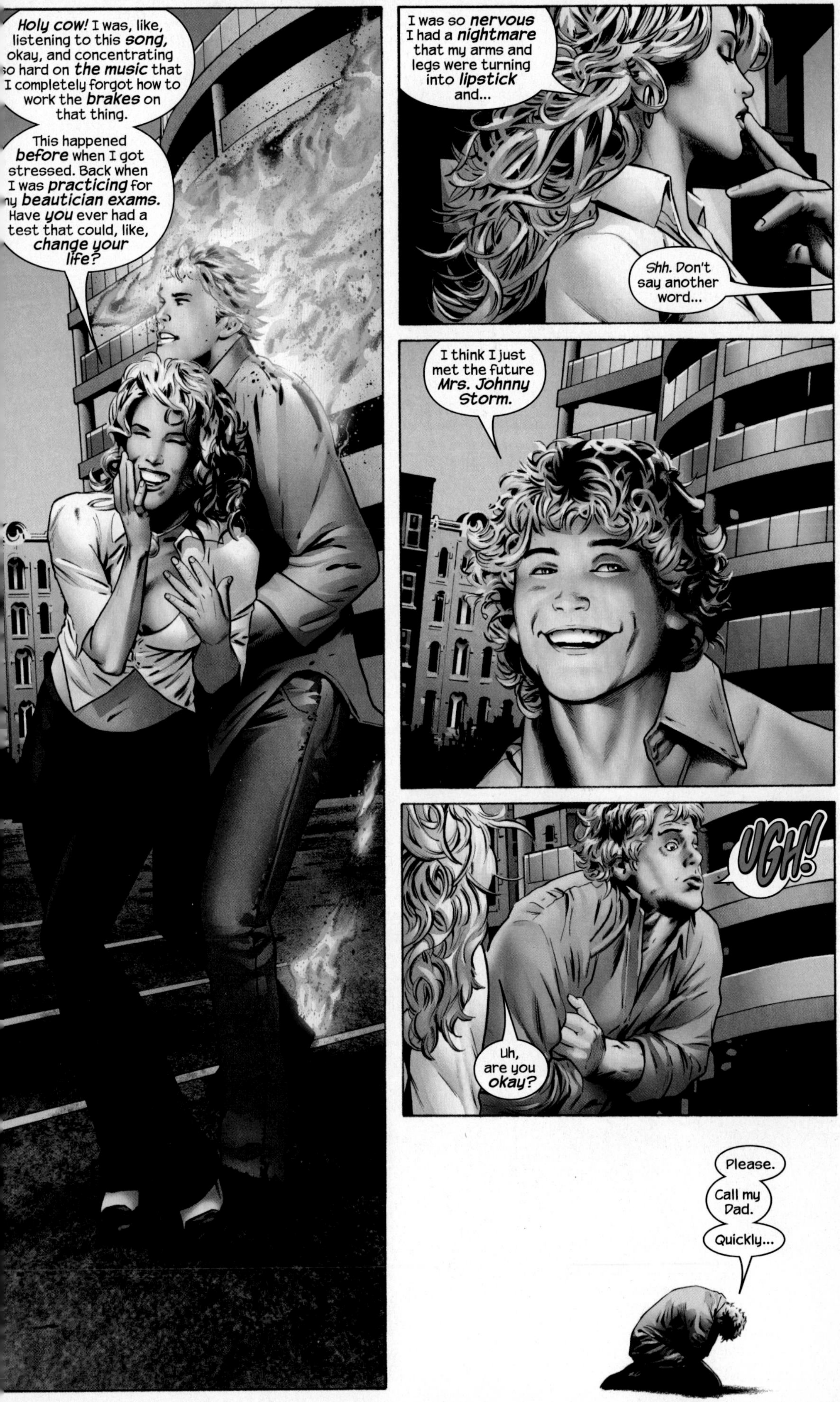
Holy cow! I was, like, listening to this song, okay, and concentrating so hard on the music that I completely forgot how to work the brakes on that thing.
This happened before when I got stressed. Back when I was practicing for my beautician exams. Have you ever had a test that could, like, change your life?
I was so nervous I had a nightmare that my arms and legs were turning into lipstick and...
Shh. Don't say another word...
I think I just met the future Mrs. Johnny Storm.
UGH!
Uh, are you okay?
Please.
Call my Dad.
Quickly...

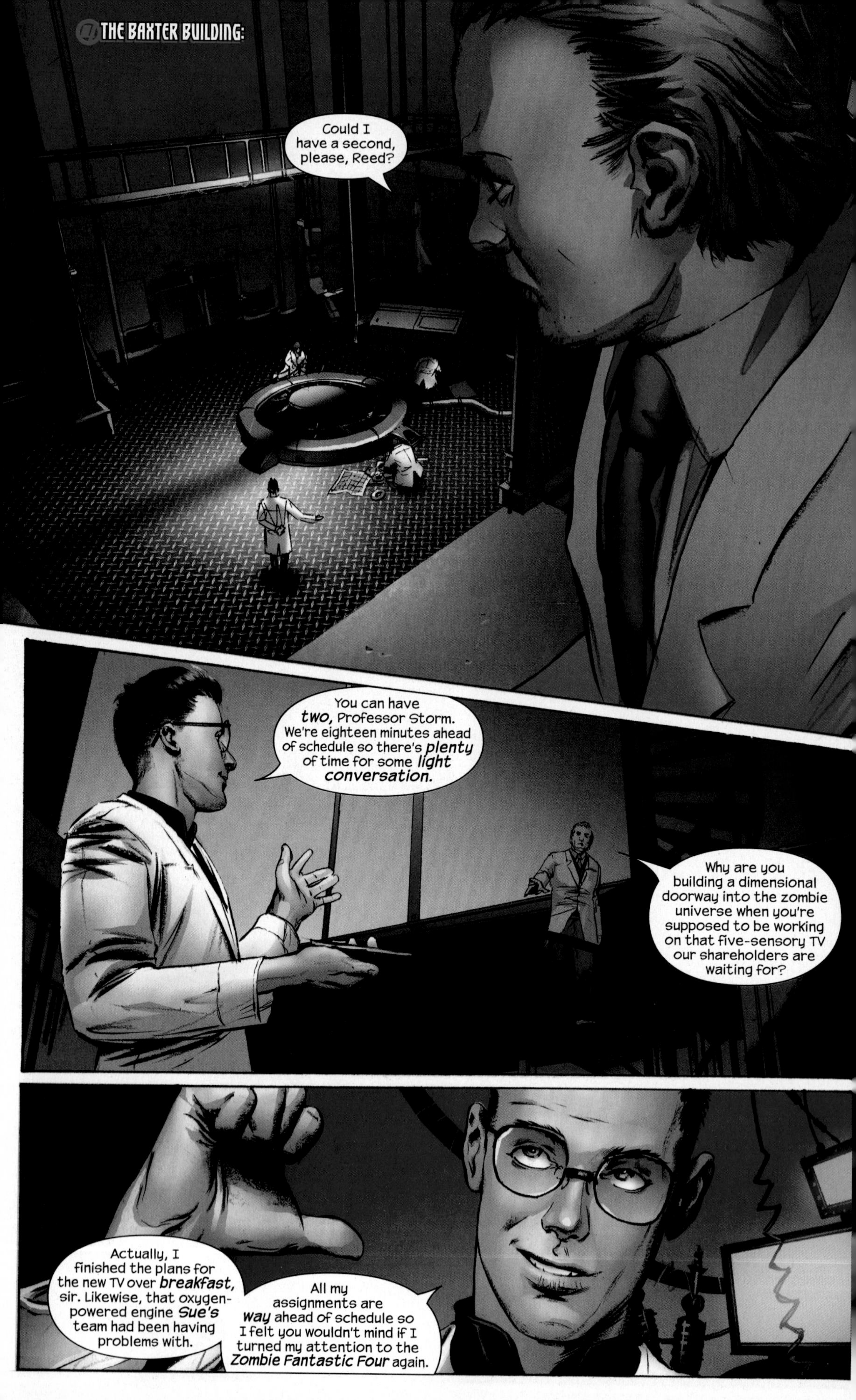
THE BAXTER BUILDING:
Could I have a second, please, Reed?
You can have two, Professor Storm. We're eighteen minutes ahead of schedule so there's plenty of time for some light conversation.
Why are you building a dimensional doorway into the zombie universe when you're supposed to be working on that five-sensory TV our shareholders are waiting for?
Actually, I finished the plans for the new TV over breakfast, sir. Likewise, that oxygen-powered engine Sue's team had been having problems with.
All my assignments are way ahead of schedule so I felt you wouldn't mind if I turned my attention to the Zombie Fantastic Four again.

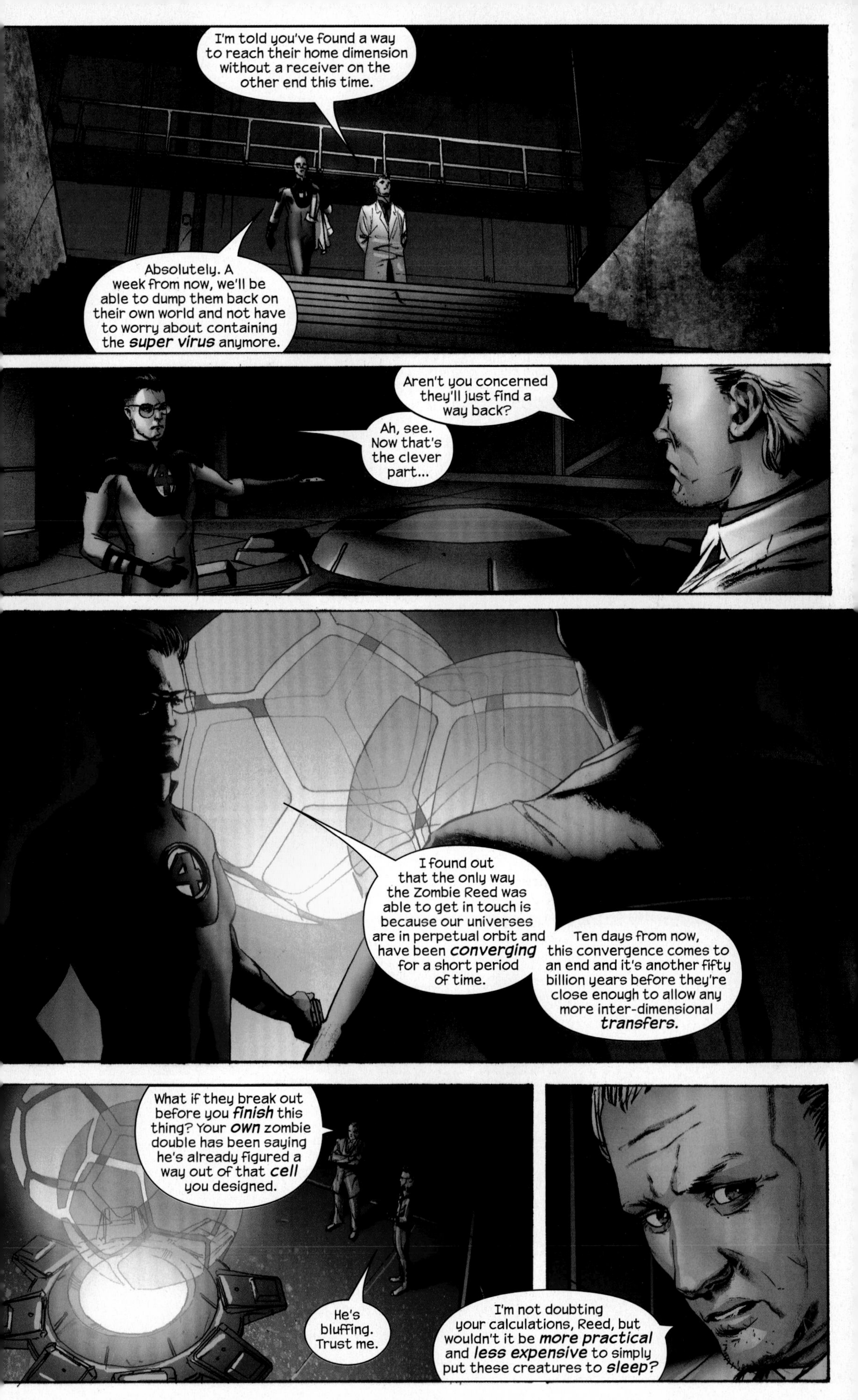
I'm told you've found a way to reach their home dimension without a receiver on the other end this time.
Absolutely. A week from now, we'll be able to dump them back on their own world and not have to worry about containing the super virus anymore.
Aren't you concerned they'll just find a way back?
Ah, see. Now that's the clever part...
I found out that the only way the Zombie Reed was able to get in touch is because our universes are in perpetual orbit and have been converging for a short period of time.
Ten days from now, this convergence comes to an end and it's another fifty billion years before they're close enough to allow any more inter-dimensional transfers.
What if they break out before you finish this thing? Your own zombie double has been saying he's already figured a way out of that cell you designed.
He's bluffing. Trust me.
I'm not doubting your calculations, Reed, but wouldn't it be more practical and less expensive to simply put these creatures to sleep?

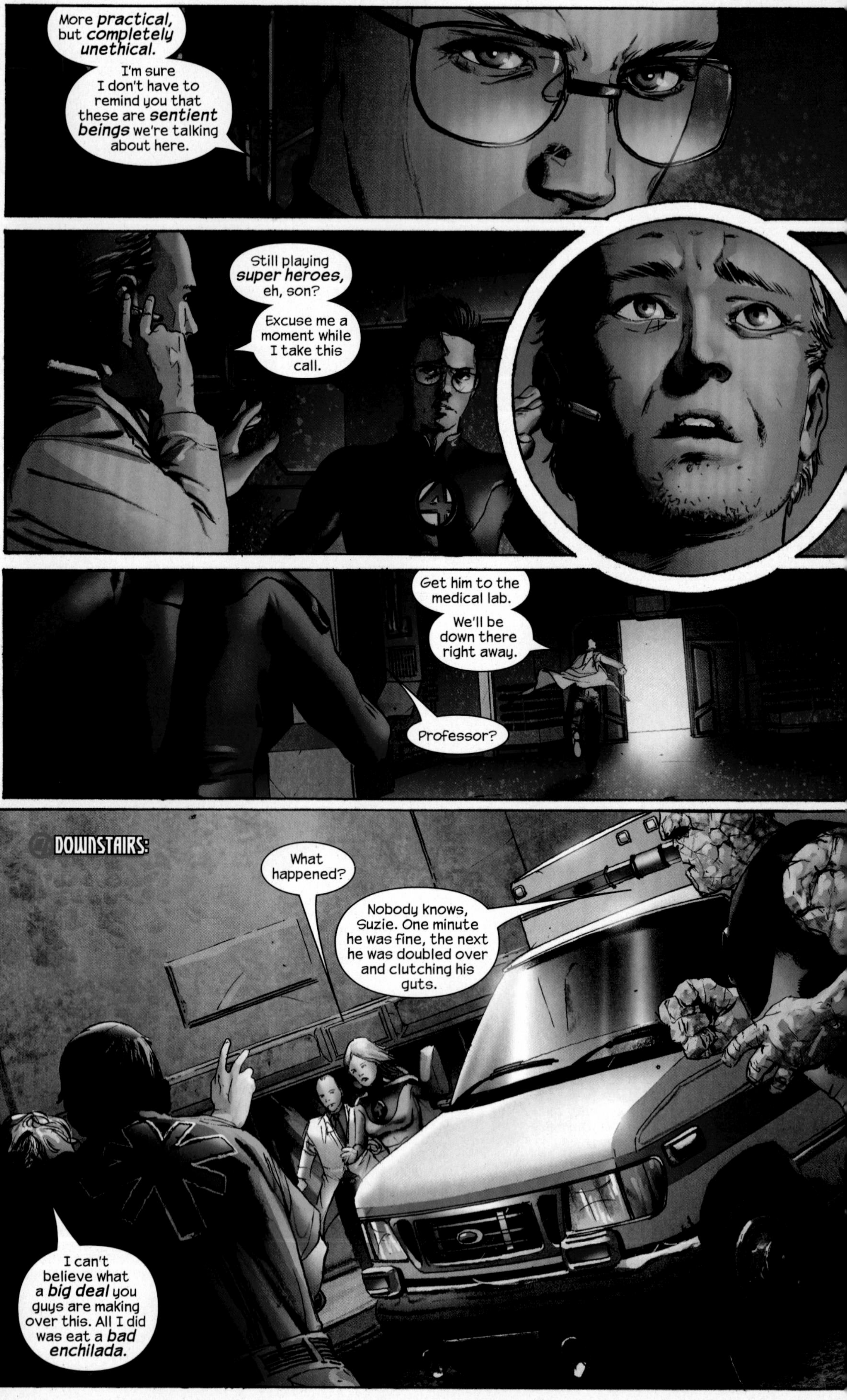
More practical, but completely unethical.
I'm sure I don't have to remind you that these are sentient beings we're talking about here.
Still playing super heroes, eh, son?
Excuse me a moment while I take this call.
Get him to the medical lab.
We'll be down there right away.
Professor?
DOWNSTAIRS:
What happened?
Nobody knows, Suzie. One minute he was fine, the next he was doubled over and clutching his guts.
I can't believe what a big deal you guys are making over this. All I did was eat a bad enchilada.

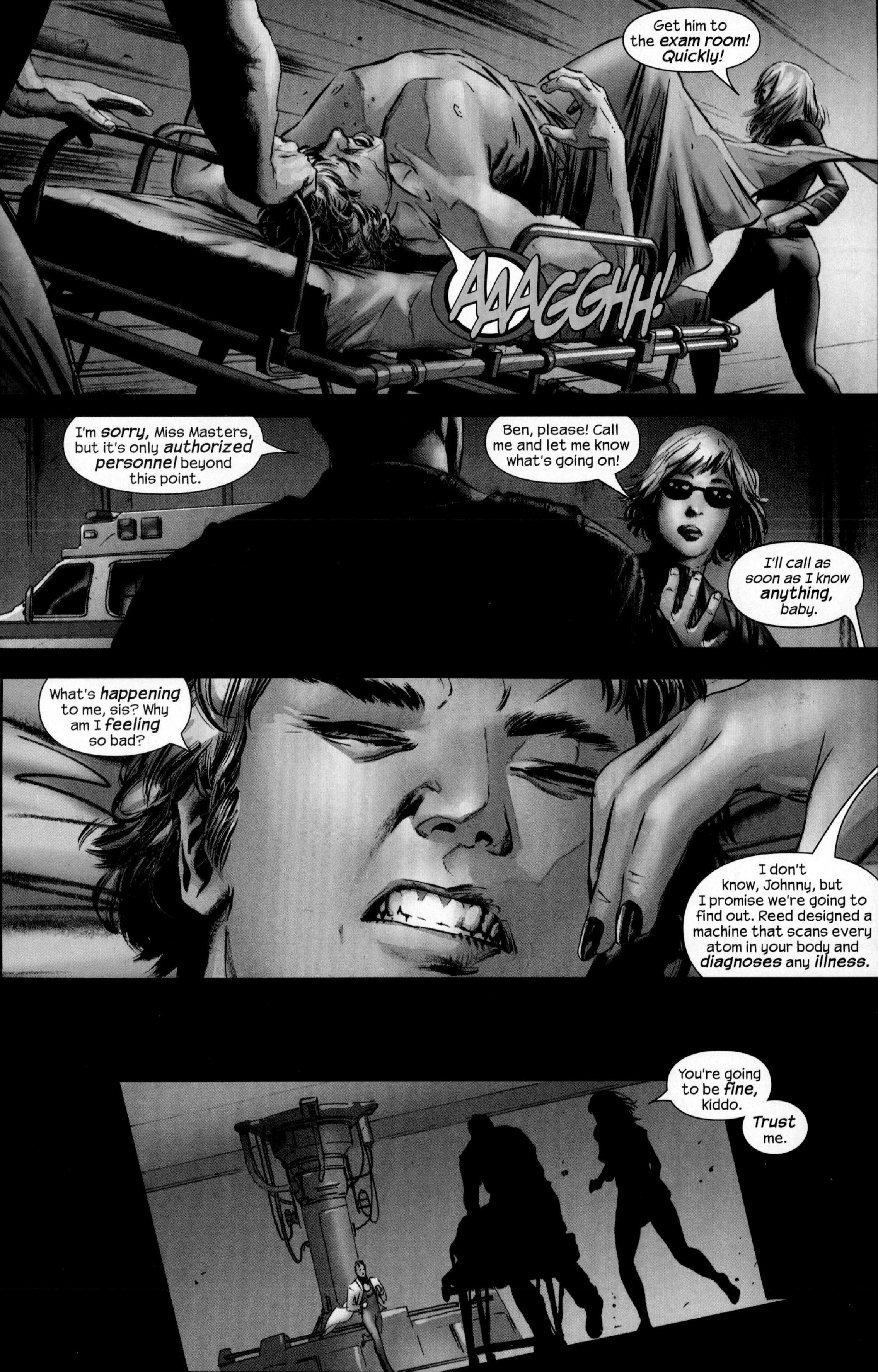
Get him to the exam room! Quickly!
AAAGGHH!
I'm sorry, Miss Masters, but it's only authorized personnel beyond this point.
Ben, please! Call me and let me know what's going on!
I'll call as soon as I know anything, baby.
What's happening to me, sis? Why am I feeling so bad?
I don't know, Johnny, but I promise we're going to find out. Reed designed a machine that scans every atom in your body and diagnoses any illness.
You're going to be fine, kiddo.
Trust me.

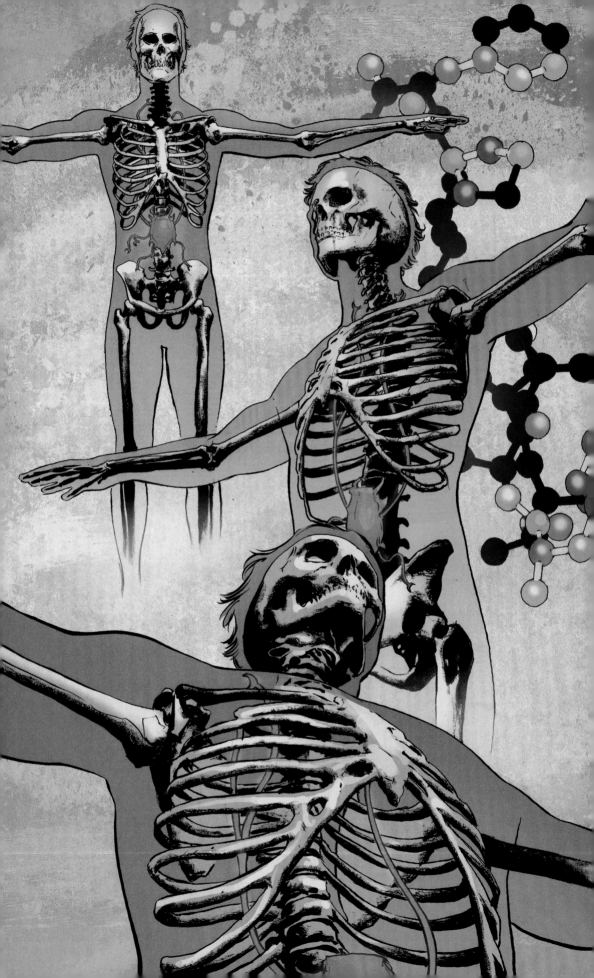

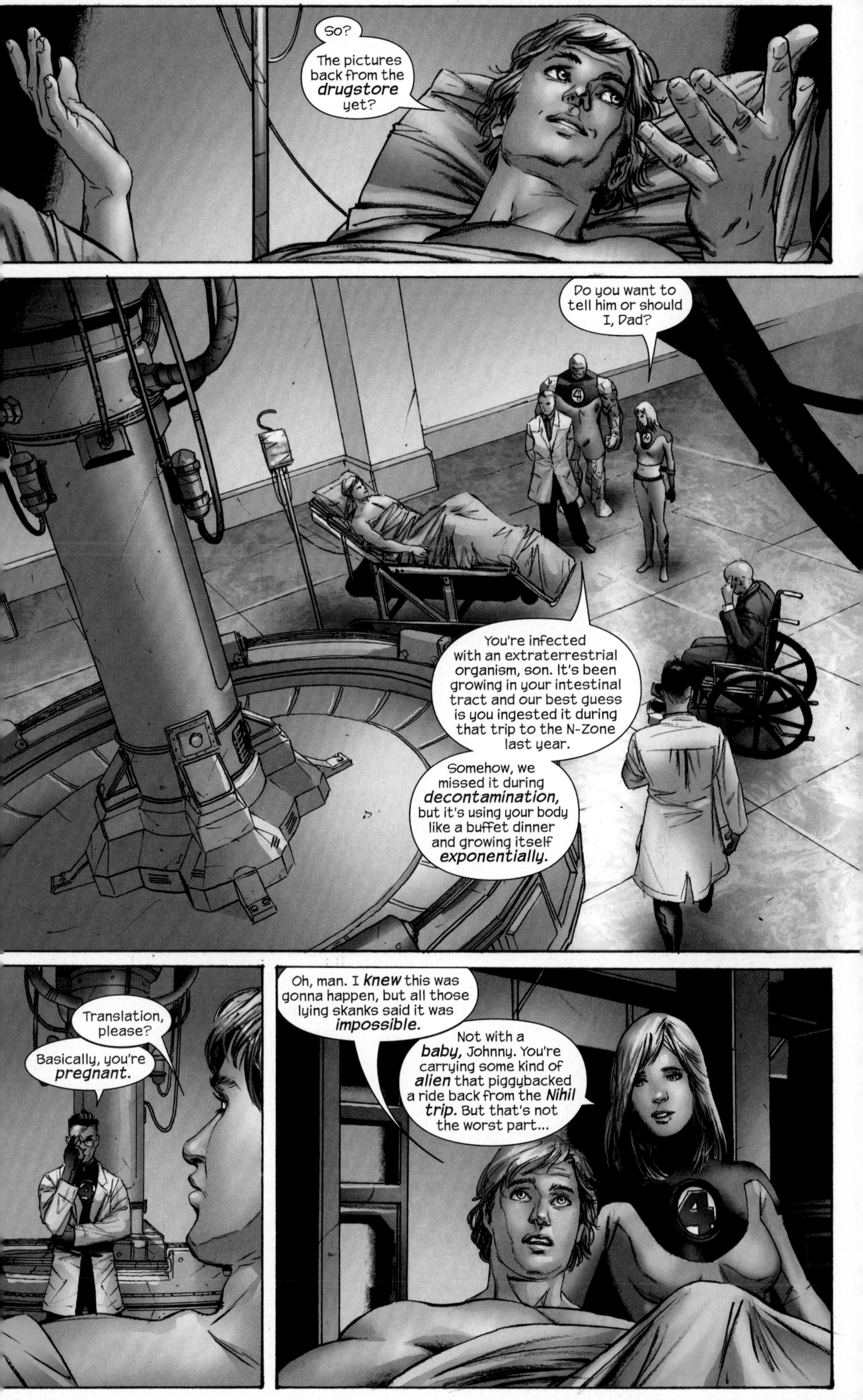

So?
The pictures back from the *drugstore* yet?
Do you want to tell him or should I, Dad?
You're infected with an extraterrestrial organism, son. It's been growing in your intestinal tract and our best guess is you ingested it during that trip to the N-Zone last year.
Somehow, we missed it during *decontamination,* but it's using your body like a buffet dinner and growing itself *exponentially.*
Translation, please?
Basically, you're *pregnant.*
Oh, man. I *knew* this was gonna happen, but all those lying skanks said it was *impossible.*
Not with a *baby,* Johnny. You're carrying some kind of *alien* that piggybacked a ride back from the *Nihil trip.* But that's not the worst part...

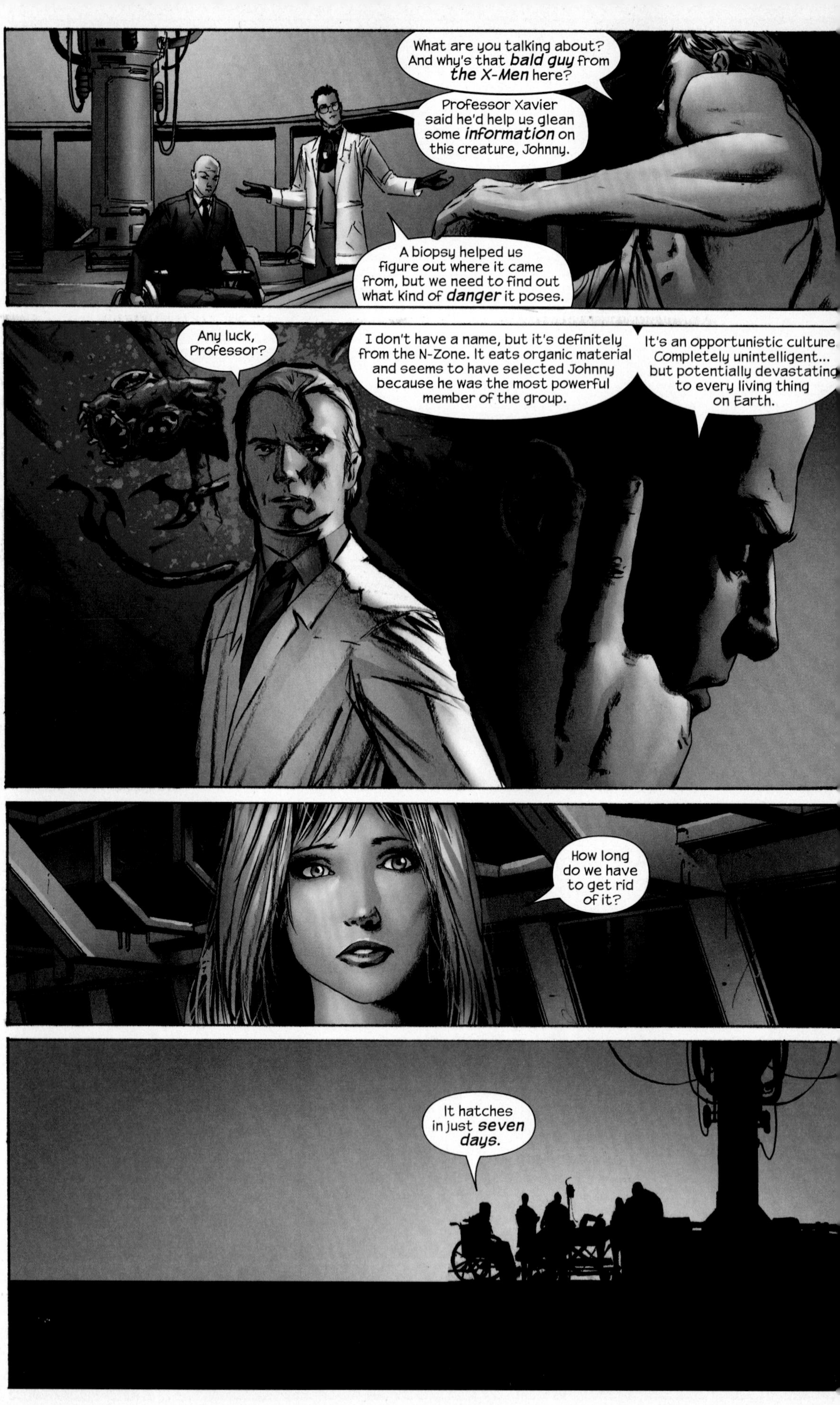
What are you talking about? And why's that *bald guy* from *the X-Men* here?
Professor Xavier said he'd help us glean some *information* on this creature, Johnny.
A biopsy helped us figure out where it came from, but we need to find out what kind of *danger* it poses.
Any luck, Professor?
I don't have a name, but it's definitely from the N-Zone. It eats organic material and seems to have selected Johnny because he was the most powerful member of the group.
It's an opportunistic culture Completely unintelligent... but potentially devastating to every living thing on Earth.
How long do we have to get rid of it?
It hatches in just *seven days.*

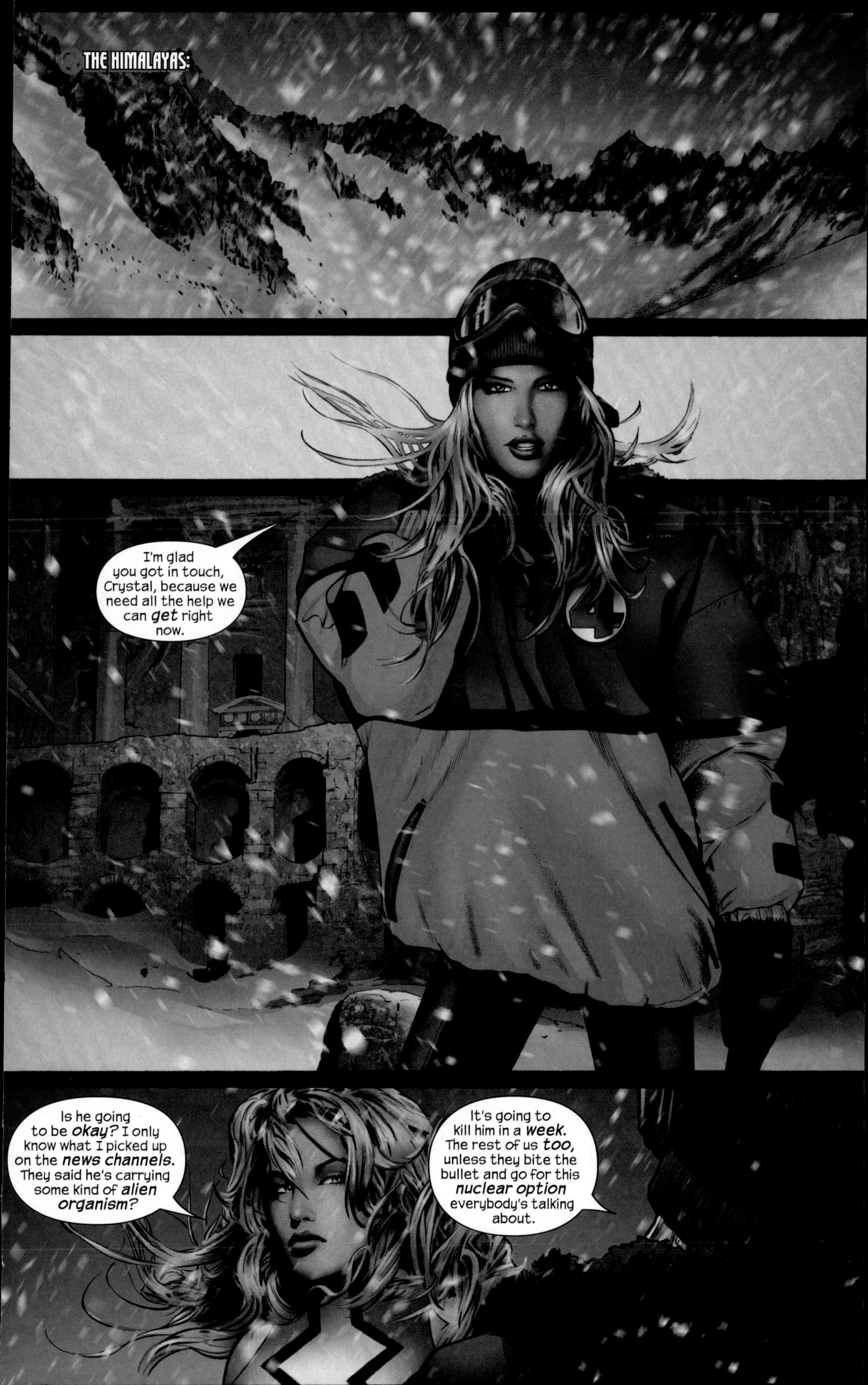
THE HIMALAYAS:
I'm glad you got in touch, Crystal, because we need all the help we can get right now.
Is he going to be okay? I only know what I picked up on the news channels. They said he's carrying some kind of alien organism?
It's going to kill him in a week. The rest of us too, unless they bite the bullet and go for this nuclear option everybody's talking about.

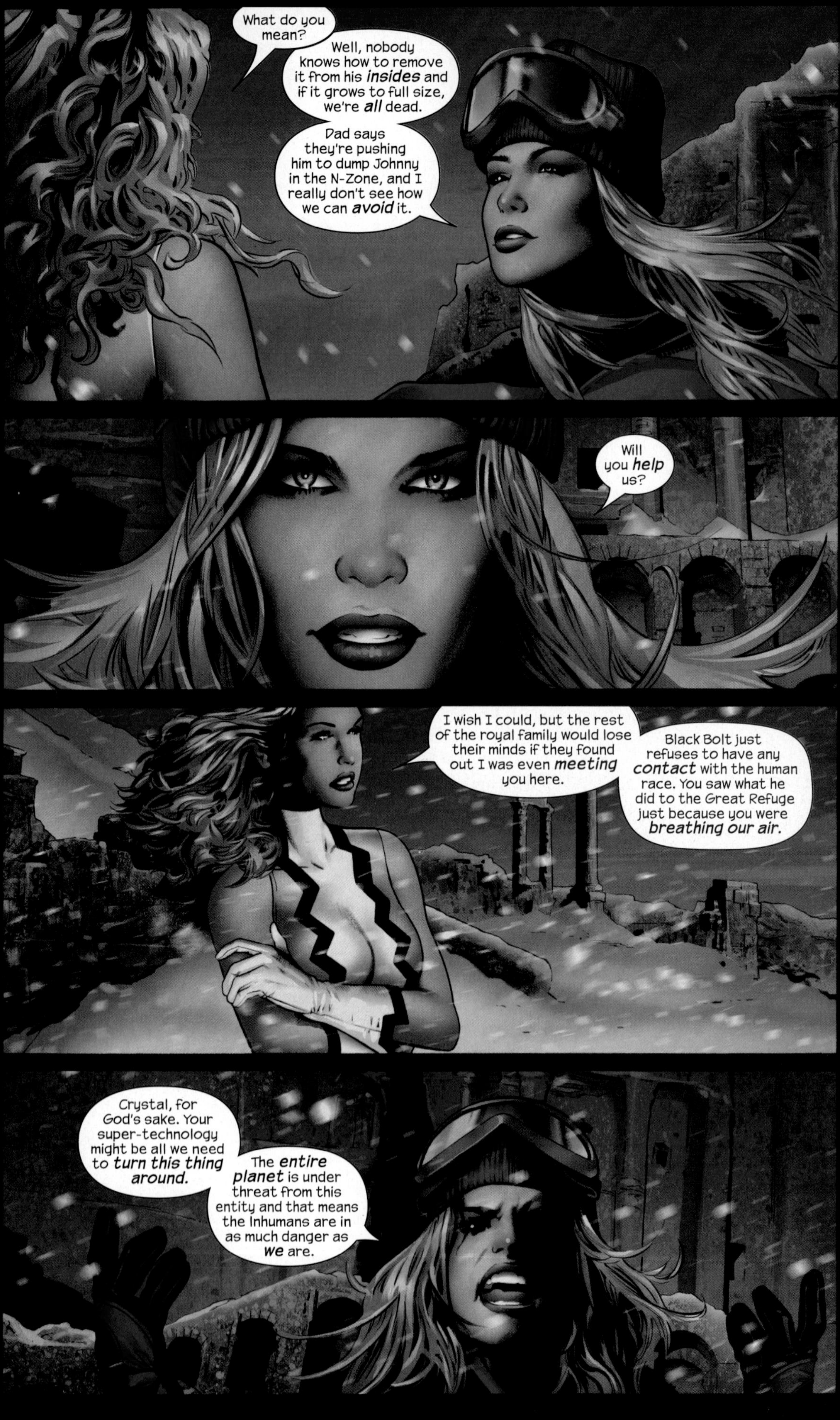

What do you mean?
Well, nobody knows how to remove it from his *insides* and if it grows to full size, we're *all* dead.
Dad says they're pushing him to dump Johnny in the N-Zone, and I really don't see how we can *avoid* it.
Will you *help* us?
I wish I could, but the rest of the royal family would lose their minds if they found out I was even *meeting* you here.
Black Bolt just refuses to have any *contact* with the human race. You saw what he did to the Great Refuge just because you were *breathing our air.*
Crystal, for God's sake. Your super-technology might be all we need to *turn this thing around.*
The *entire planet* is under threat from this entity and that means the Inhumans are in as much danger as *we* are.

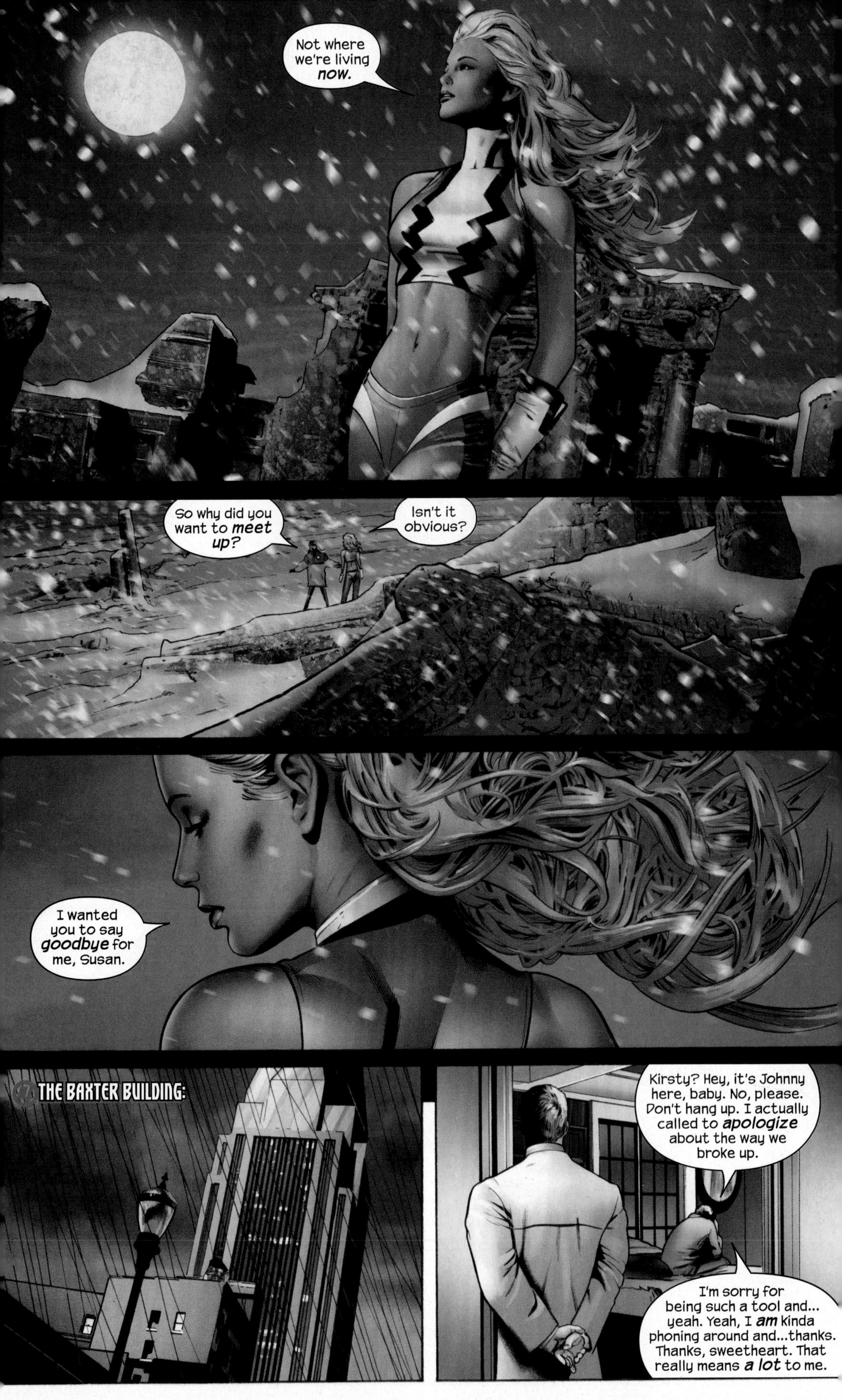
Not where we're living **now.**
So why did you want to **meet up?**
Isn't it obvious?
I wanted you to say **goodbye** for me, Susan.
THE BAXTER BUILDING:
Kirsty? Hey, it's Johnny here, baby. No, please. Don't hang up. I actually called to **apologize** about the way we broke up.
I'm sorry for being such a tool and... yeah. Yeah, I **am** kinda phoning around and...thanks. Thanks, sweetheart. That really means **a lot** to me.

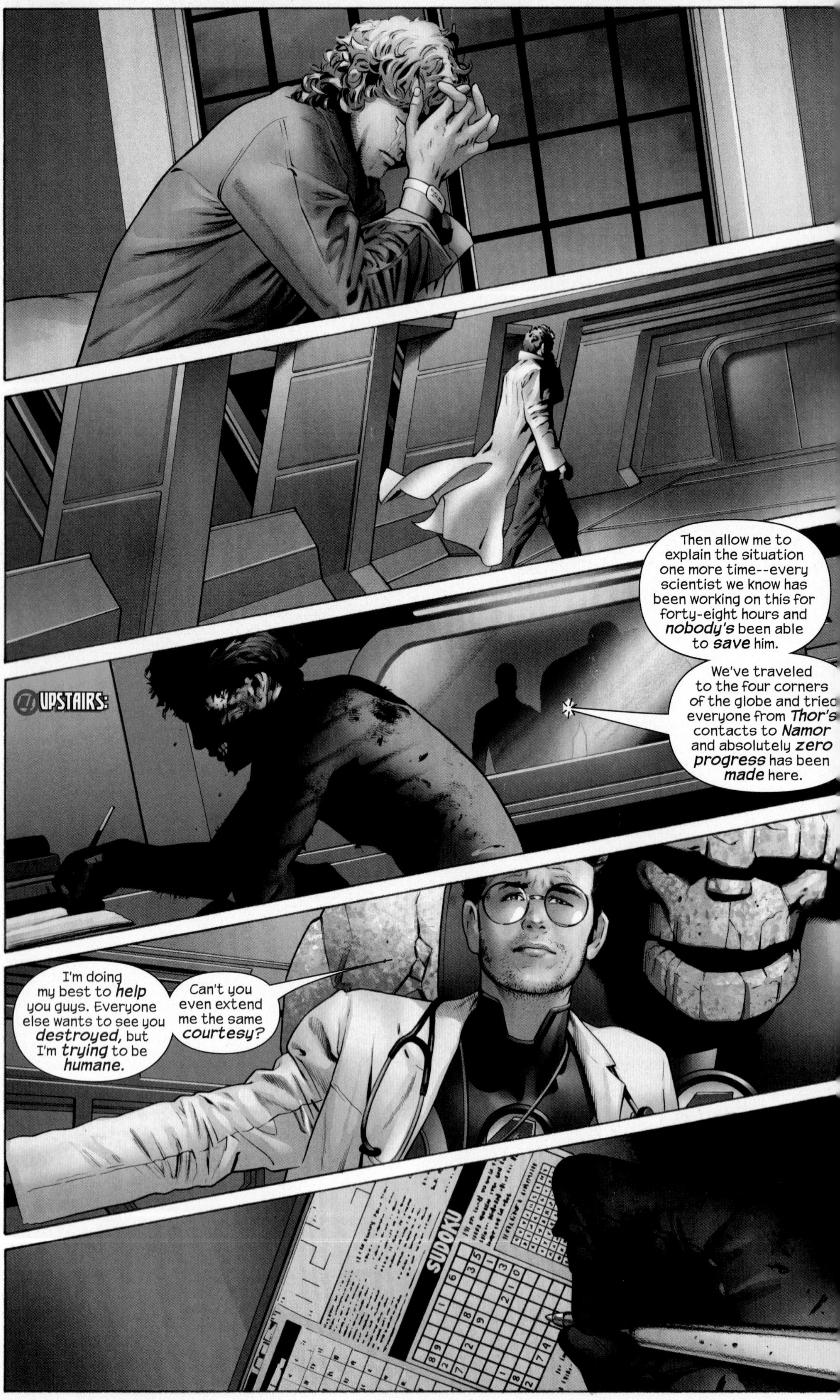
UPSTAIRS:
Then allow me to explain the situation one more time--every scientist we know has been working on this for forty-eight hours and nobody's been able to save him.
We've traveled to the four corners of the globe and tried everyone from Thor's contacts to Namor and absolutely zero progress has been made here.
I'm doing my best to help you guys. Everyone else wants to see you destroyed, but I'm trying to be humane.
Can't you even extend me the same courtesy?
SUDOKU

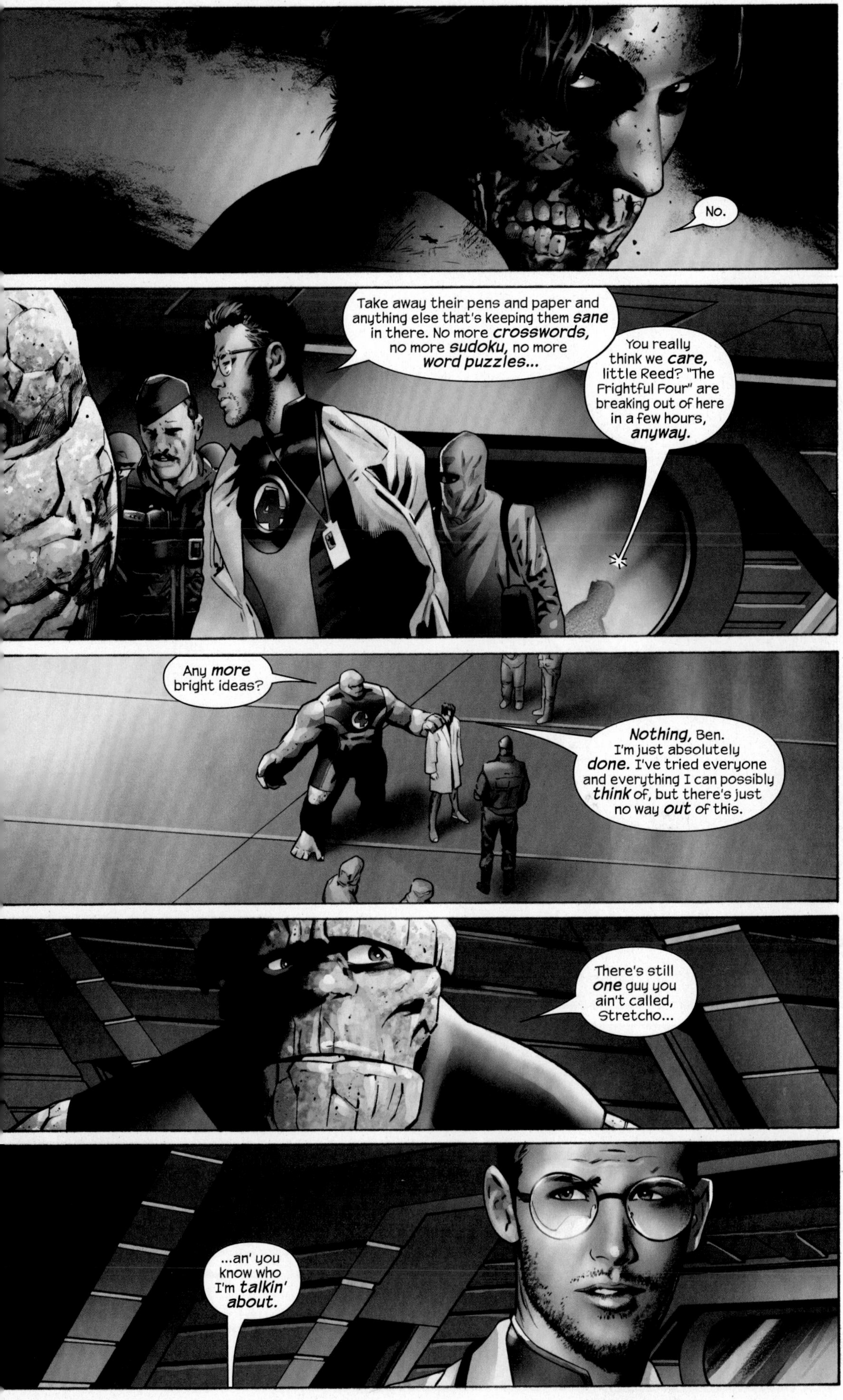

No.
Take away their pens and paper and anything else that's keeping them *sane* in there. No more *crosswords,* no more *sudoku,* no more *word puzzles...*
You really think we *care,* little Reed? "The Frightful Four" are breaking out of here in a few hours, *anyway.*
Any *more* bright ideas?
Nothing, Ben. I'm just absolutely *done.* I've tried everyone and everything I can possibly *think* of, but there's just no way *out* of this.
There's still *one* guy you ain't called, Stretcho...
...an' you know who I'm *talkin'* *about.*

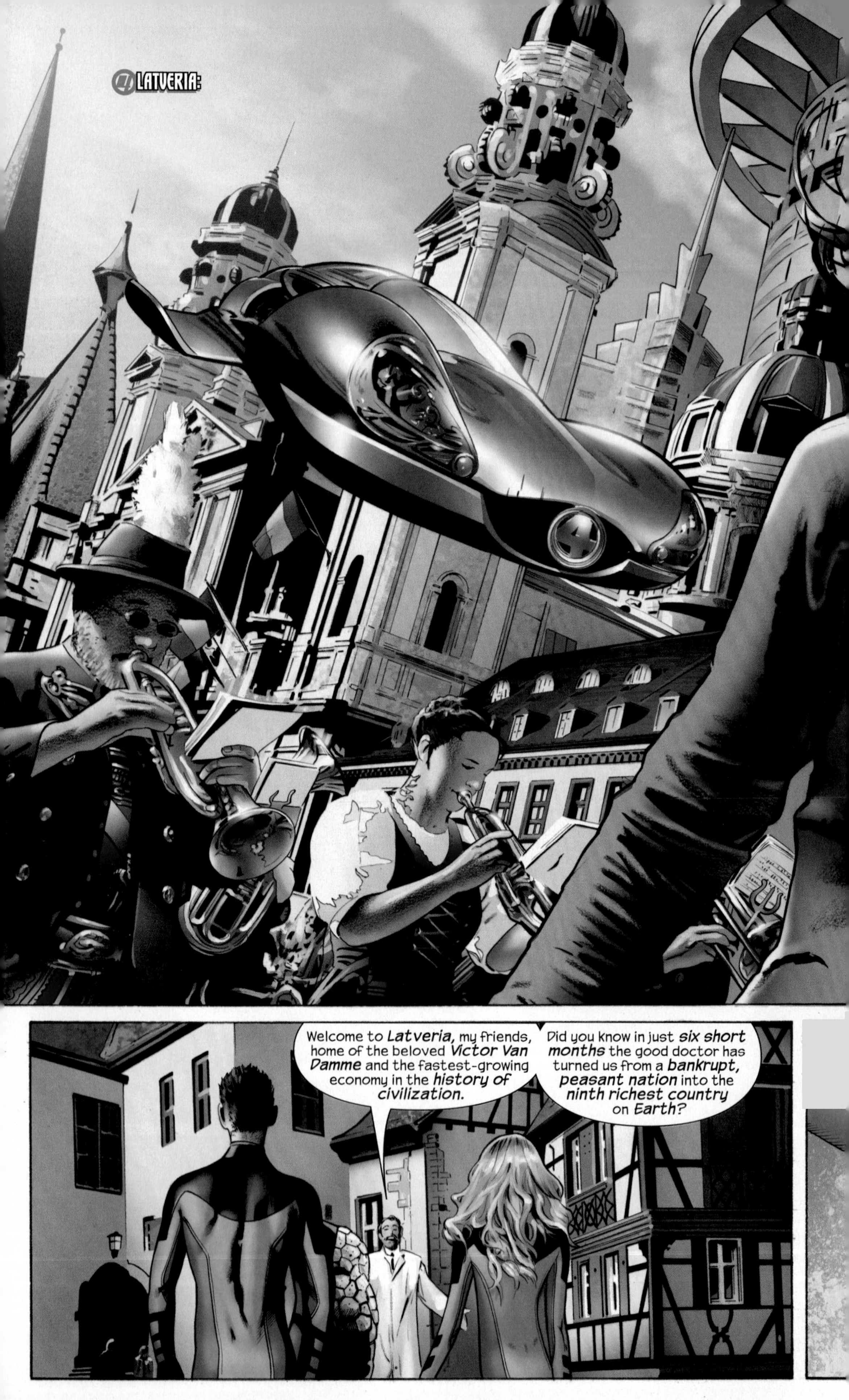
LATVERIA:
Welcome to Latveria, my friends, home of the beloved Victor Van Damme and the fastest-growing economy in the history of civilization.
Did you know in just six short months the good doctor has turned us from a bankrupt, peasant nation into the ninth richest country on Earth?

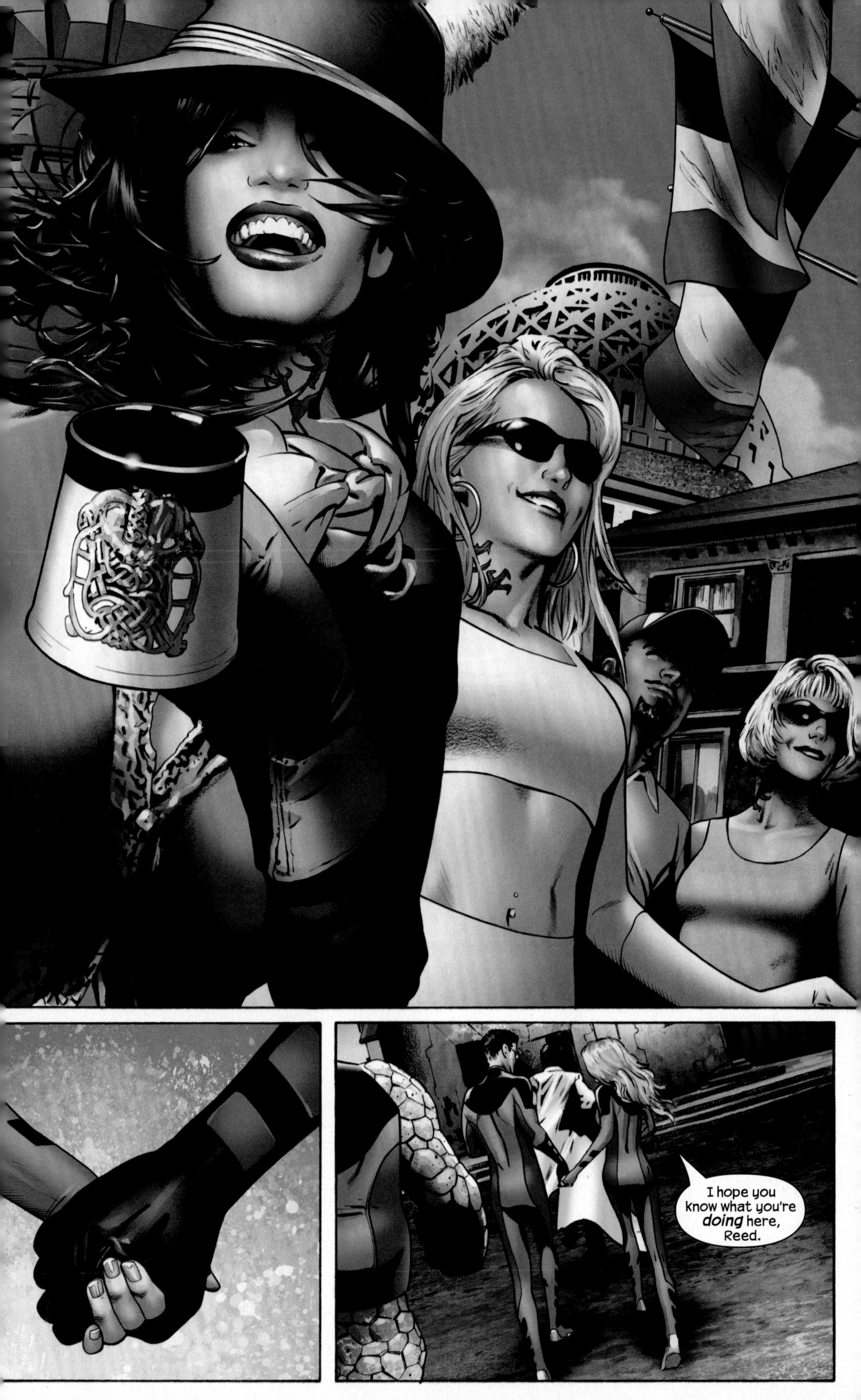
I hope you know what you're *doing* here, Reed.

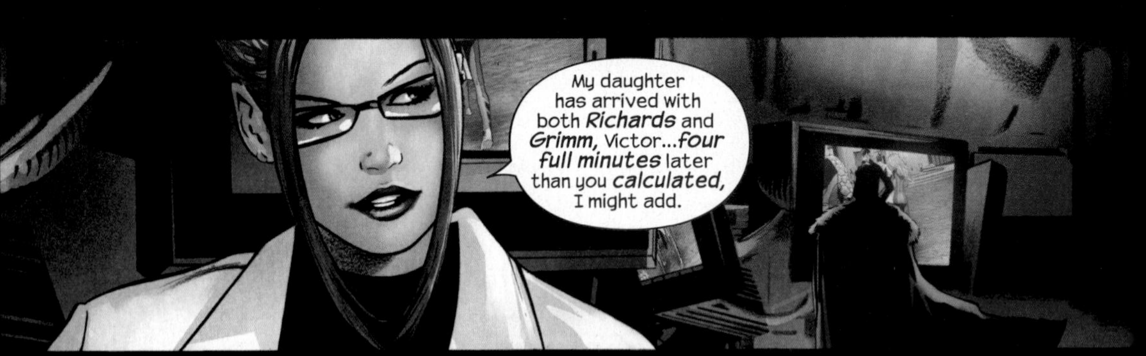
My daughter has arrived with both Richards and Grimm, Victor...four full minutes later than you calculated, I might add.

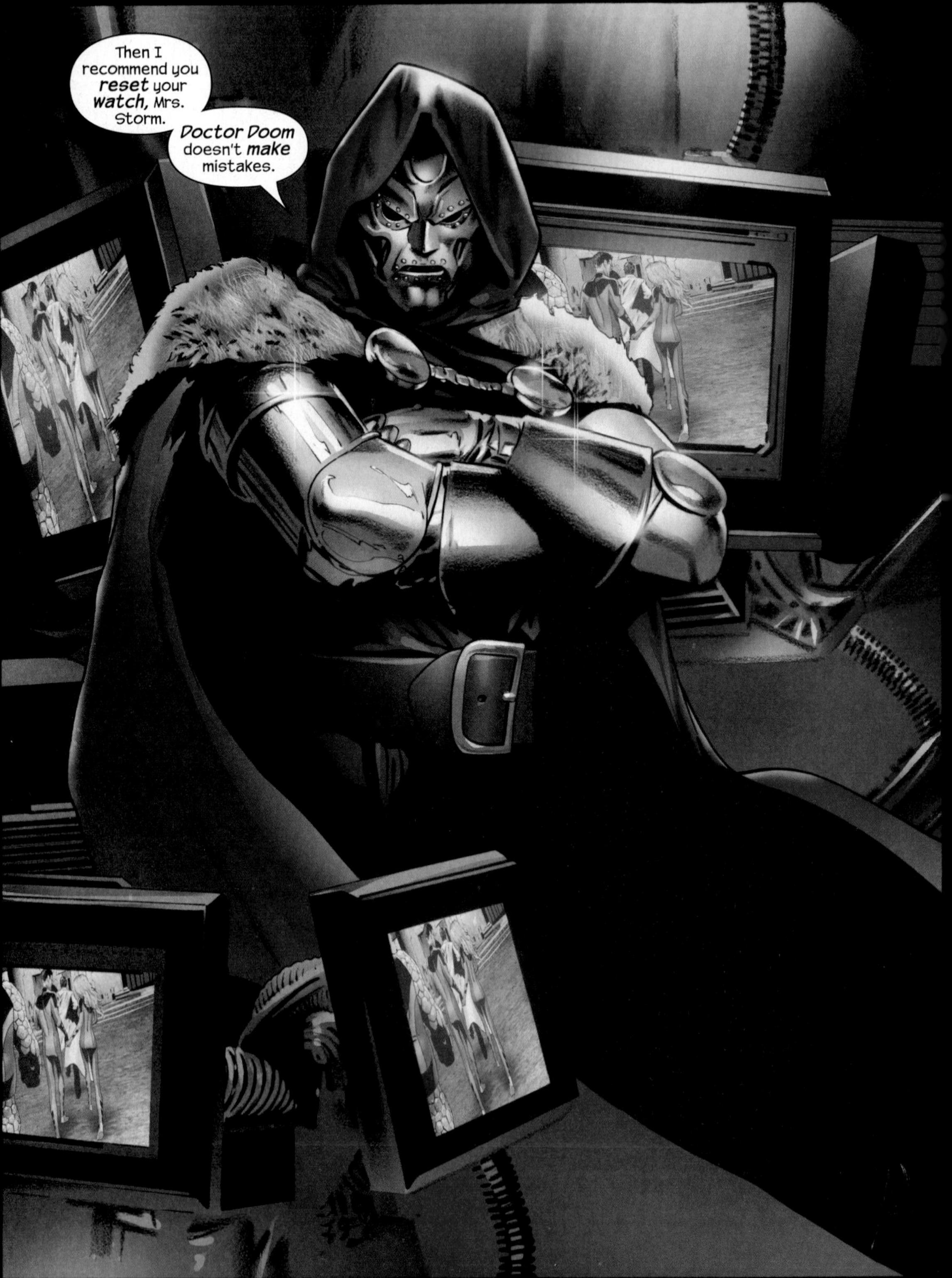
Then I recommend you reset your watch, Mrs. Storm.
Doctor Doom doesn't make mistakes.

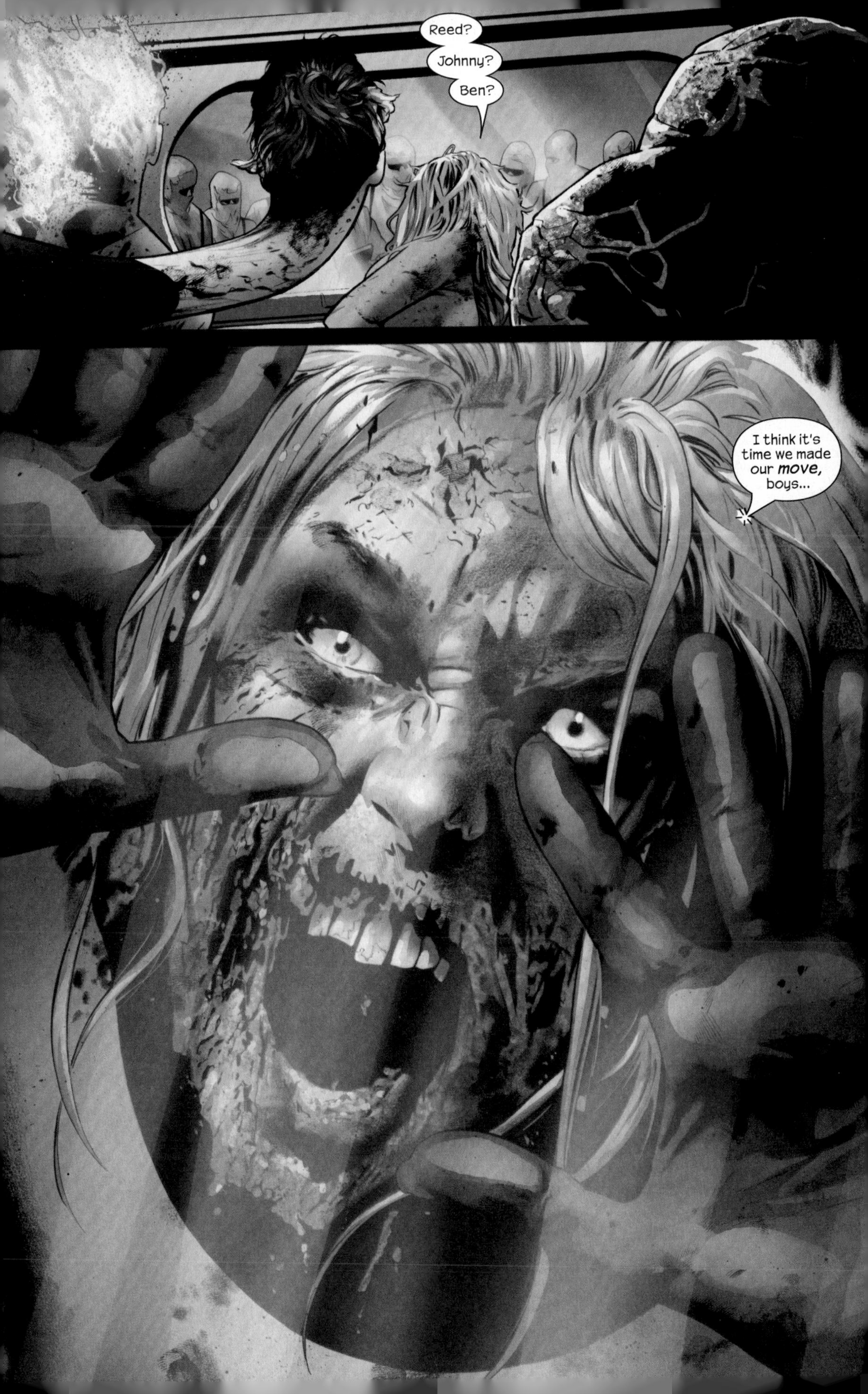
Reed?
Johnny?
Ben?
I think it's time we made our *move,* boys...

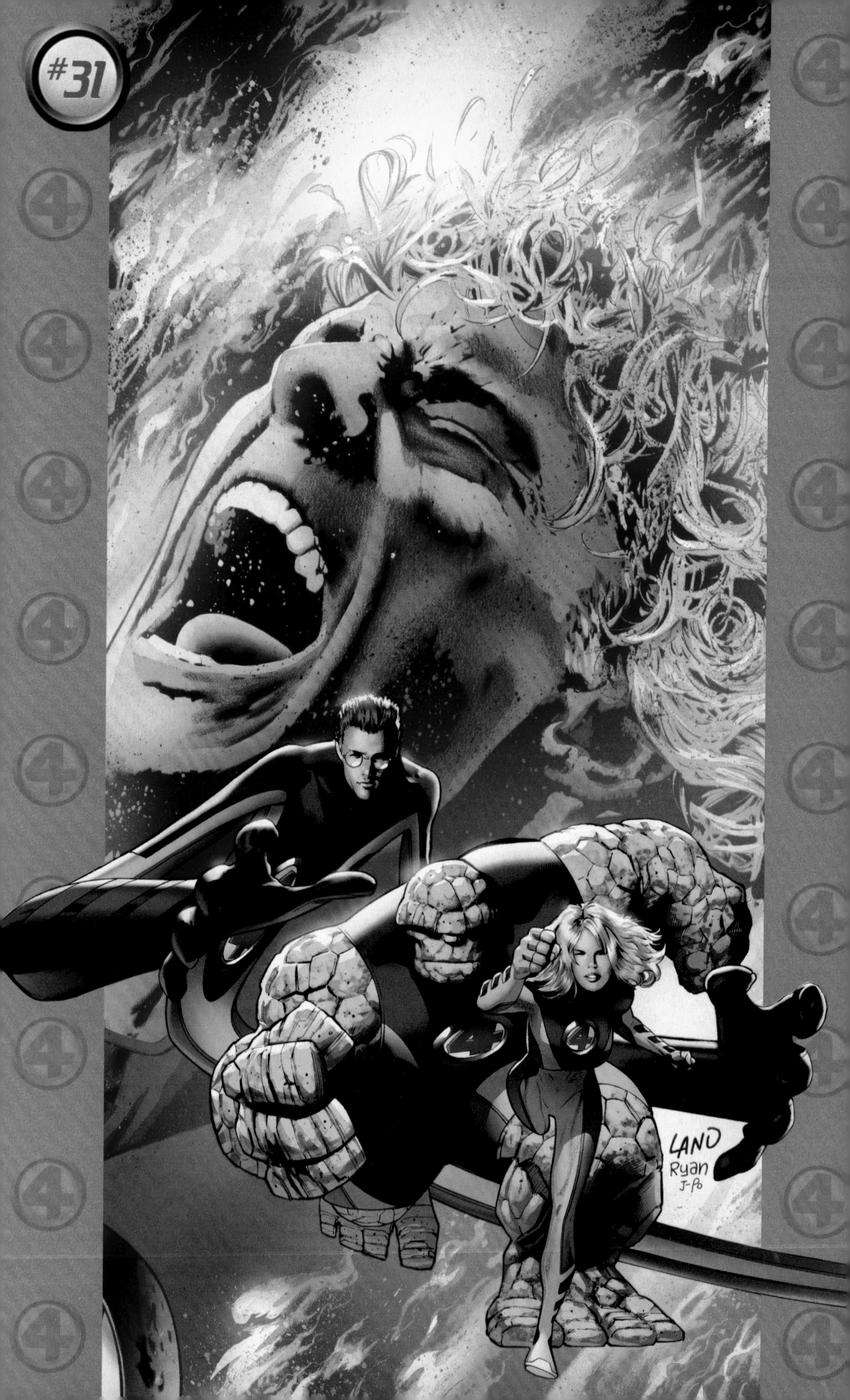
#31
LAND
Ryan
J-Po

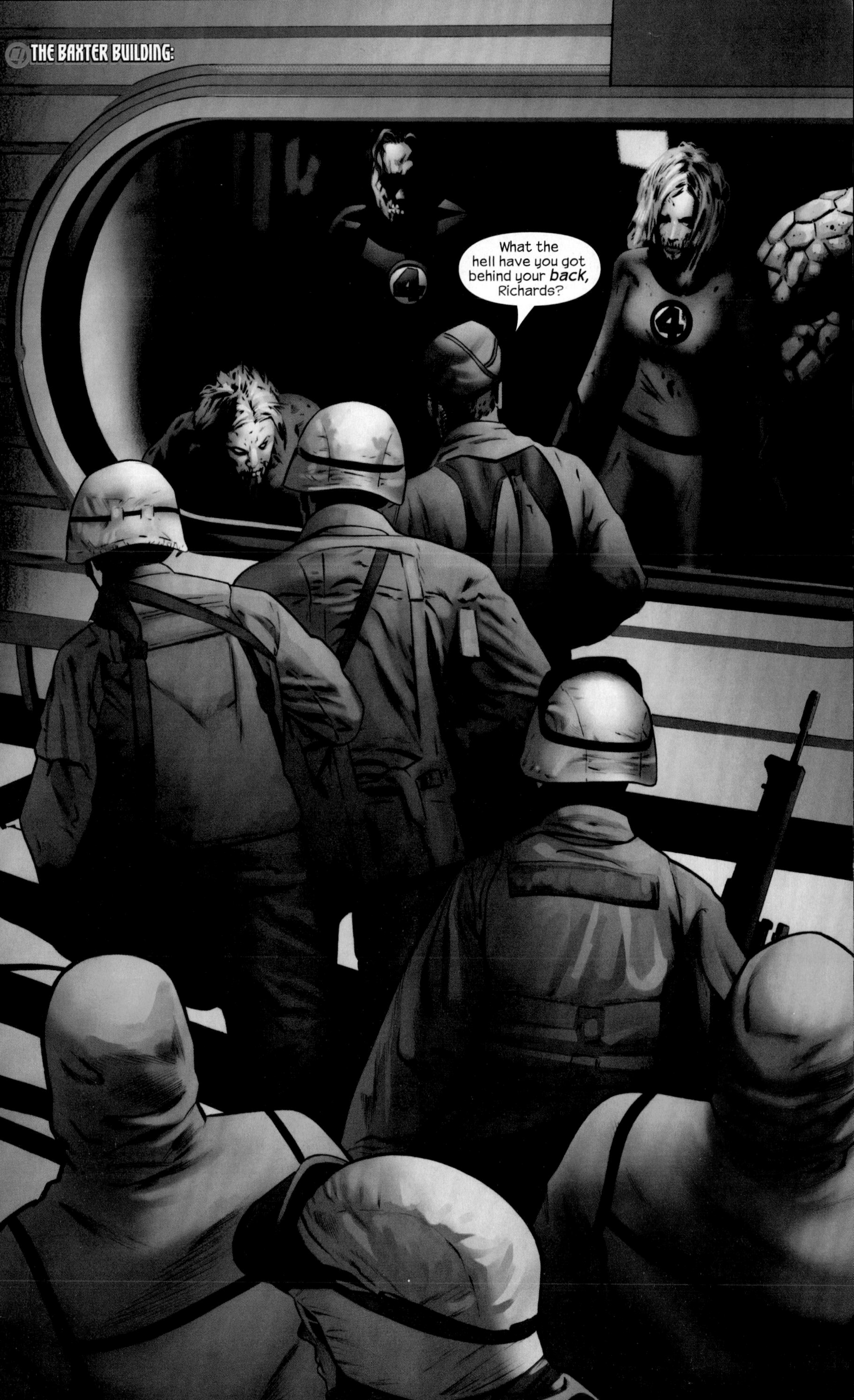
THE BAXTER BUILDING:
What the hell have you got behind your back, Richards?

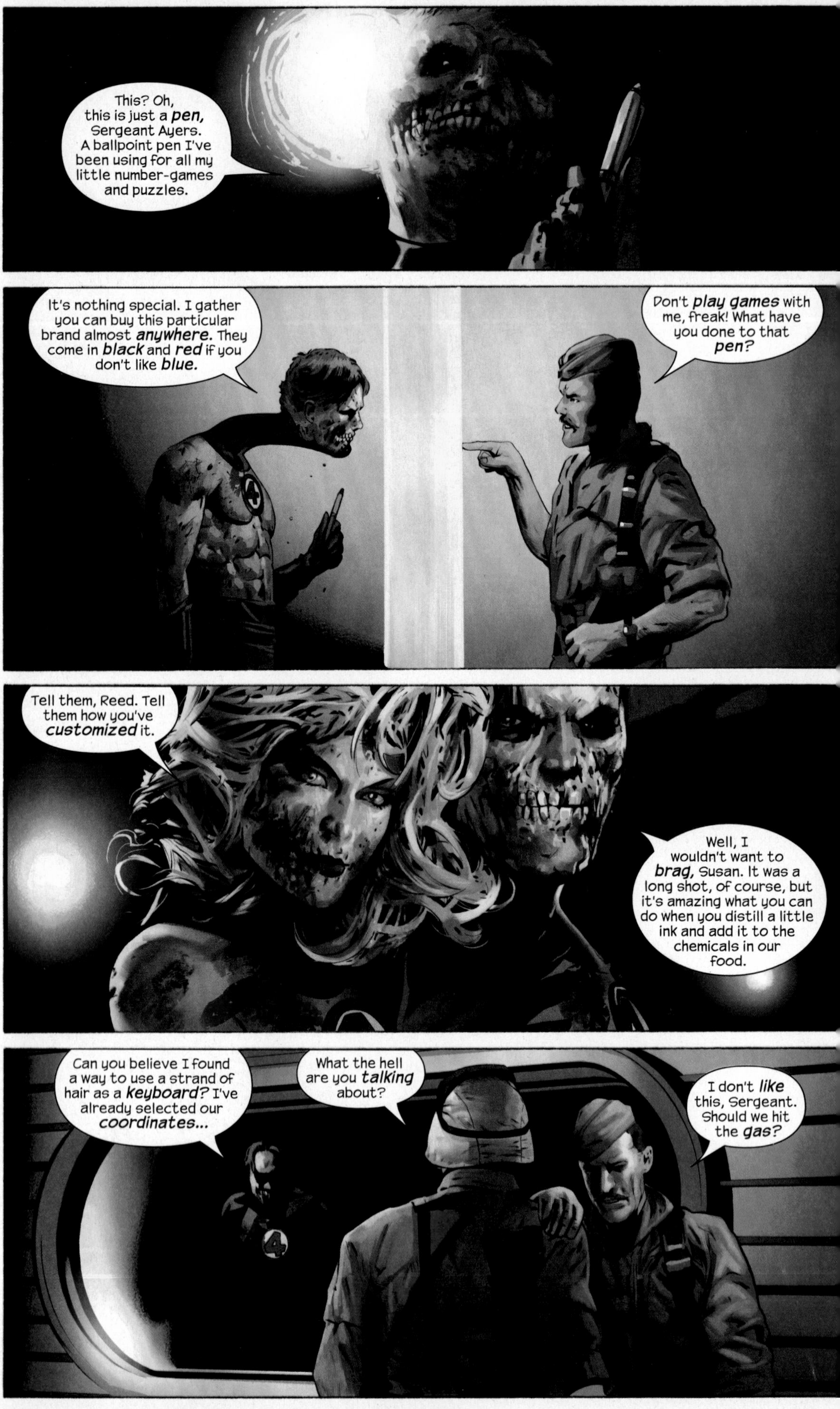
This? Oh, this is just a pen, Sergeant Ayers. A ballpoint pen I've been using for all my little number-games and puzzles.
It's nothing special. I gather you can buy this particular brand almost anywhere. They come in black and red if you don't like blue.
Don't play games with me, freak! What have you done to that pen?
Tell them, Reed. Tell them how you've customized it.
Well, I wouldn't want to brag, Susan. It was a long shot, of course, but it's amazing what you can do when you distill a little ink and add it to the chemicals in our food.
Can you believe I found a way to use a strand of hair as a keyboard? I've already selected our coordinates...
What the hell are you talking about?
I don't like this, Sergeant. Should we hit the gas?

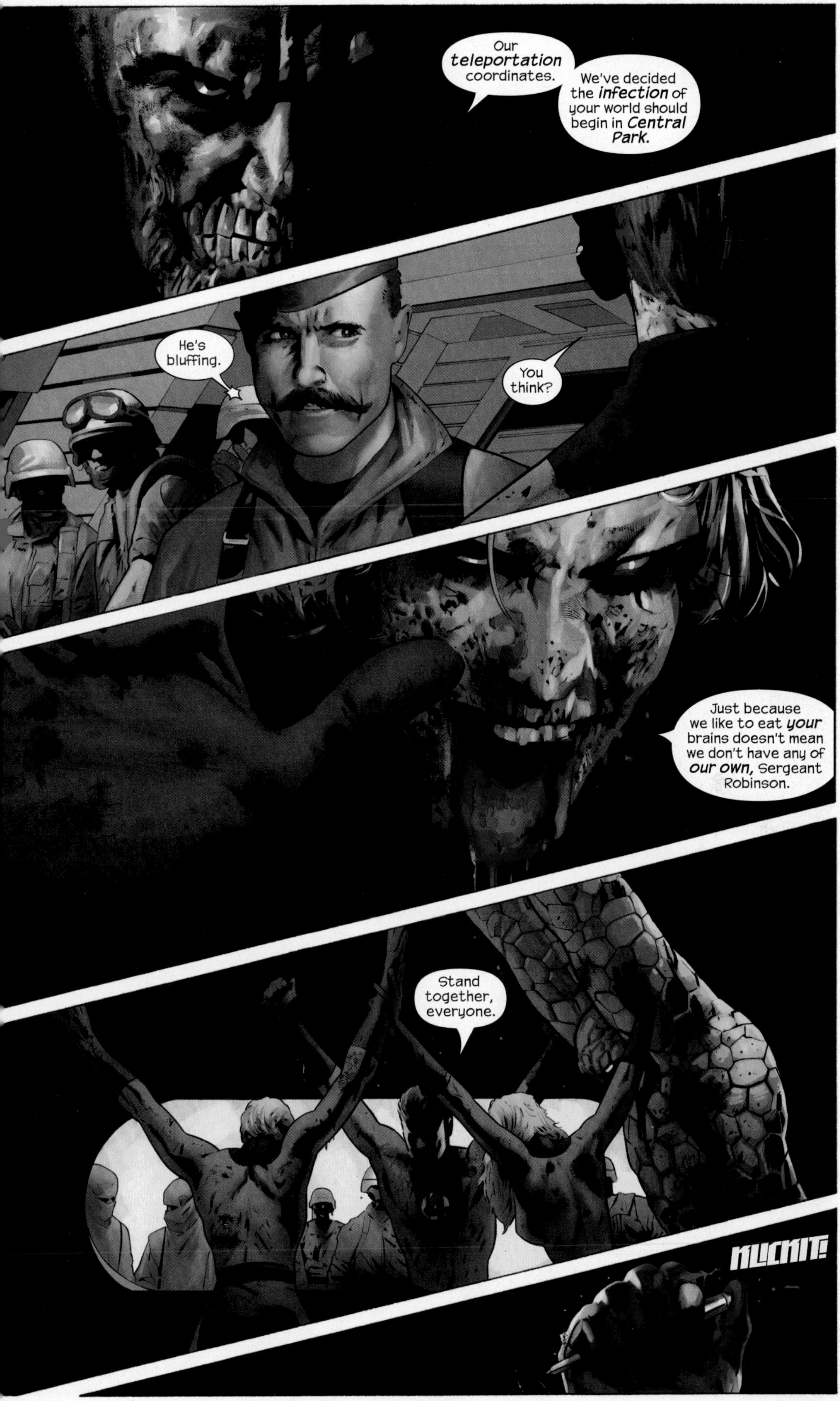

Our teleportation coordinates.
We've decided the infection of your world should begin in Central Park.
He's bluffing.
You think?
Just because we like to eat your brains doesn't mean we don't have any of our own, Sergeant Robinson.
Stand together, everyone.
KLICKIT!

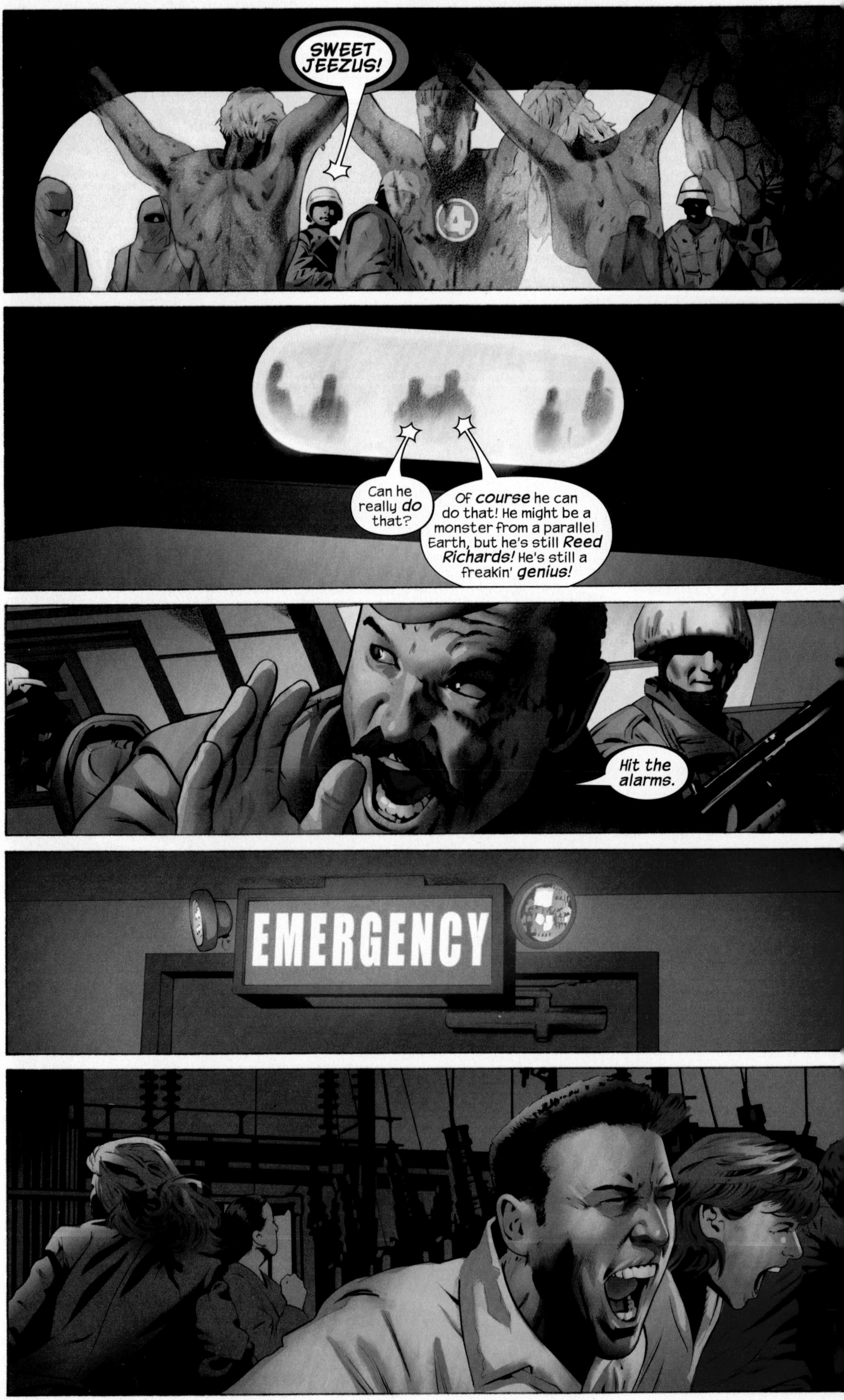
SWEET JEEZUS!
Can he really do that?
Of course he can do that! He might be a monster from a parallel Earth, but he's still Reed Richards! He's still a freakin' genius!
Hit the alarms.
EMERGENCY

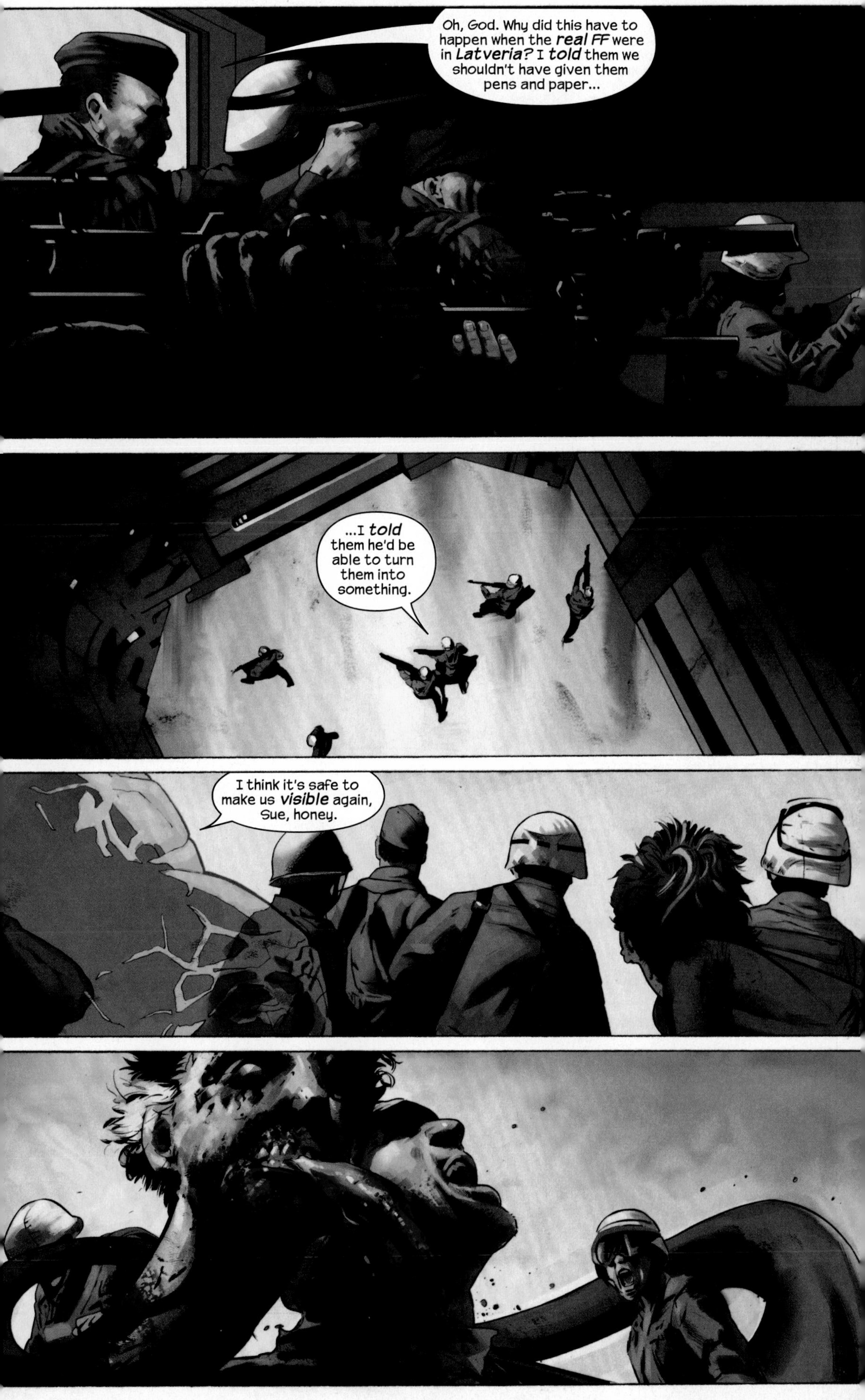
Oh, God. Why did this have to happen when the *real FF* were in *Latveria?* I *told* them we shouldn't have given them pens and paper...
...I *told* them he'd be able to turn them into something.
I think it's safe to make us *visible* again, Sue, honey.

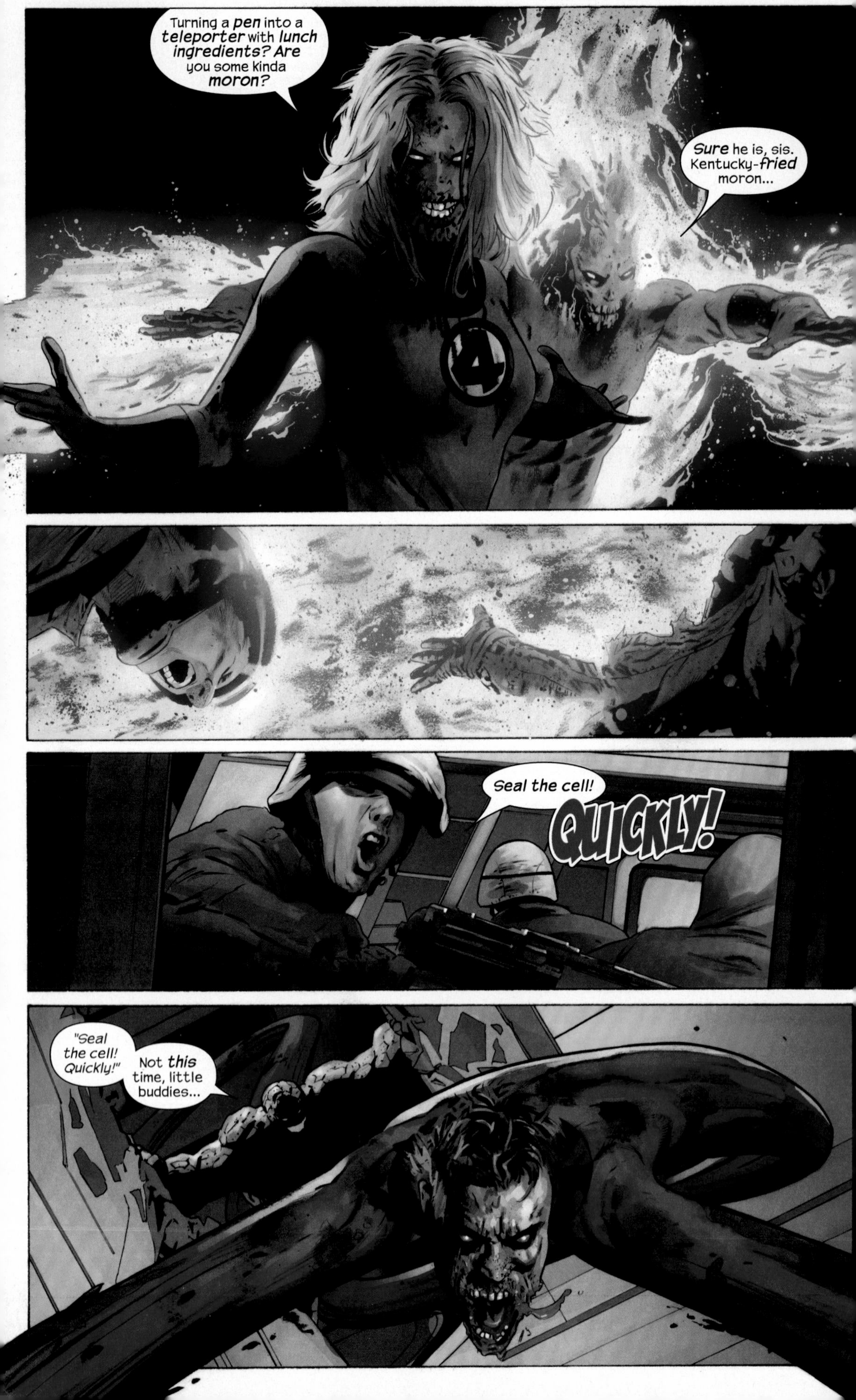
Turning a pen into a teleporter with lunch ingredients? Are you some kinda moron?
Sure he is, sis. Kentucky-fried moron...
Seal the cell!
QUICKLY!
"Seal the cell! Quickly!"
Not this time, little buddies...

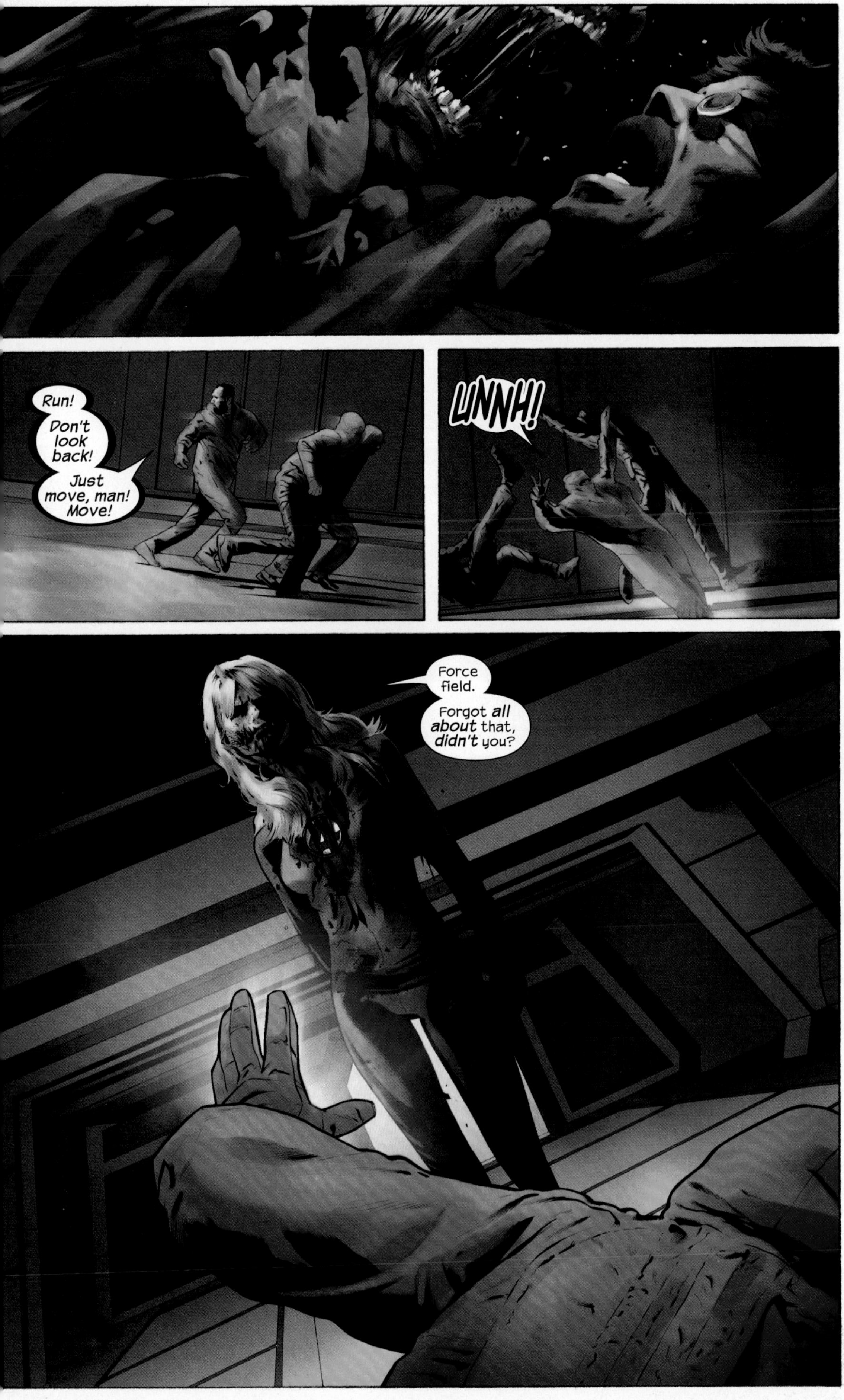
Run! Don't look back! Just move, man! Move!
UNNH!
Force field.
Forgot all about that, didn't you?

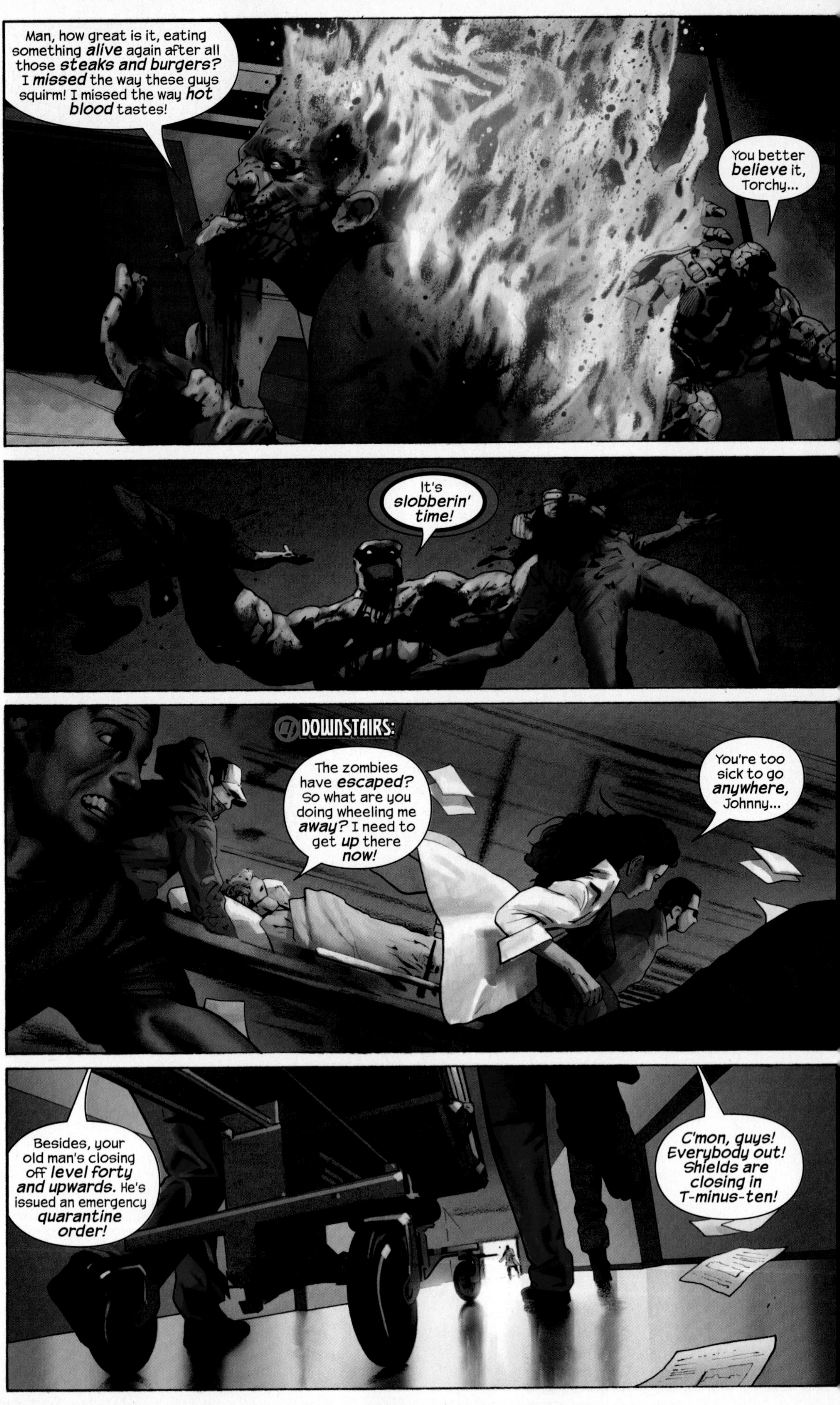
Man, how great is it, eating something *alive* again after all those *steaks and burgers?* I *missed* the way these guys squirm! I missed the way *hot blood* tastes!
You better *believe* it, Torchy...
It's *slobberin' time!*
DOWNSTAIRS:
The zombies have *escaped?* So what are you doing wheeling me *away?* I need to get *up* there *now!*
You're too sick to go *anywhere,* Johnny...
Besides, your old man's closing off *level forty and upwards.* He's issued an emergency *quarantine order!*
C'mon, guys! Everybody out! Shields are closing in T-minus-ten!

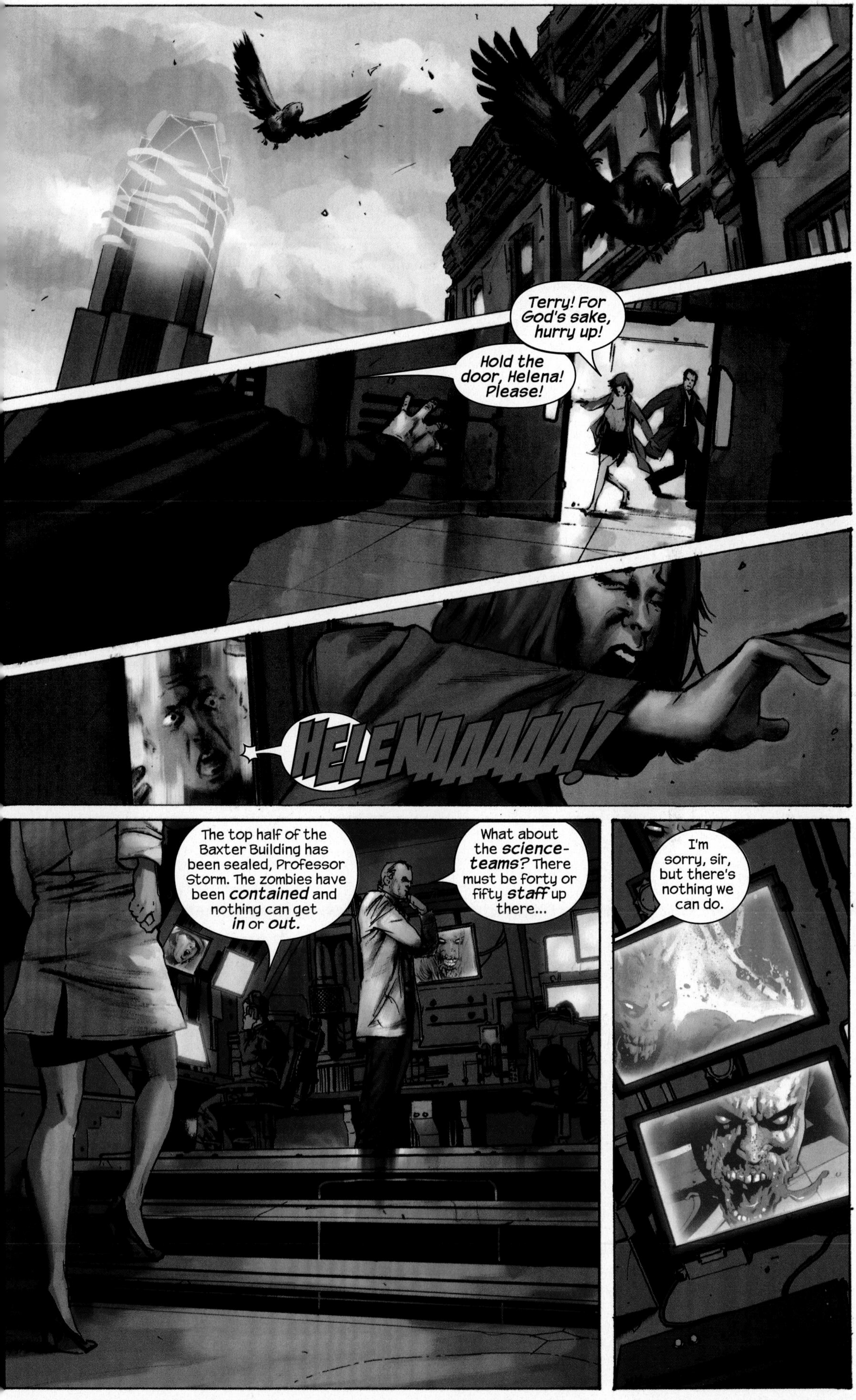
Terry! For God's sake, hurry up!
Hold the door, Helena! Please!
HELENAAAAA!
The top half of the Baxter Building has been sealed, Professor Storm. The zombies have been *contained* and nothing can get *in* or *out*.
What about the *science-teams?* There must be forty or fifty *staff* up there...
I'm sorry, sir, but there's nothing we can do.

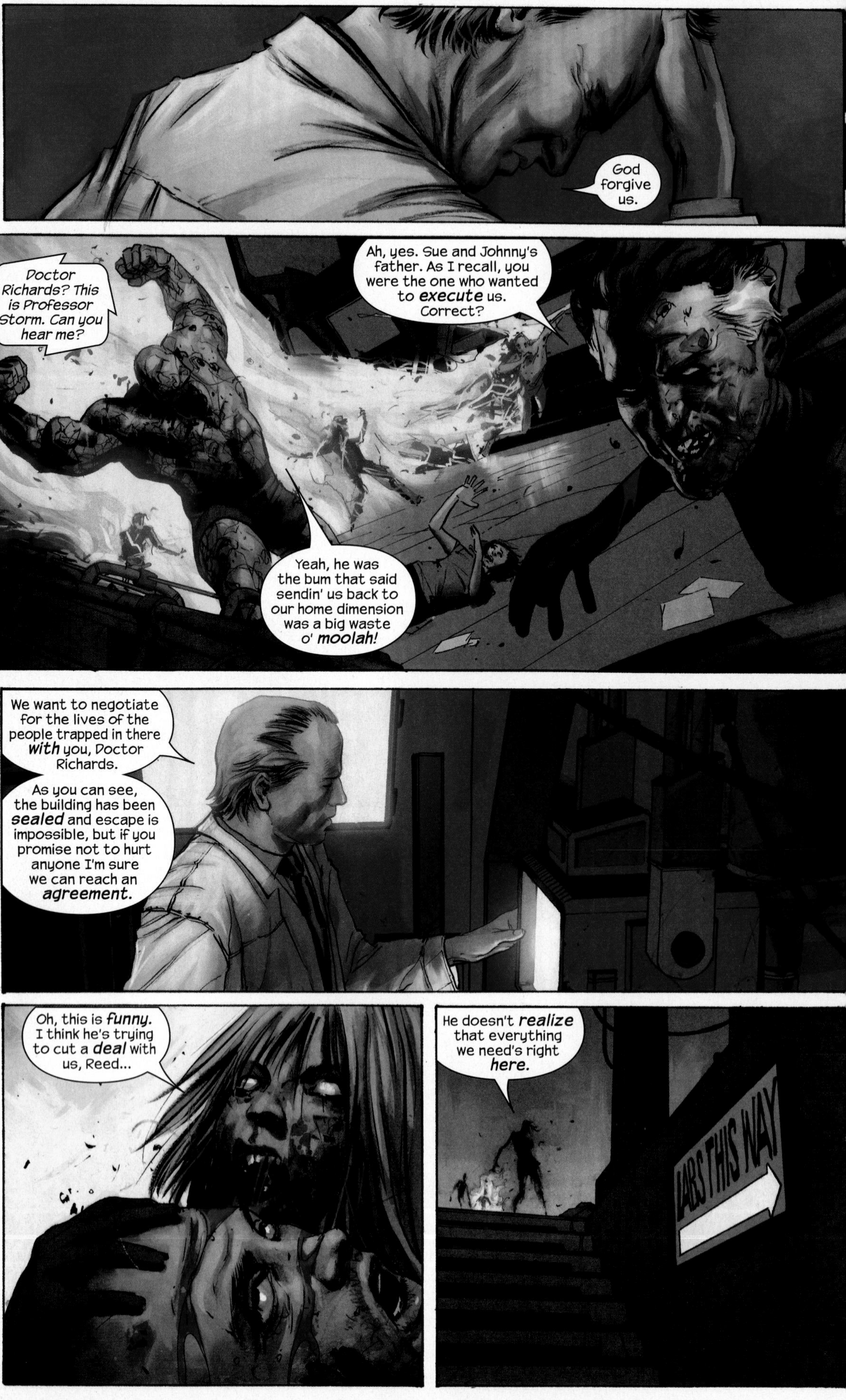

God forgive us.
Doctor Richards? This is Professor Storm. Can you hear me?
Ah, yes. Sue and Johnny's father. As I recall, you were the one who wanted to execute us. Correct?
Yeah, he was the bum that said sendin' us back to our home dimension was a big waste o' moolah!
We want to negotiate for the lives of the people trapped in there with you, Doctor Richards.
As you can see, the building has been sealed and escape is impossible, but if you promise not to hurt anyone I'm sure we can reach an agreement.
Oh, this is funny. I think he's trying to cut a deal with us, Reed...
He doesn't realize that everything we need's right here.
LABS THIS WAY

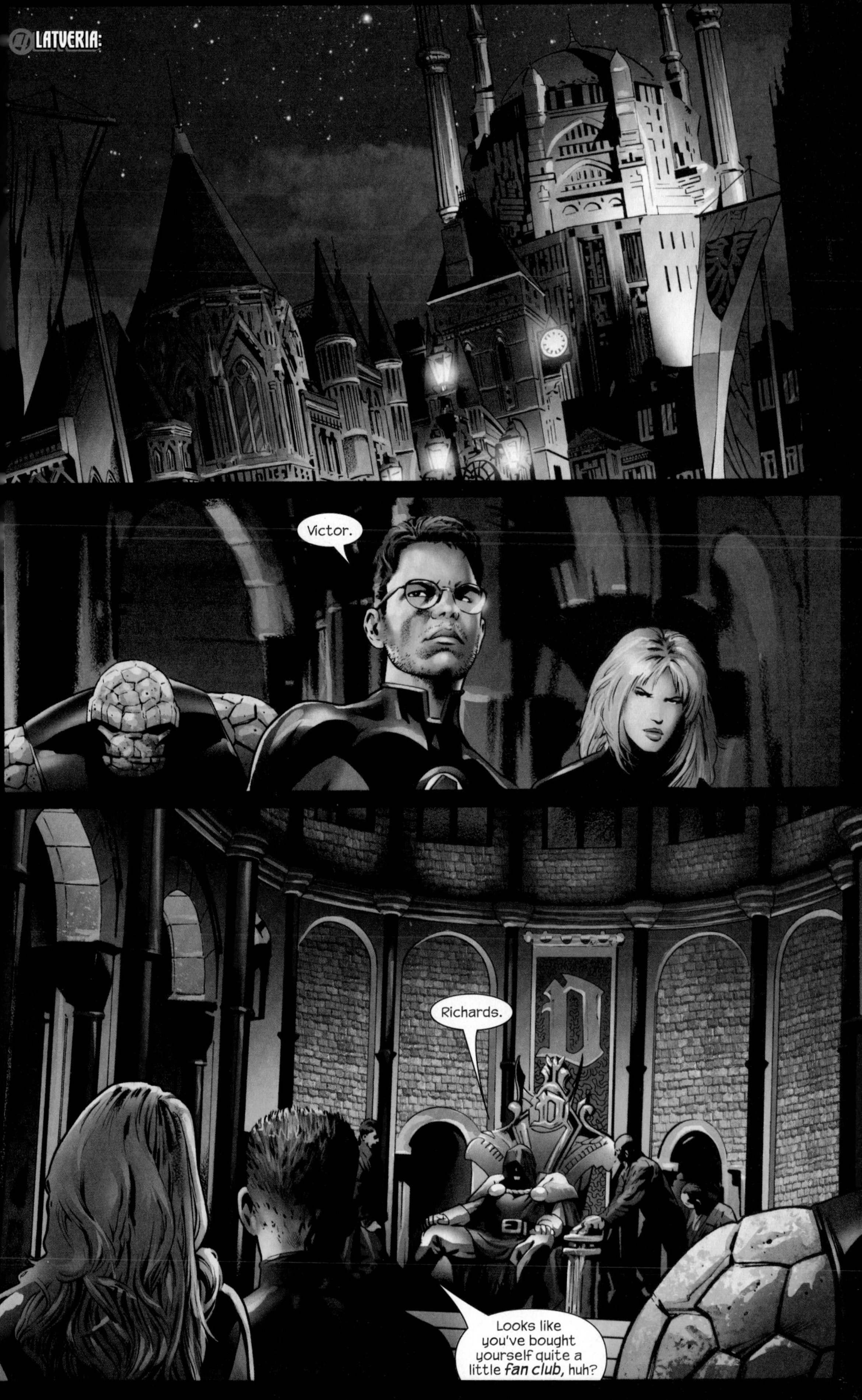
LATVERIA:
Victor.
Richards.
Looks like you've bought yourself quite a little fan club, huh?

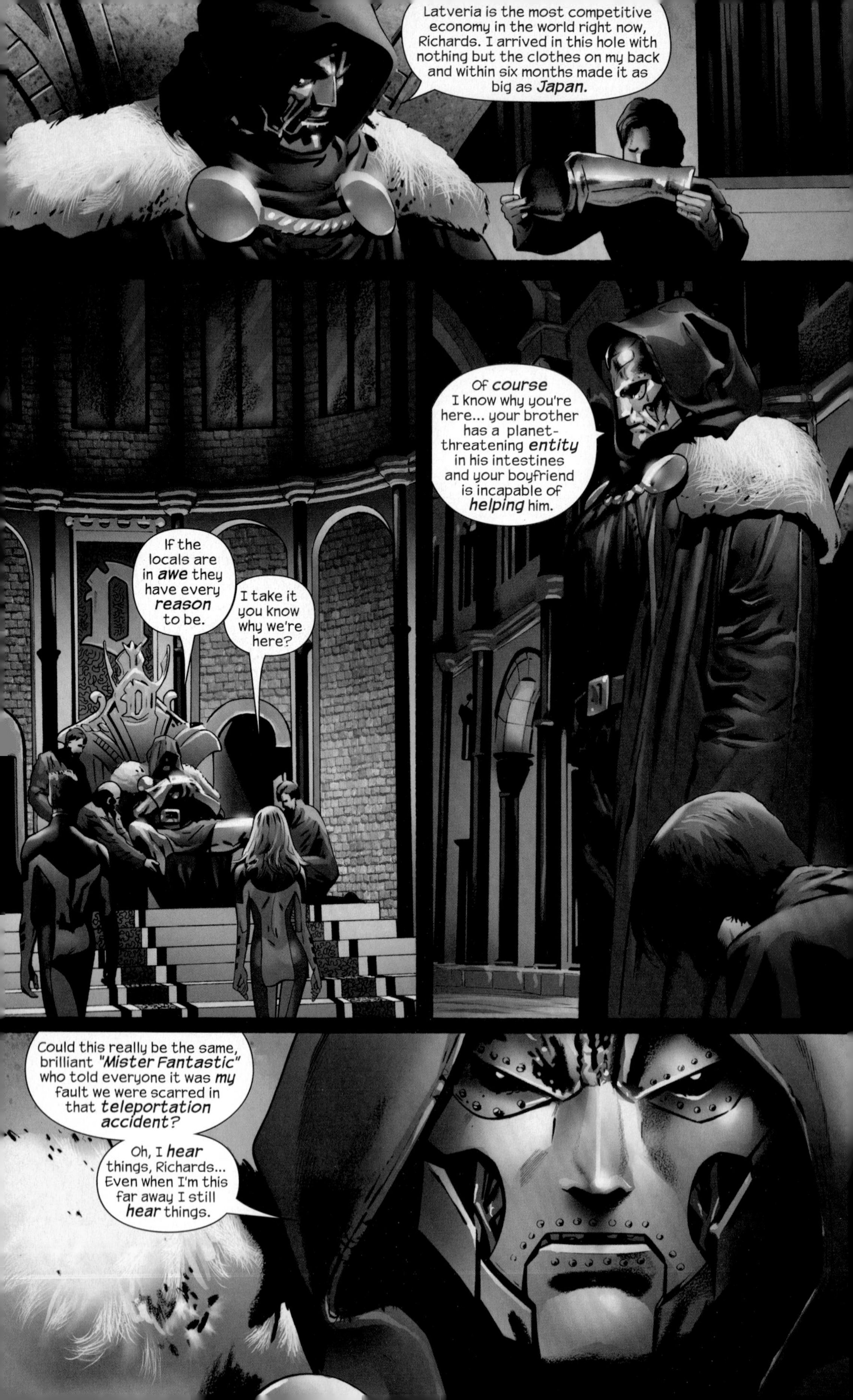
Latveria is the most competitive economy in the world right now, Richards. I arrived in this hole with nothing but the clothes on my back and within six months made it as big as Japan.
If the locals are in awe they have every reason to be.
I take it you know why we're here?
Of course I know why you're here... your brother has a planet-threatening entity in his intestines and your boyfriend is incapable of helping him.
Could this really be the same, brilliant "Mister Fantastic" who told everyone it was my fault we were scarred in that teleportation accident?
Oh, I hear things, Richards... Even when I'm this far away I still hear things.

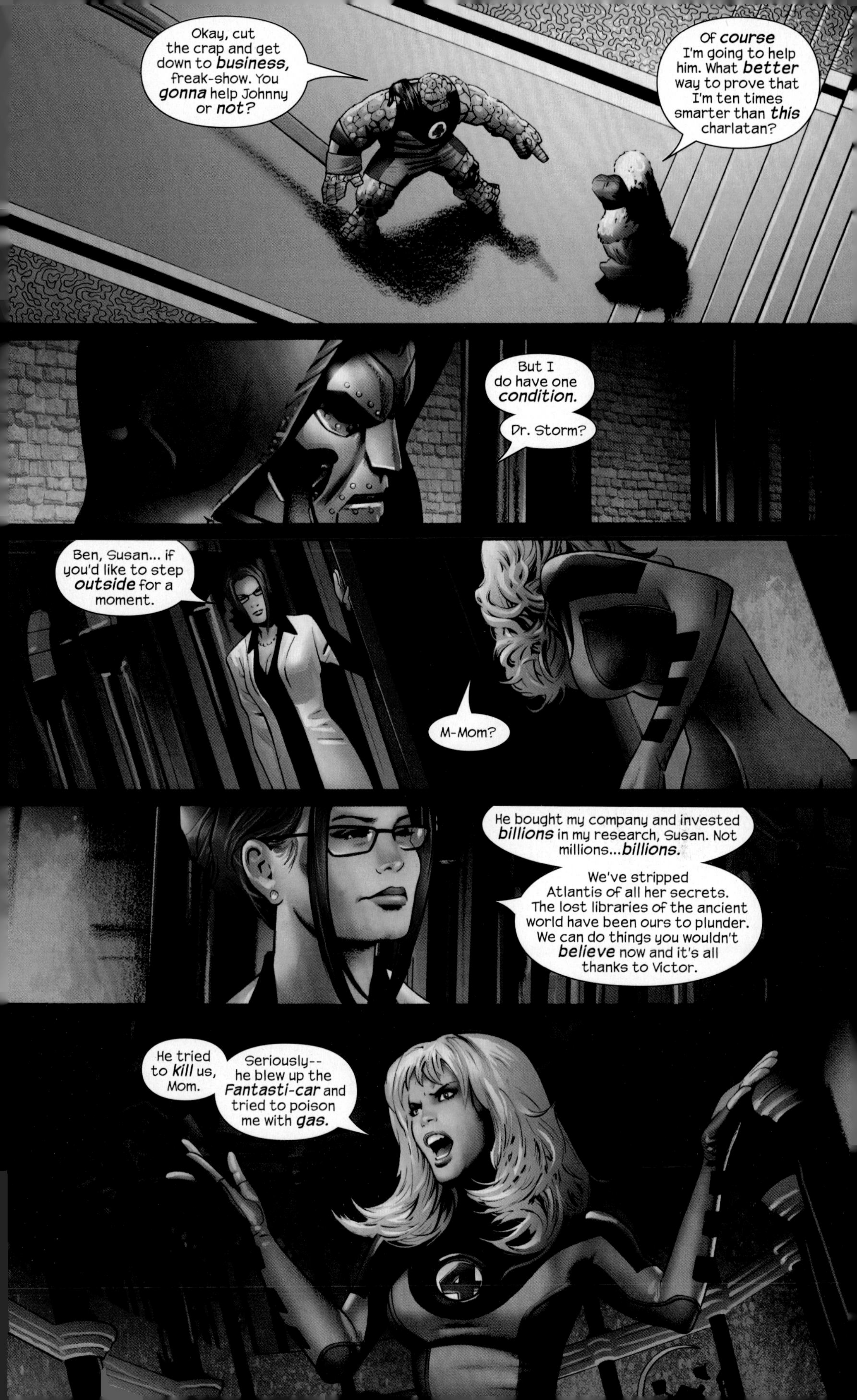
Okay, cut the crap and get down to business, freak-show. You gonna help Johnny or not?
Of course I'm going to help him. What better way to prove that I'm ten times smarter than this charlatan?
But I do have one condition.
Dr. Storm?
Ben, Susan... if you'd like to step outside for a moment.
M-Mom?
He bought my company and invested billions in my research, Susan. Not millions...billions.
We've stripped Atlantis of all her secrets. The lost libraries of the ancient world have been ours to plunder. We can do things you wouldn't believe now and it's all thanks to Victor.
He tried to kill us, Mom.
Seriously-- he blew up the Fantasti-car and tried to poison me with gas.

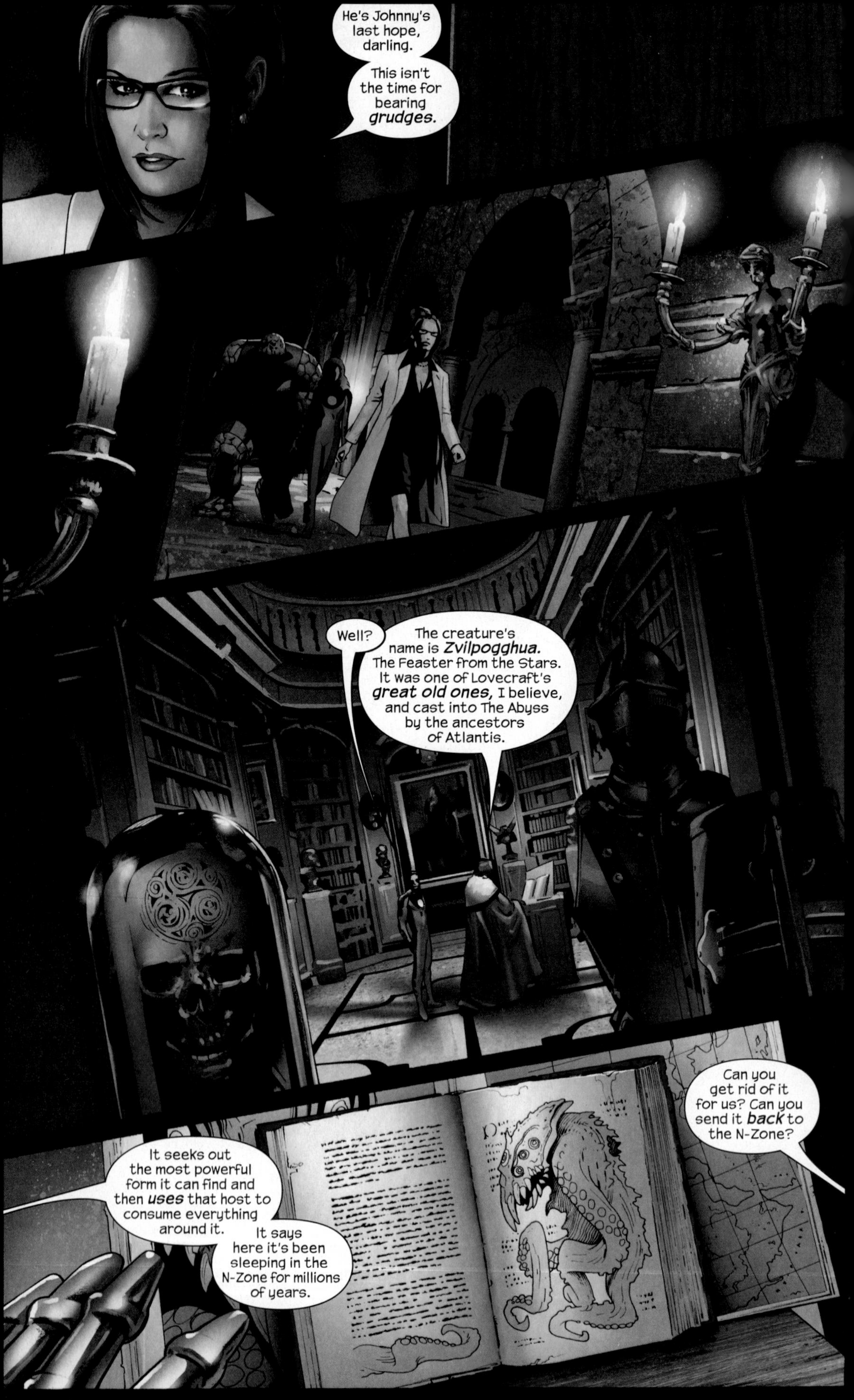
He's Johnny's last hope, darling.
This isn't the time for bearing *grudges.*
Well?
The creature's name is *Zvilpogghua.* The Feaster from the Stars. It was one of Lovecraft's *great old ones,* I believe, and cast into The Abyss by the ancestors of Atlantis.
It seeks out the most powerful form it can find and then *uses* that host to consume everything around it.
It says here it's been sleeping in the N-Zone for millions of years.
Can you get rid of it for us? Can you send it *back* to the N-Zone?

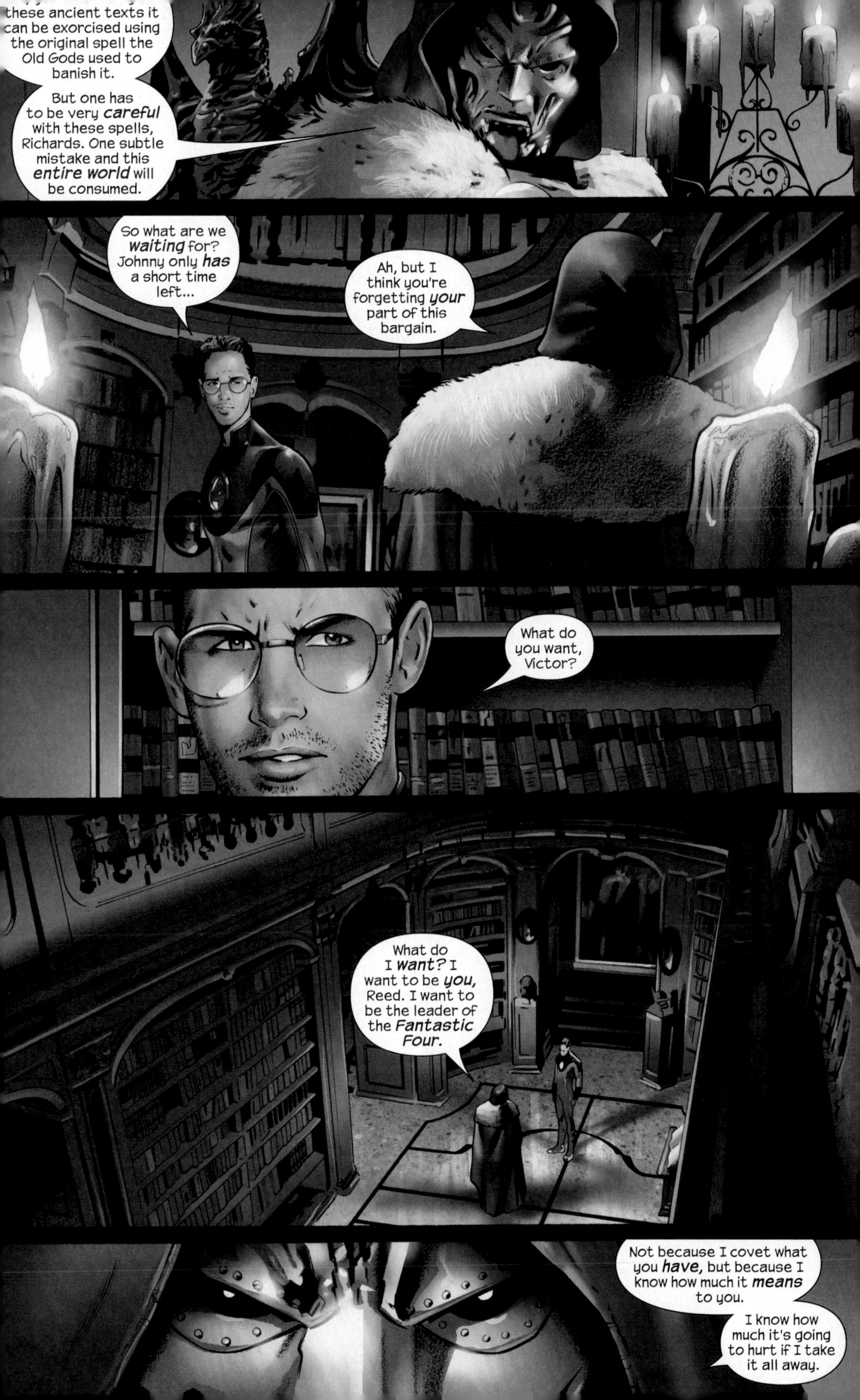
these ancient texts it can be exorcised using the original spell the Old Gods used to banish it.
But one has to be very *careful* with these spells, Richards. One subtle mistake and this *entire world* will be consumed.
So what are we *waiting* for? Johnny only *has* a short time left...
Ah, but I think you're forgetting *your* part of this bargain.
What do you want, Victor?
What do I *want?* I want to be *you,* Reed. I want to be the leader of the *Fantastic Four.*
Not because I covet what you *have,* but because I know how much it *means* to you.
I know how much it's going to hurt if I take it all away.

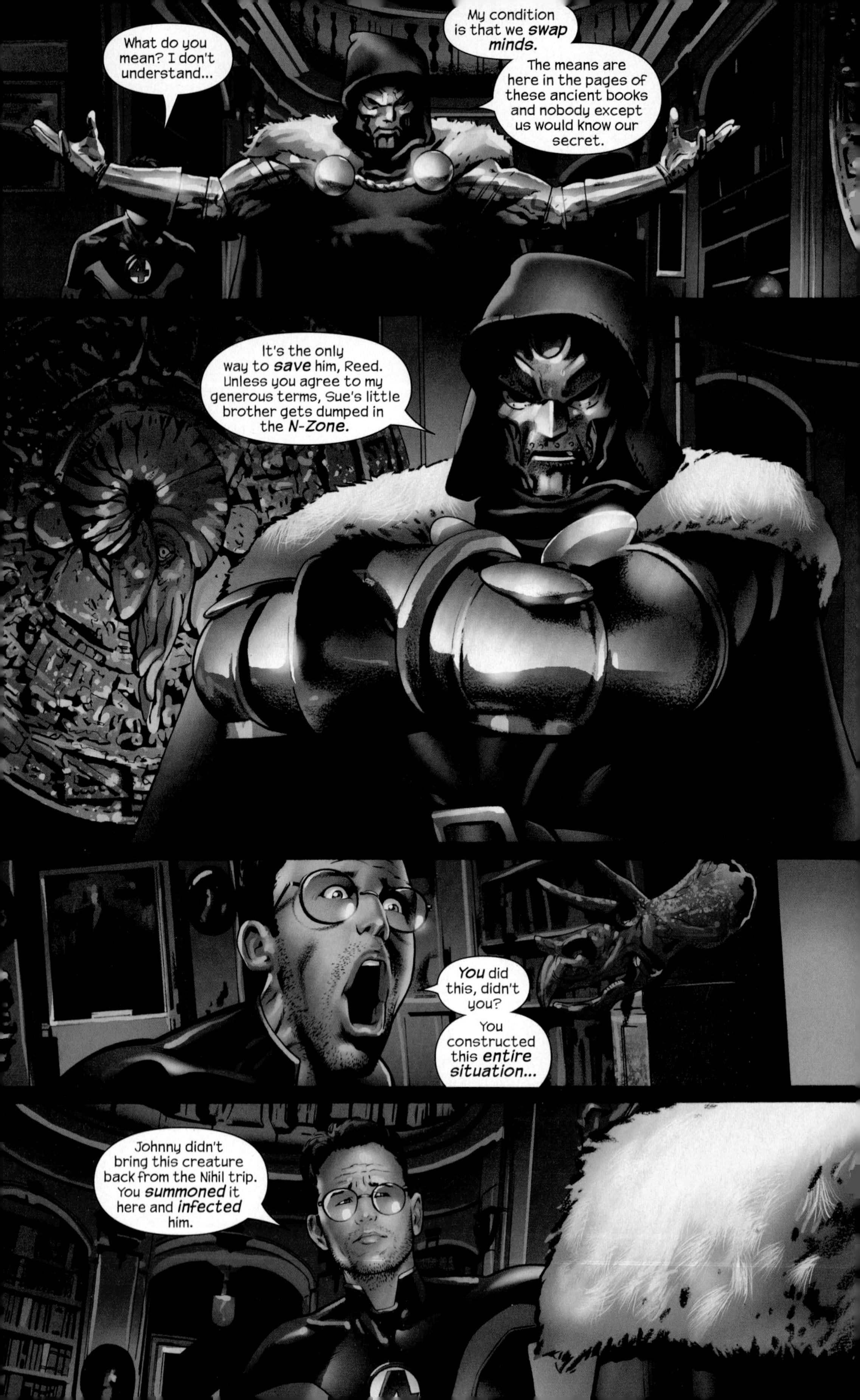
What do you mean? I don't understand...
My condition is that we *swap minds.*
The means are here in the pages of these ancient books and nobody except us would know our secret.
It's the only way to *save* him, Reed. Unless you agree to my generous terms, Sue's little brother gets dumped in the *N-Zone.*
You did this, didn't you?
You constructed this *entire situation...*
Johnny didn't bring this creature back from the Nihil trip. You *summoned* it here and *infected* him.

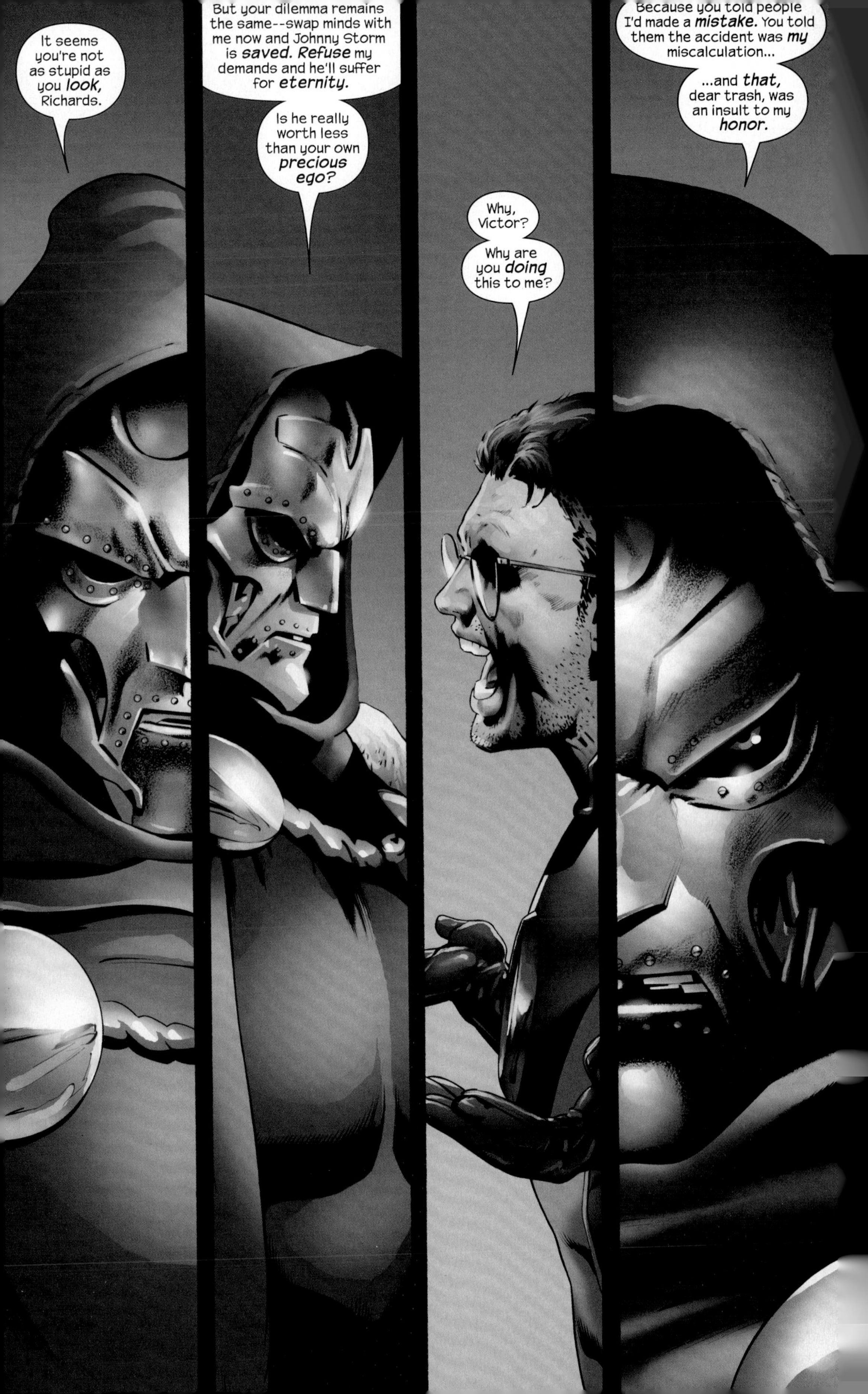
It seems you're not as stupid as you look, Richards.
But your dilemma remains the same--swap minds with me now and Johnny Storm is saved. Refuse my demands and he'll suffer for eternity.
Is he really worth less than your own precious ego?
Why, Victor?
Why are you doing this to me?
Because you told people I'd made a mistake. You told them the accident was my miscalculation...
...and that, dear trash, was an insult to my honor.

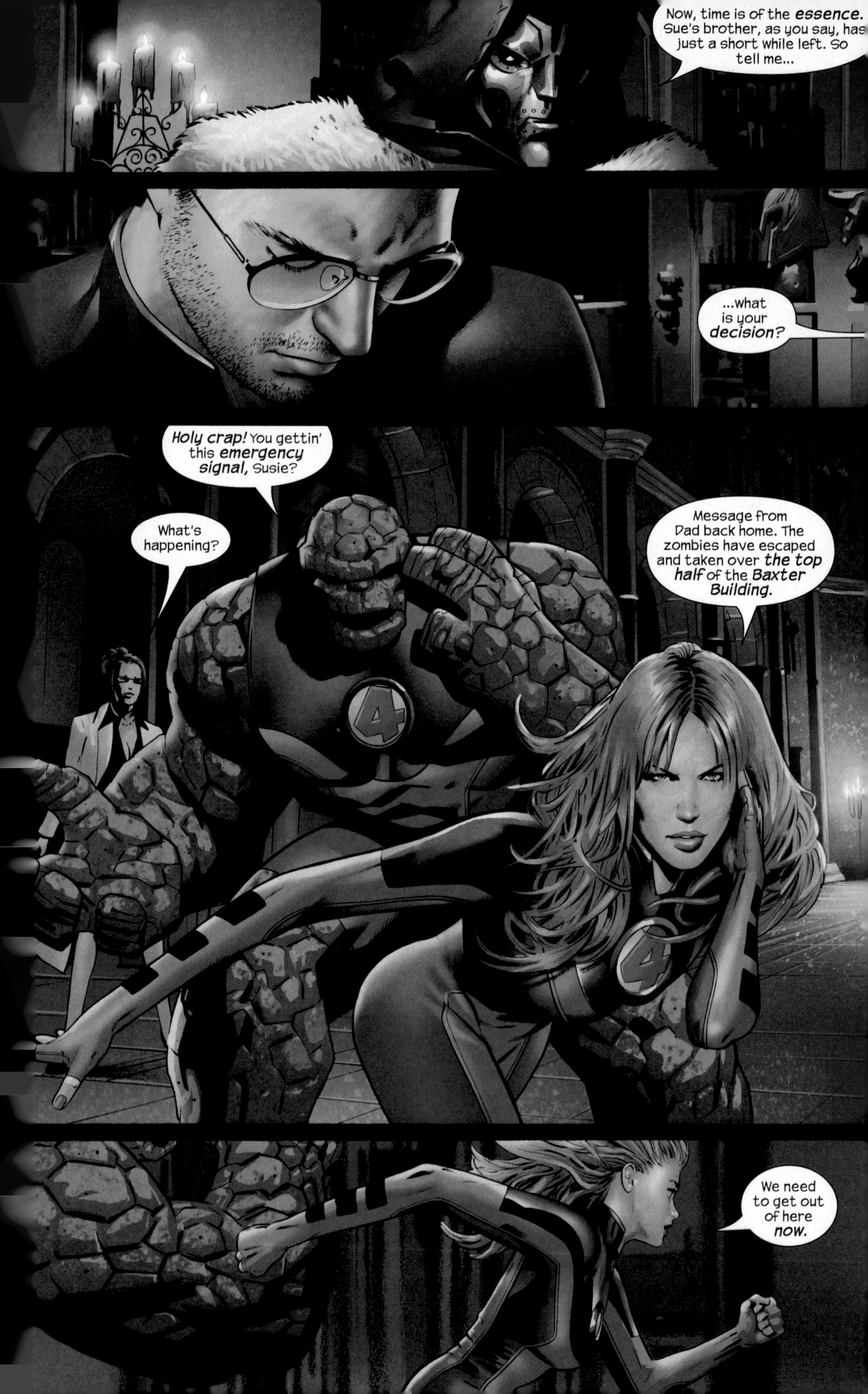
Now, time is of the essence. Sue's brother, as you say, has just a short while left. So tell me...
...what is your decision?
Holy crap! You gettin' this emergency signal, Susie?
What's happening?
Message from Dad back home. The zombies have escaped and taken over the top half of the Baxter Building.
We need to get out of here now.

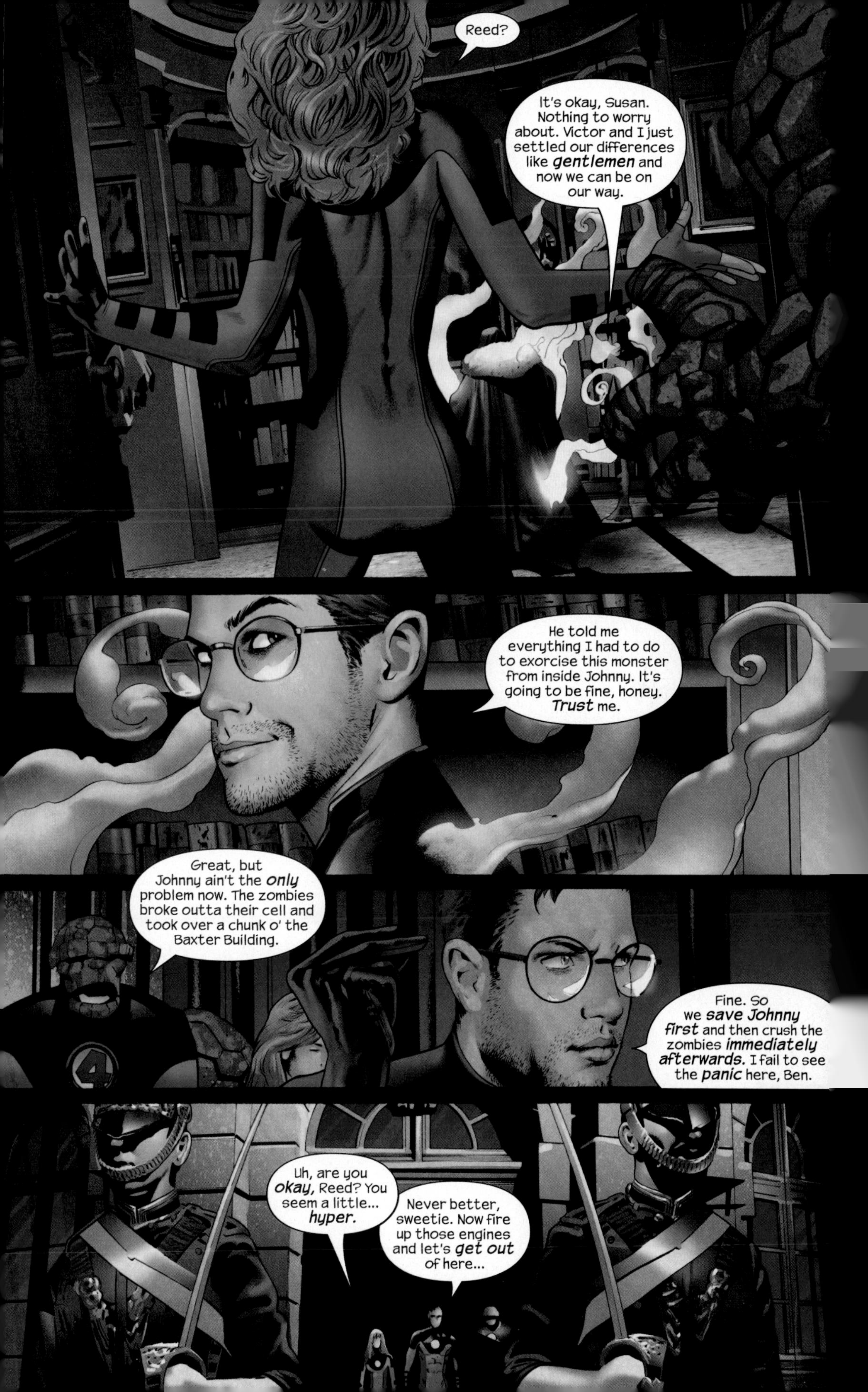

Reed?
It's okay, Susan. Nothing to worry about. Victor and I just settled our differences like *gentlemen* and now we can be on our way.
He told me everything I had to do to exorcise this monster from inside Johnny. It's going to be fine, honey. *Trust* me.
Great, but Johnny ain't the *only* problem now. The zombies broke outta their cell and took over a chunk o' the Baxter Building.
Fine. So we *save Johnny first* and then crush the zombies *immediately afterwards.* I fail to see the *panic* here, Ben.
Uh, are you *okay,* Reed? You seem a little... *hyper.*
Never better, sweetie. Now fire up those engines and let's *get out* of here...

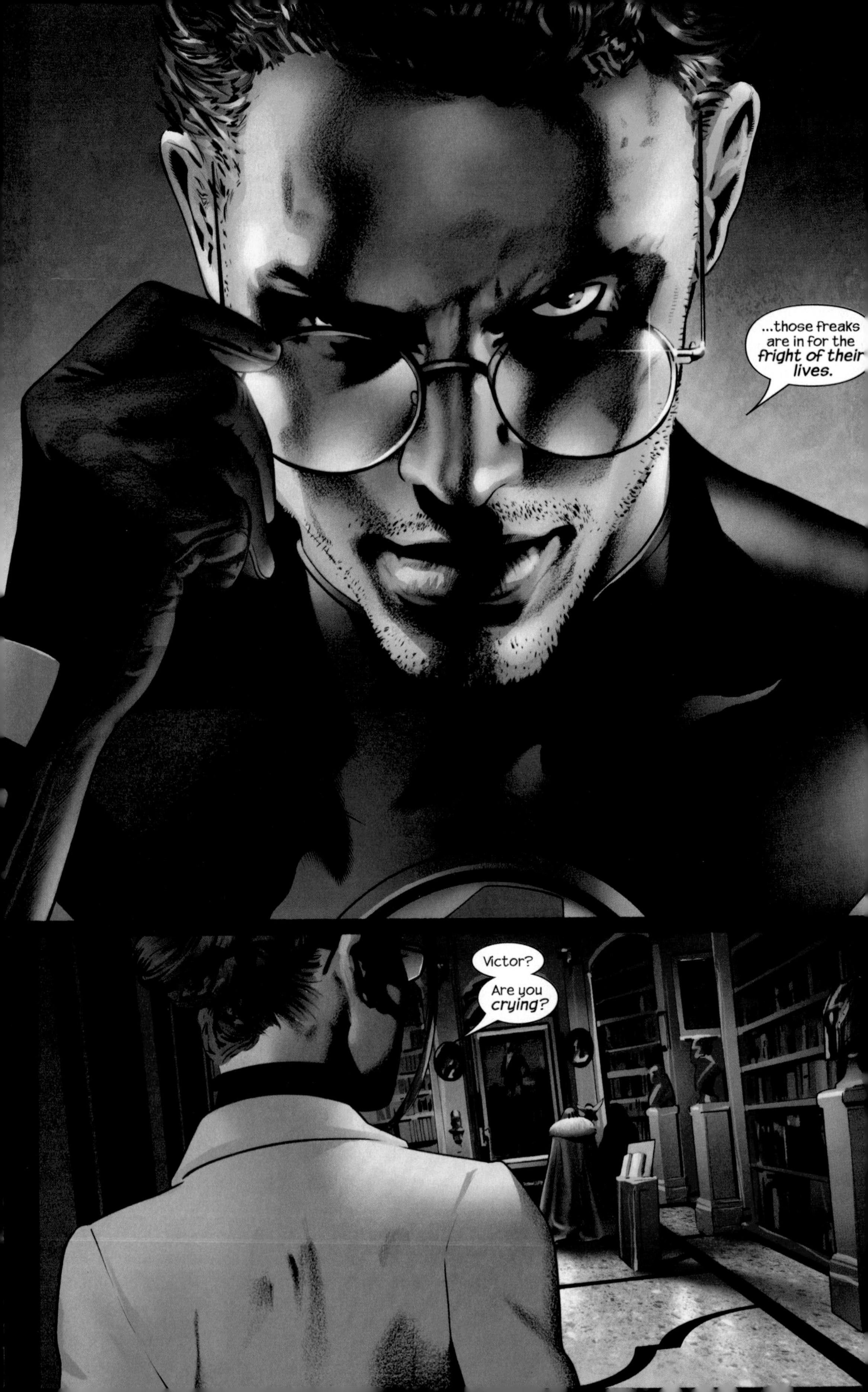
...those freaks are in for the fright of their lives.
Victor?
Are you crying?

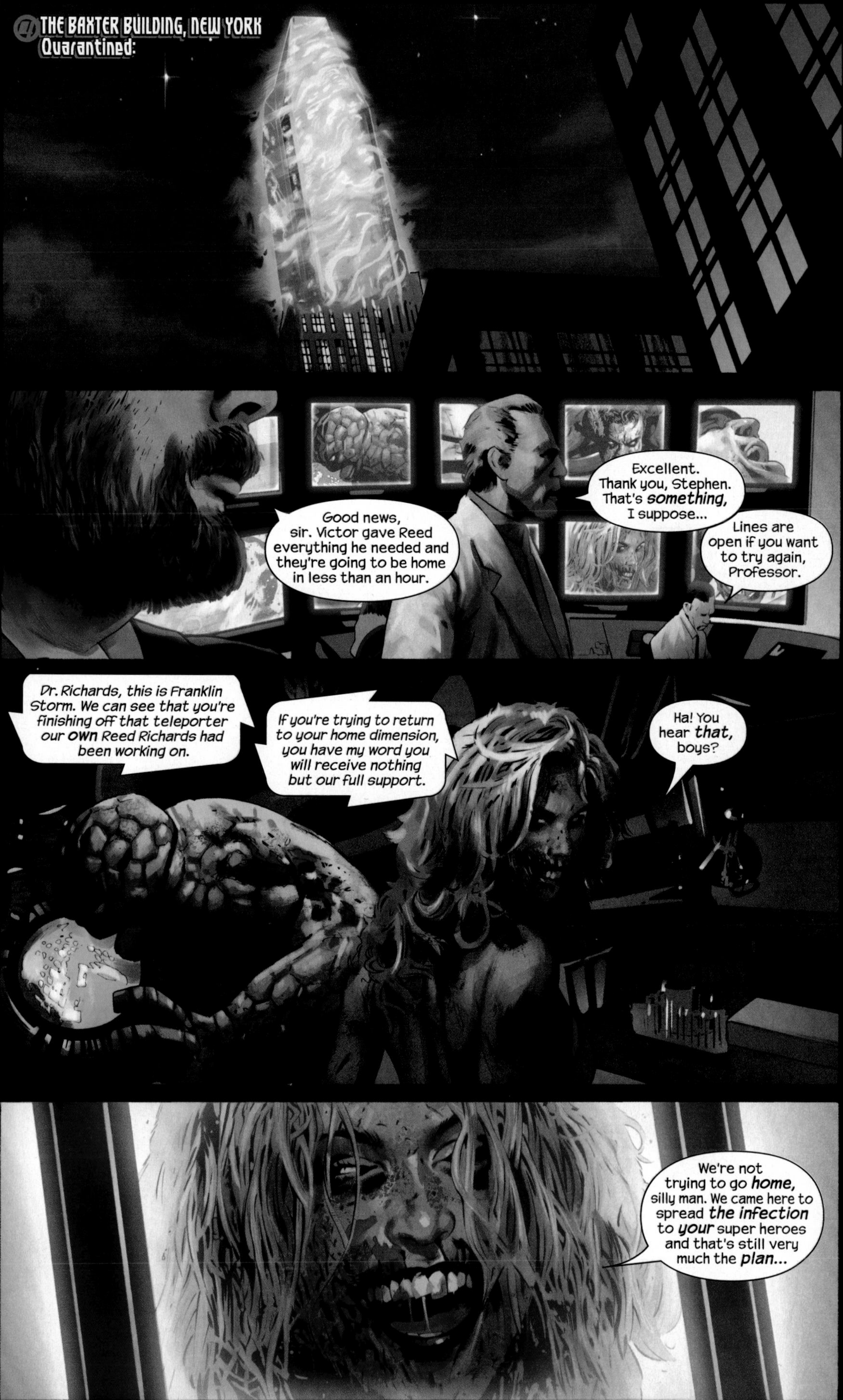
THE BAXTER BUILDING, NEW YORK Quarantined:
Good news, sir. Victor gave Reed everything he needed and they're going to be home in less than an hour.
Excellent. Thank you, Stephen. That's *something,* I suppose...
Lines are open if you want to try again, Professor.
Dr. Richards, this is Franklin Storm. We can see that you're finishing off that teleporter our **own** Reed Richards had been working on.
If you're trying to return to your home dimension, you have my word you will receive nothing but our full support.
Ha! You hear *that,* boys?
We're not trying to go ***home,*** silly man. We came here to spread ***the infection*** to ***your*** super heroes and that's still very much the ***plan...***

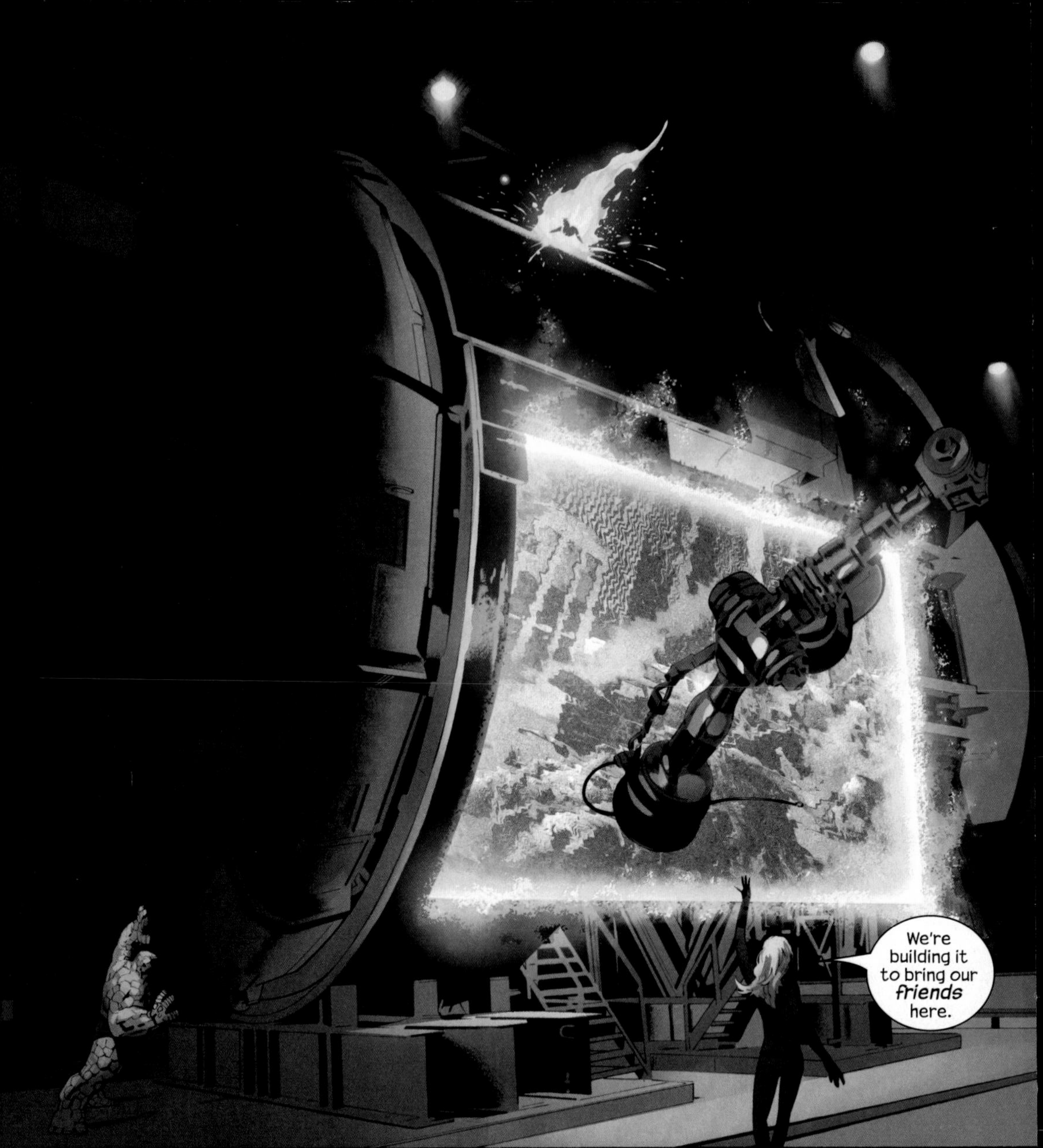
We're building it to bring our *friends* here.

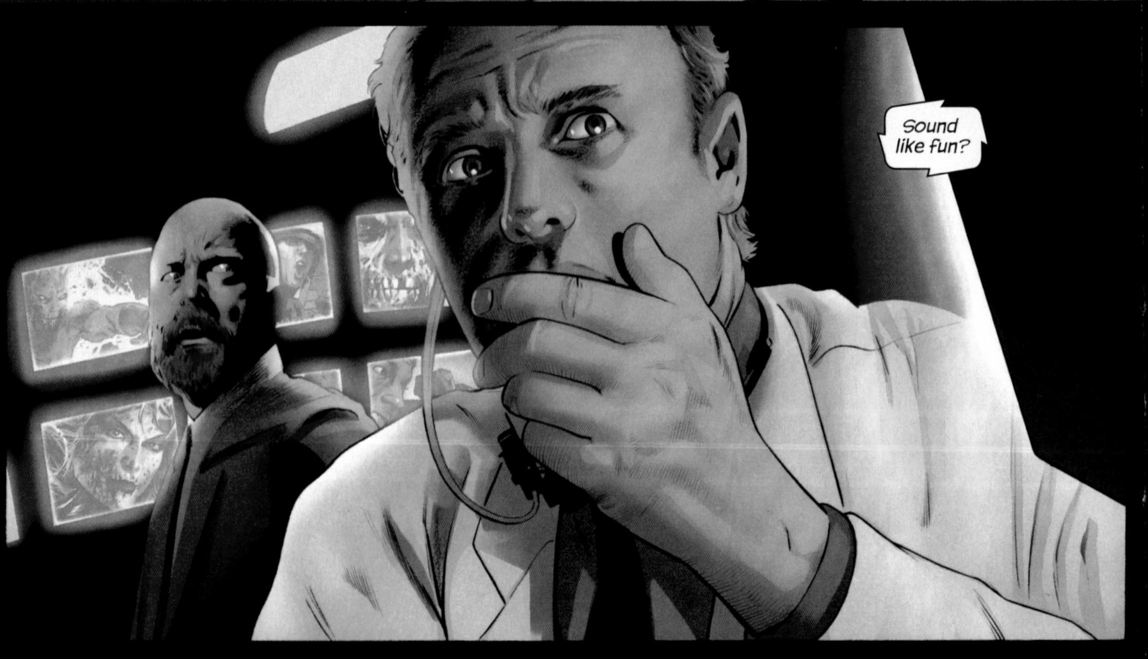
Sound like fun?

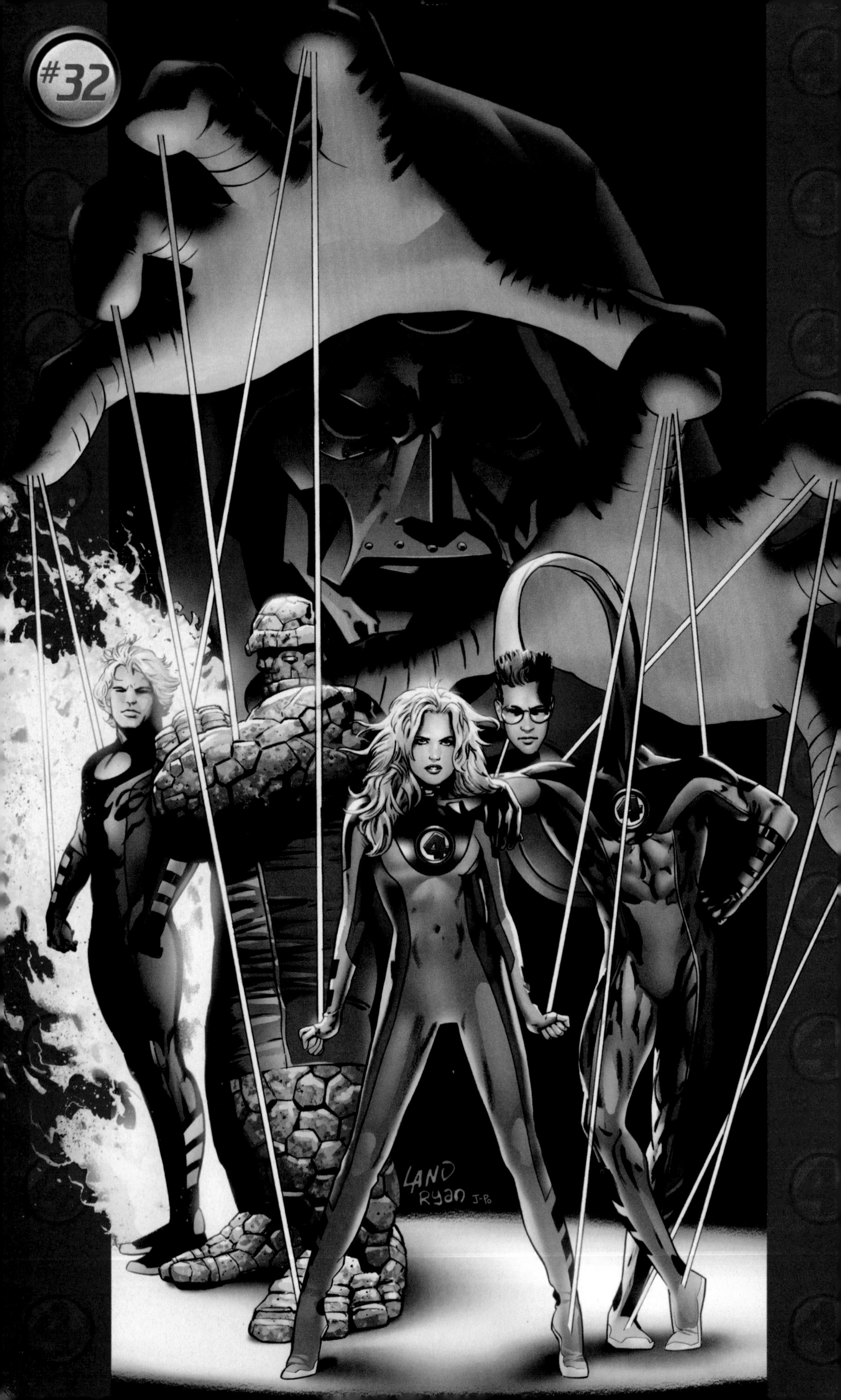
#32
LAND
RYAN J-Po

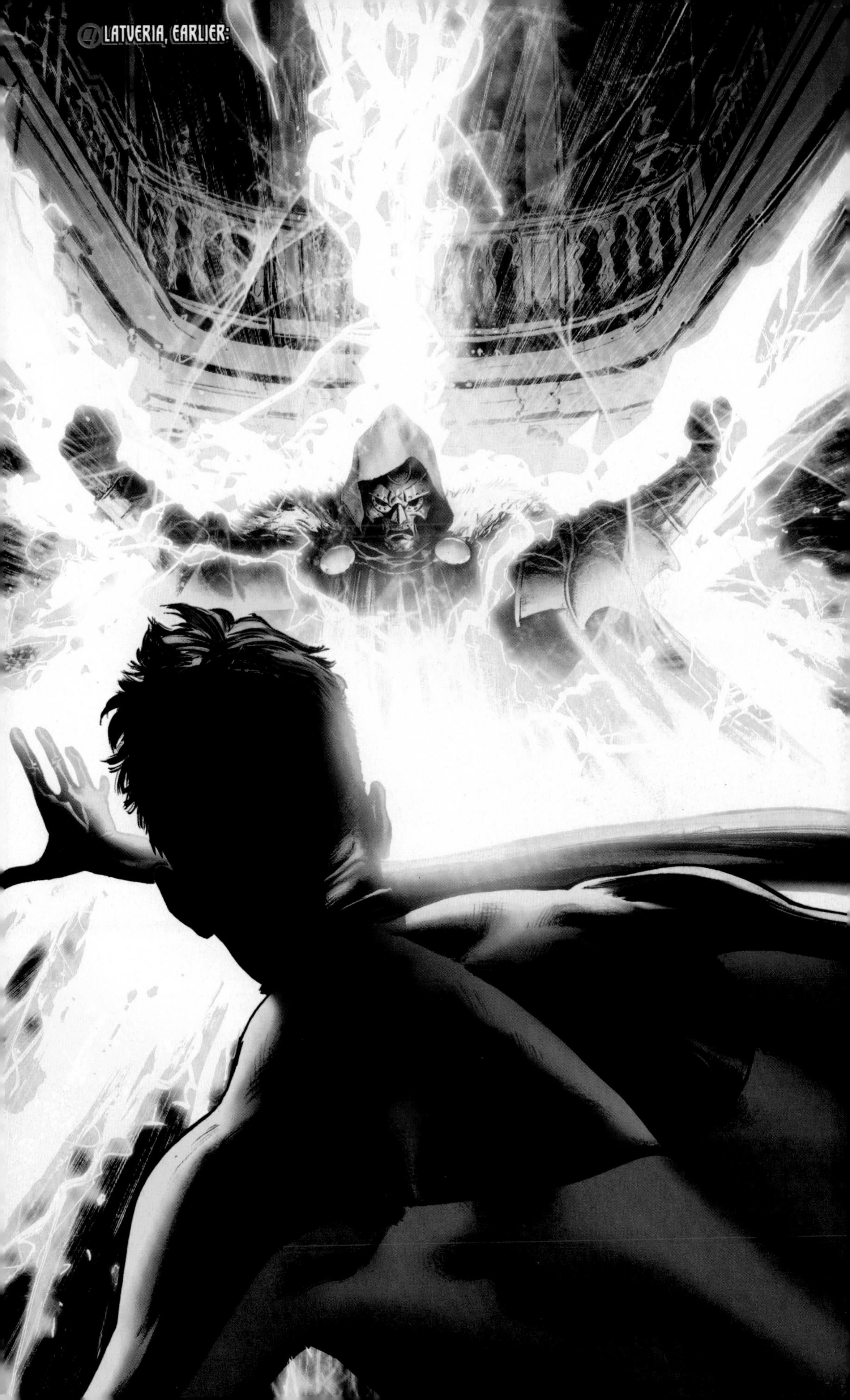
LATVERIA, EARLIER:

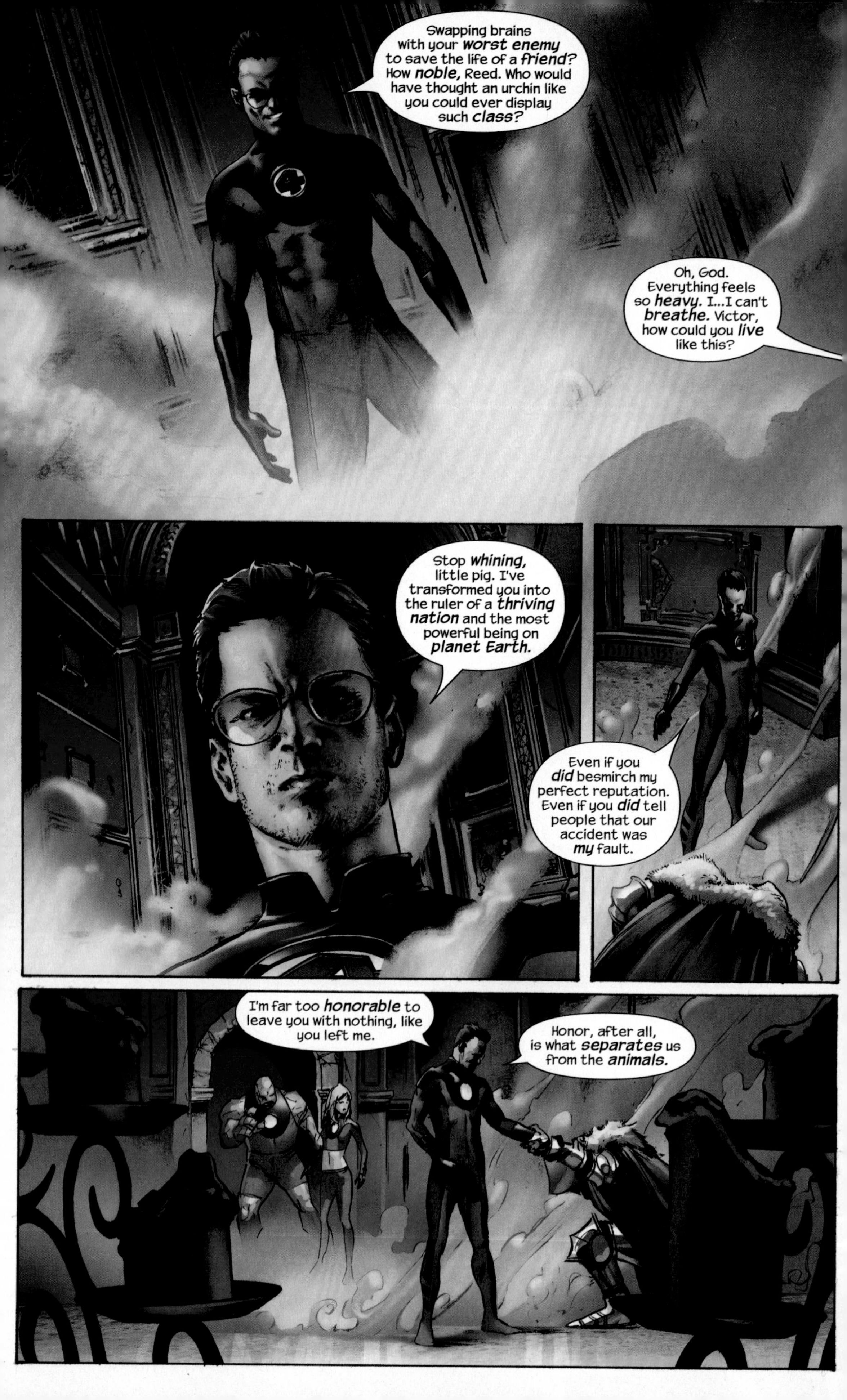
Swapping brains with your worst enemy to save the life of a friend? How noble, Reed. Who would have thought an urchin like you could ever display such class?
Oh, God. Everything feels so heavy. I...I can't breathe. Victor, how could you live like this?
Stop whining, little pig. I've transformed you into the ruler of a thriving nation and the most powerful being on planet Earth.
Even if you did besmirch my perfect reputation. Even if you did tell people that our accident was my fault.
I'm far too honorable to leave you with nothing, like you left me.
Honor, after all, is what separates us from the animals.

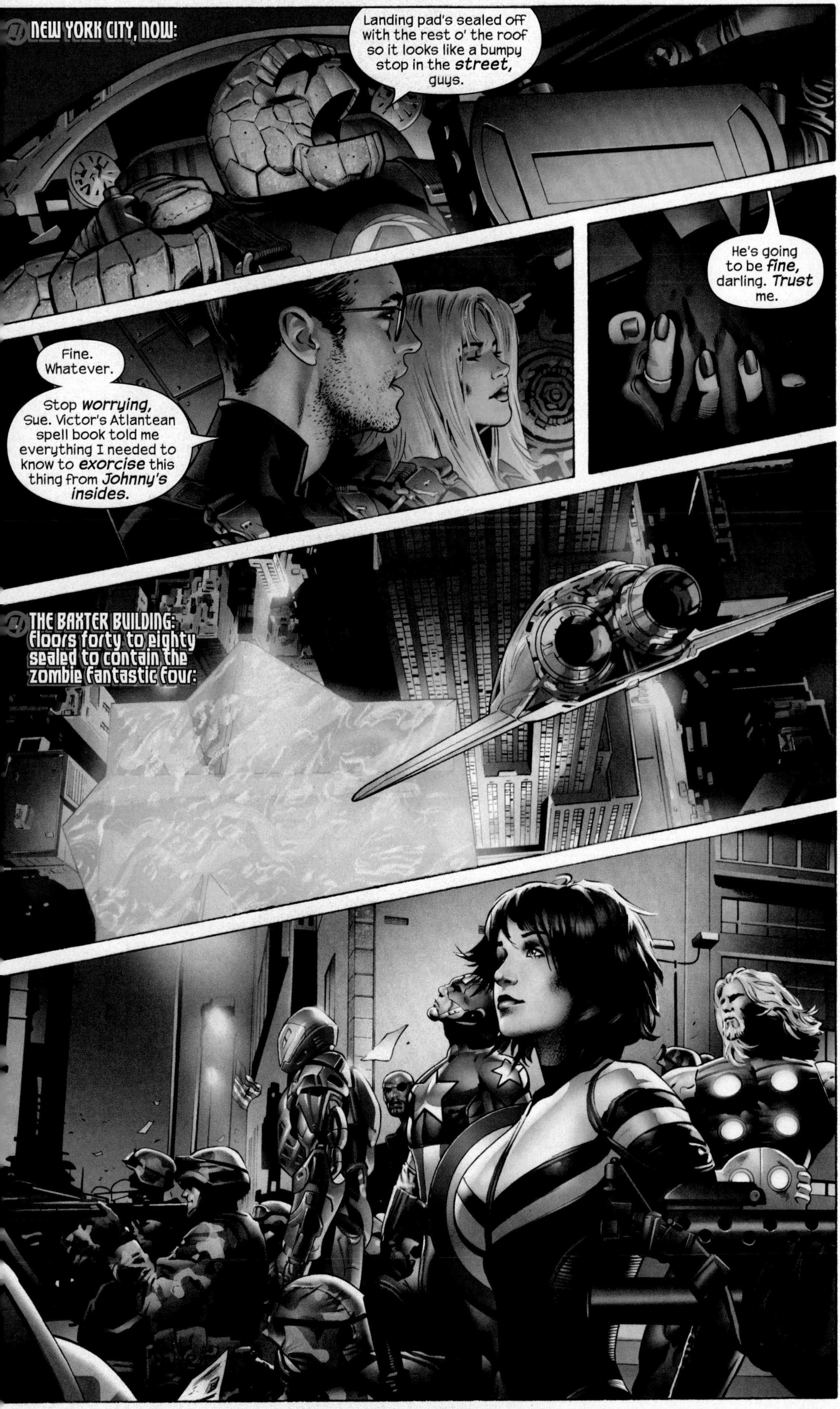
NEW YORK CITY, NOW:
Landing pad's sealed off with the rest o' the roof so it looks like a bumpy stop in the street, guys.
Fine. Whatever.
Stop worrying, Sue. Victor's Atlantean spell book told me everything I needed to know to exorcise this thing from Johnny's insides.
He's going to be fine, darling. Trust me.
THE BAXTER BUILDING: Floors forty to eighty sealed to contain the zombie Fantastic Four:

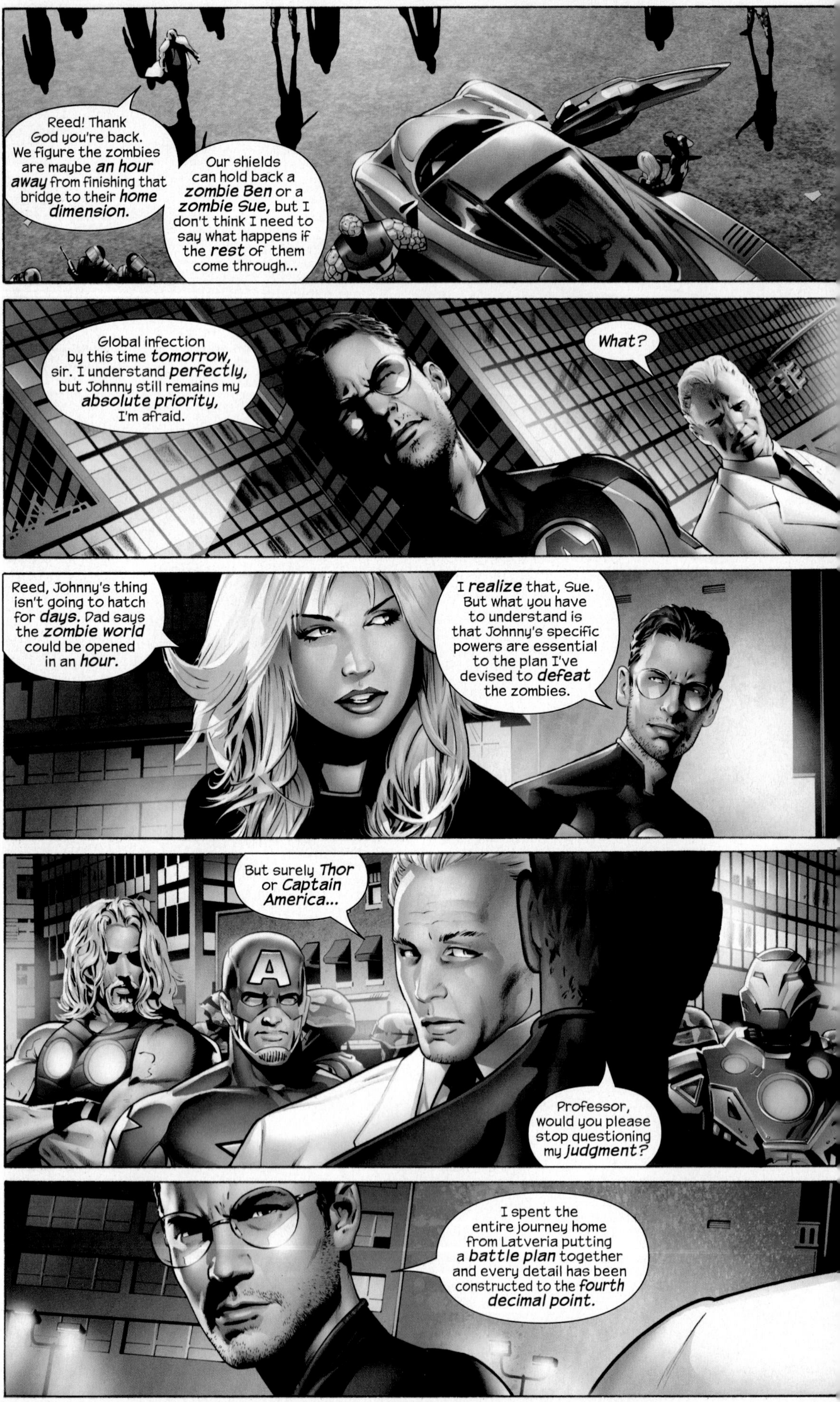

Reed! Thank God you're back. We figure the zombies are maybe an hour away from finishing that bridge to their home dimension.
Our shields can hold back a zombie Ben or a zombie Sue, but I don't think I need to say what happens if the rest of them come through...
Global infection by this time tomorrow, sir. I understand perfectly, but Johnny still remains my absolute priority, I'm afraid.
What?
Reed, Johnny's thing isn't going to hatch for days. Dad says the zombie world could be opened in an hour.
I realize that, Sue. But what you have to understand is that Johnny's specific powers are essential to the plan I've devised to defeat the zombies.
But surely Thor or Captain America...
Professor, would you please stop questioning my judgment?
I spent the entire journey home from Latveria putting a battle plan together and every detail has been constructed to the fourth decimal point.

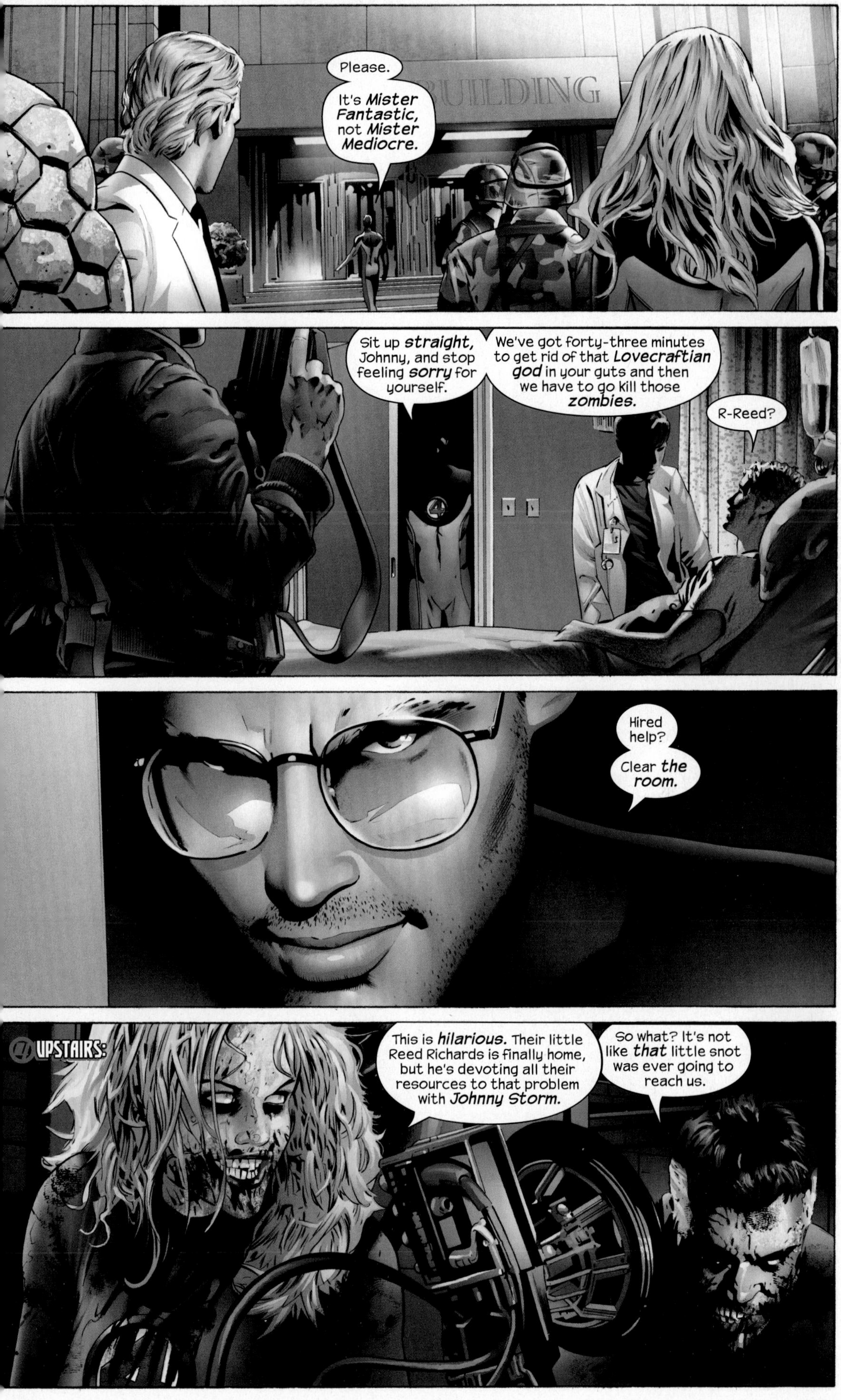
BUILDING
Please.
It's Mister Fantastic, not Mister Mediocre.
Sit up straight, Johnny, and stop feeling sorry for yourself.
We've got forty-three minutes to get rid of that Lovecraftian god in your guts and then we have to go kill those zombies.
R-Reed?
Hired help?
Clear the room.
UPSTAIRS:
This is hilarious. Their little Reed Richards is finally home, but he's devoting all their resources to that problem with Johnny Storm.
So what? It's not like that little snot was ever going to reach us.

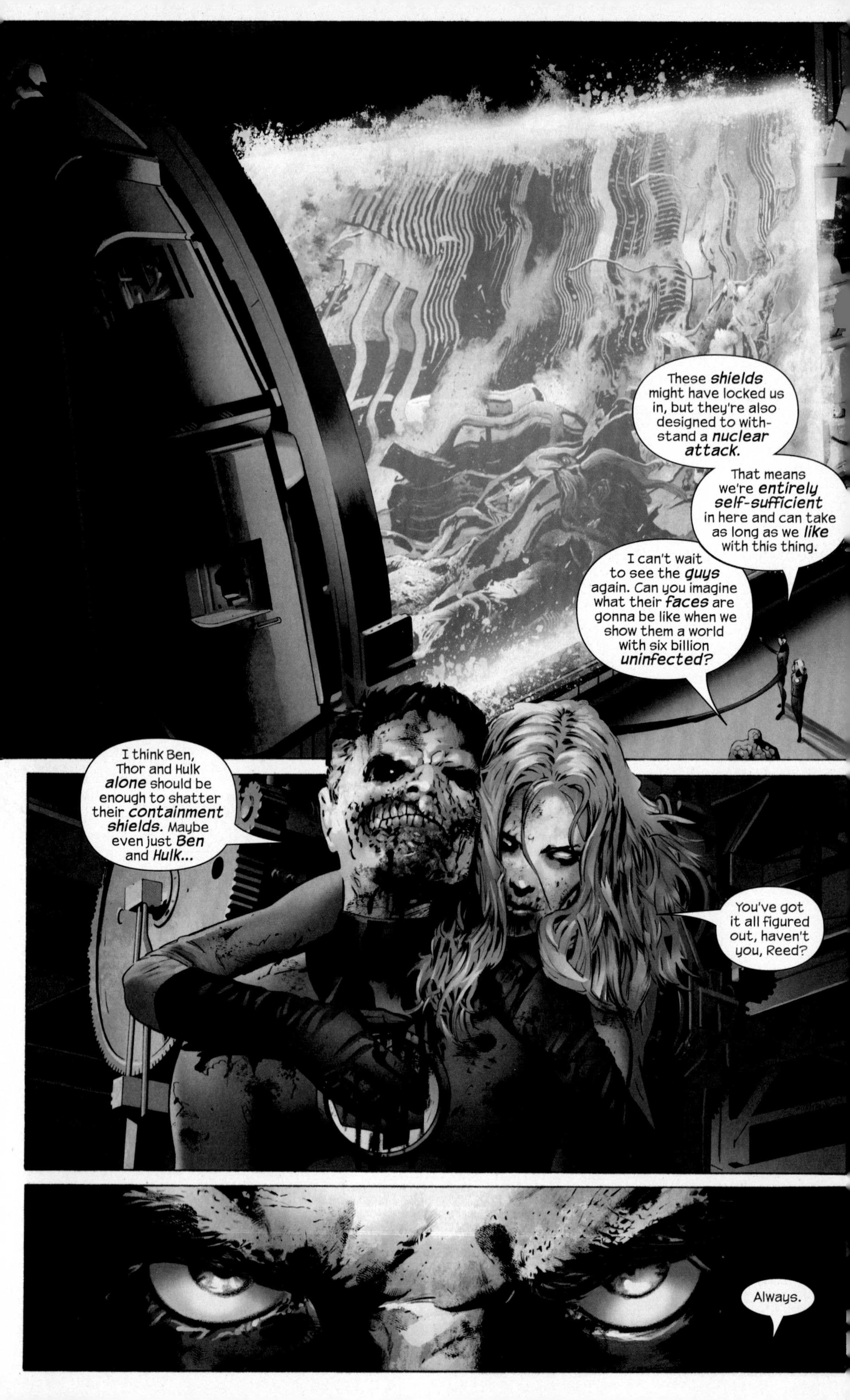
These *shields* might have locked us in, but they're also designed to with-stand a *nuclear attack.*
That means we're *entirely self-sufficient* in here and can take as long as we *like* with this thing.
I can't wait to see the *guys* again. Can you imagine what their *faces* are gonna be like when we show them a world with six billion *uninfected?*
I think Ben, Thor and Hulk *alone* should be enough to shatter their *containment shields.* Maybe even just *Ben* and *Hulk...*
You've got it all figured out, haven't you, Reed?
Always.

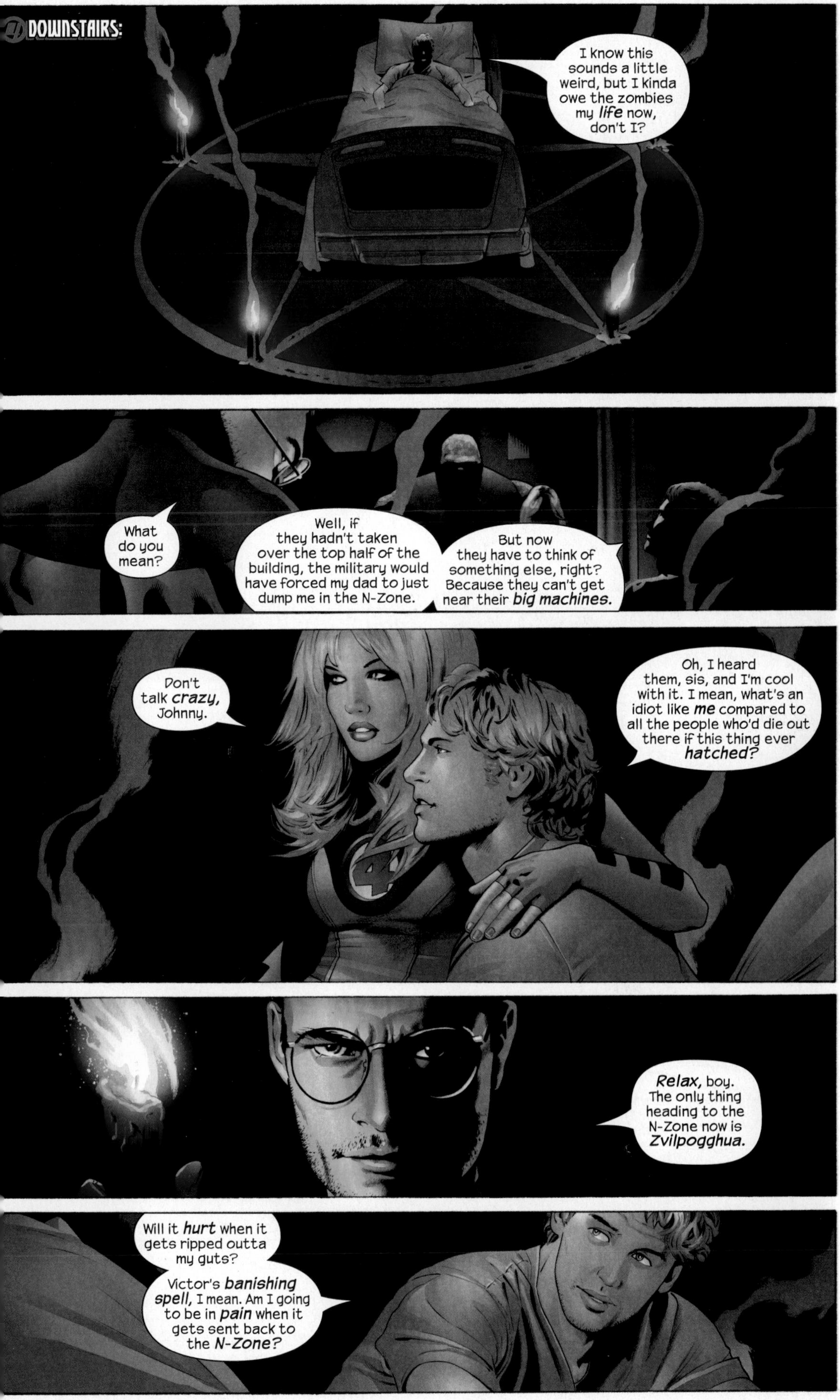
DOWNSTAIRS:
I know this sounds a little weird, but I kinda owe the zombies my *life* now, don't I?
What do you mean?
Well, if they hadn't taken over the top half of the building, the military would have forced my dad to just dump me in the N-Zone.
But now they have to think of something else, right? Because they can't get near their *big machines.*
Don't talk *crazy,* Johnny.
Oh, I heard them, sis, and I'm cool with it. I mean, what's an idiot like *me* compared to all the people who'd die out there if this thing ever *hatched?*
Relax, boy. The only thing heading to the N-Zone now is *Zvilpogghua.*
Will it *hurt* when it gets ripped outta my guts?
Victor's *banishing spell,* I mean. Am I going to be in *pain* when it gets sent back to the *N-Zone?*

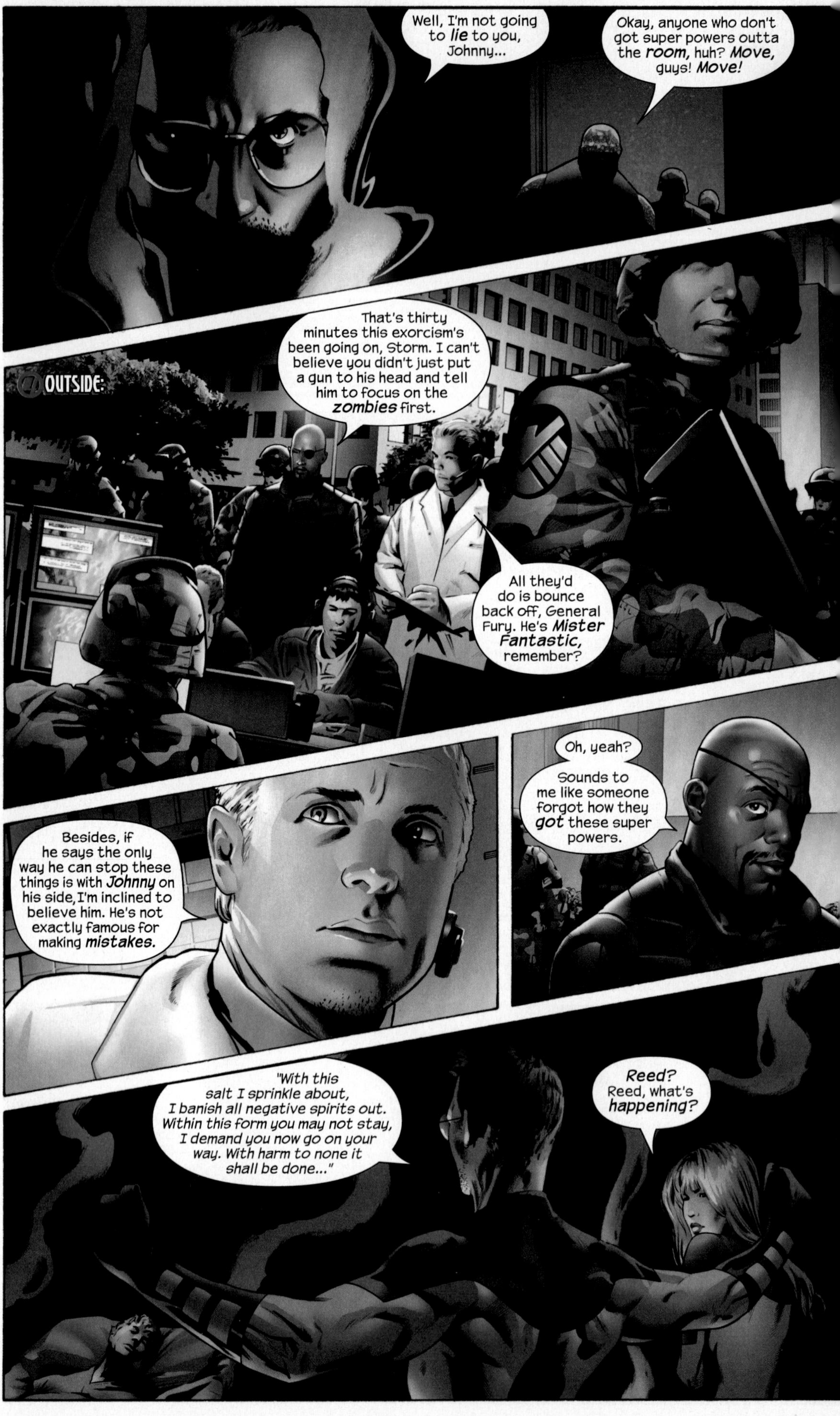

Well, I'm not going to *lie* to you, Johnny...
Okay, anyone who don't got super powers outta the *room,* huh? *Move,* guys! *Move!*
OUTSIDE:
That's thirty minutes this exorcism's been going on, Storm. I can't believe you didn't just put a gun to his head and tell him to focus on the *zombies* first.
All they'd do is bounce back off, General Fury. He's *Mister Fantastic,* remember?
Besides, if he says the only way he can stop these things is with *Johnny* on his side, I'm inclined to believe him. He's not exactly famous for making *mistakes.*
Oh, yeah?
Sounds to me like someone forgot how they *got* these super powers.
"With this salt I sprinkle about, I banish all negative spirits out. Within this form you may not stay, I demand you now go on your way. With harm to none it shall be done..."
Reed? Reed, what's *happening?*

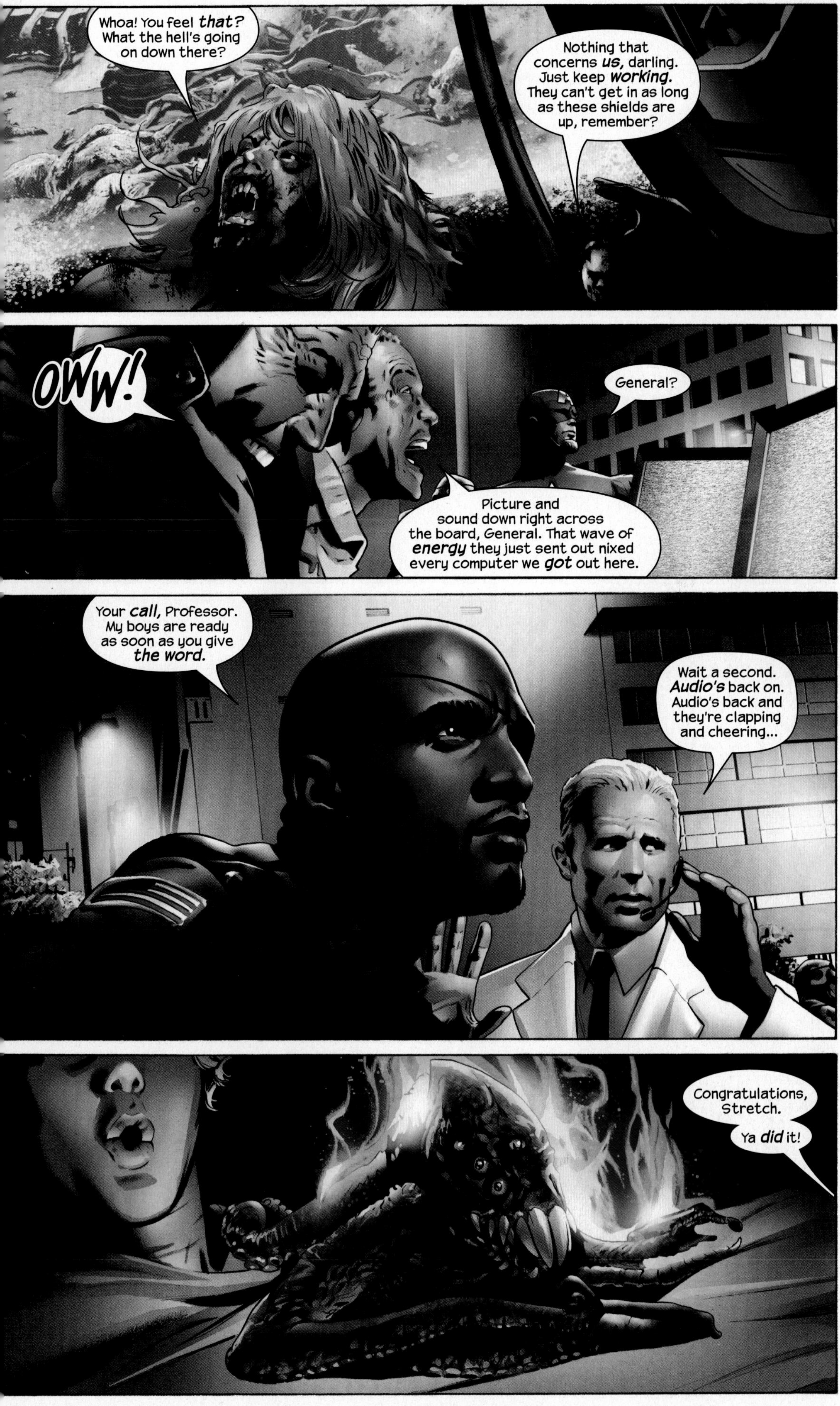
Whoa! You feel that? What the hell's going on down there?
Nothing that concerns us, darling. Just keep working. They can't get in as long as these shields are up, remember?
OWW!
General?
Picture and sound down right across the board, General. That wave of energy they just sent out nixed every computer we got out here.
Your call, Professor. My boys are ready as soon as you give the word.
Wait a second. Audio's back on. Audio's back and they're clapping and cheering...
Congratulations, Stretch.
Ya did it!

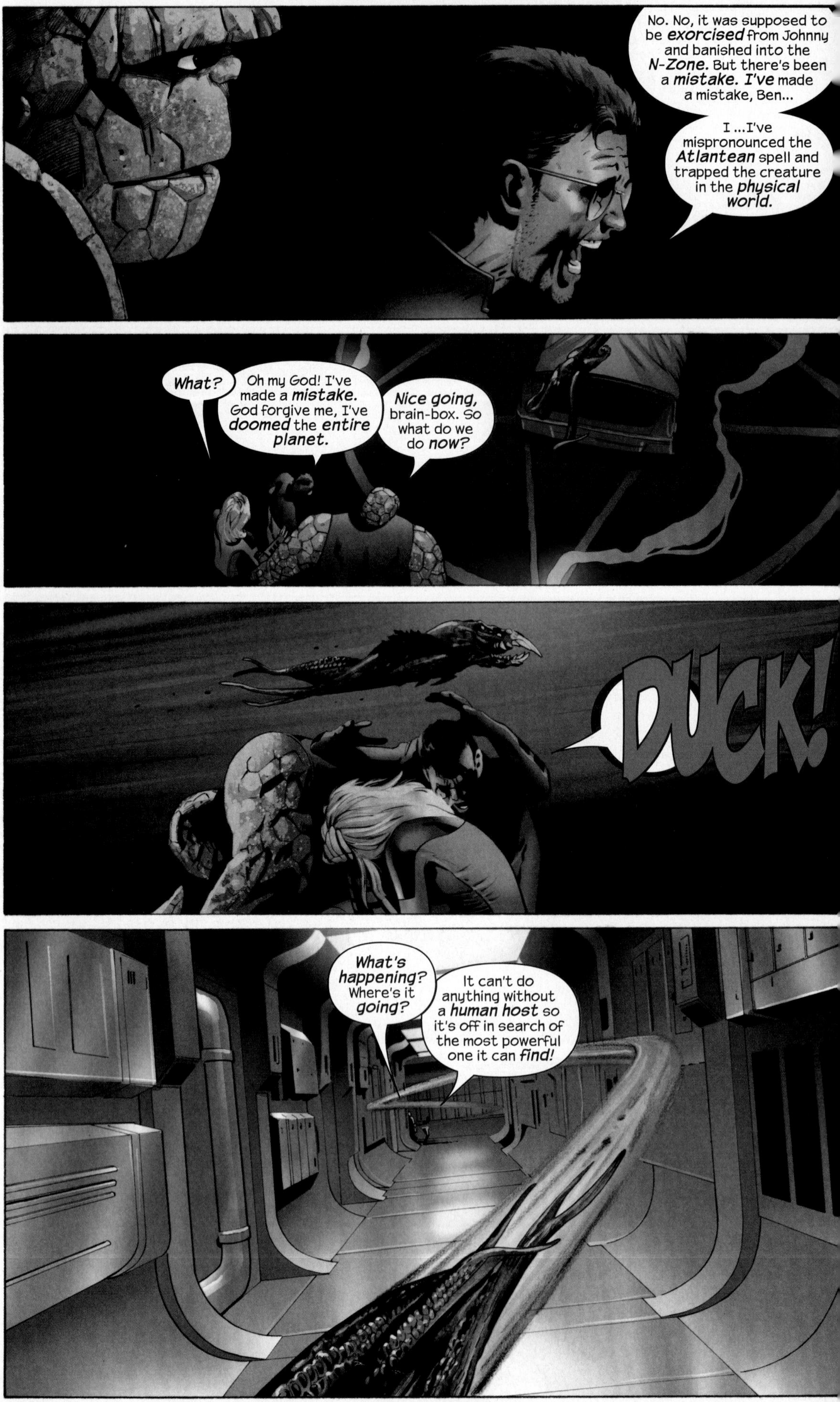
No. No, it was supposed to be *exorcised* from Johnny and banished into the *N-Zone.* But there's been a *mistake. I've* made a mistake, Ben...
I ...I've mispronounced the *Atlantean* spell and trapped the creature in the *physical world.*
What?
Oh my God! I've made a *mistake.* God forgive me, I've *doomed* the *entire planet.*
Nice going, brain-box. So what do we do *now?*
DUCK!
What's happening? Where's it *going?*
It can't do anything without a *human host* so it's off in search of the most powerful one it can *find!*

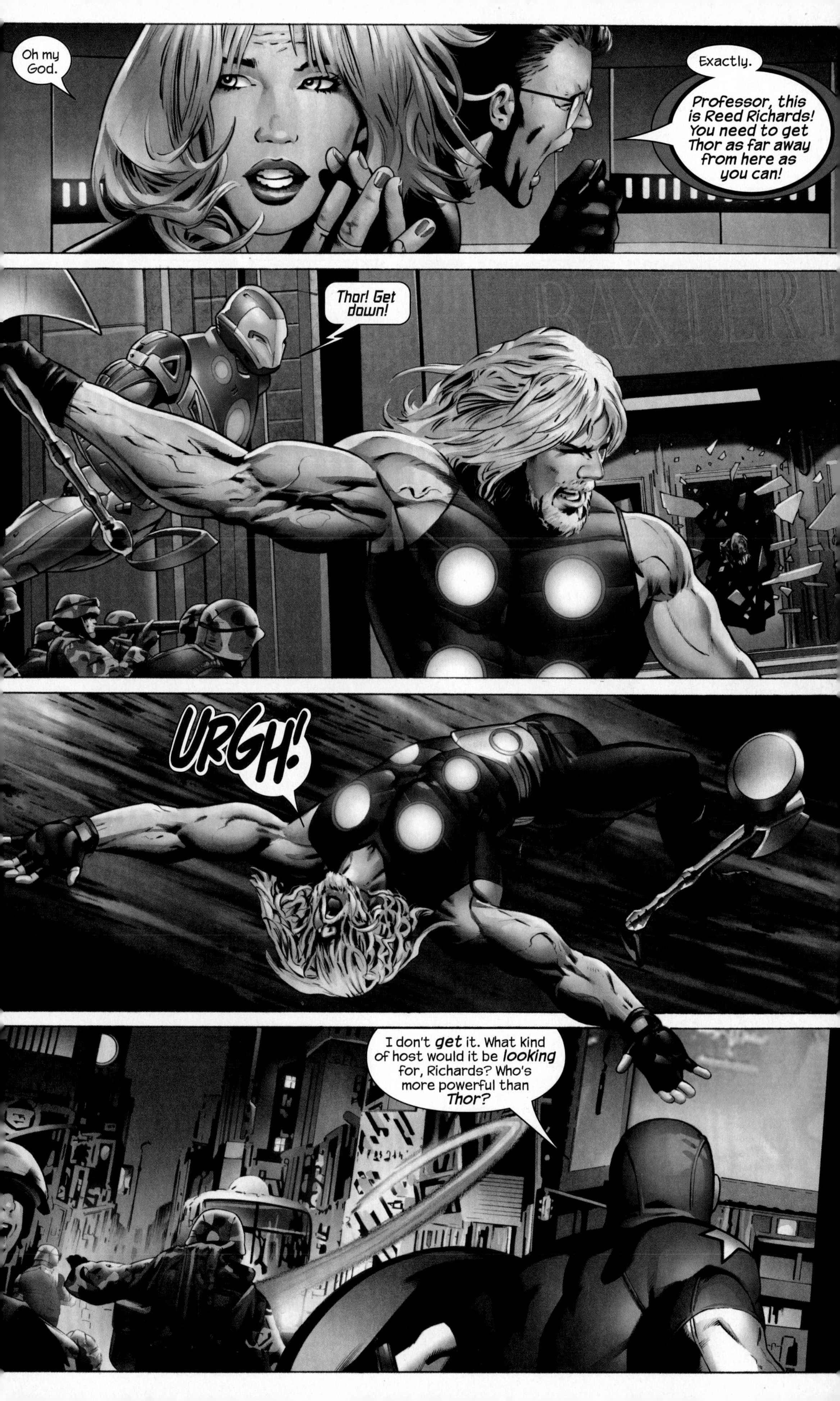
Oh my God.
Exactly.
Professor, this is Reed Richards! You need to get Thor as far away from here as you can!
Thor! Get down!
URGH!
I don't get it. What kind of host would it be looking for, Richards? Who's more powerful than Thor?

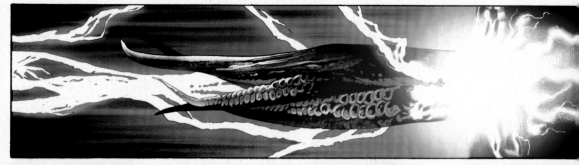

Sorry to burst your *bubble*, boys.

Now open those shields and let's *finish* this thing.

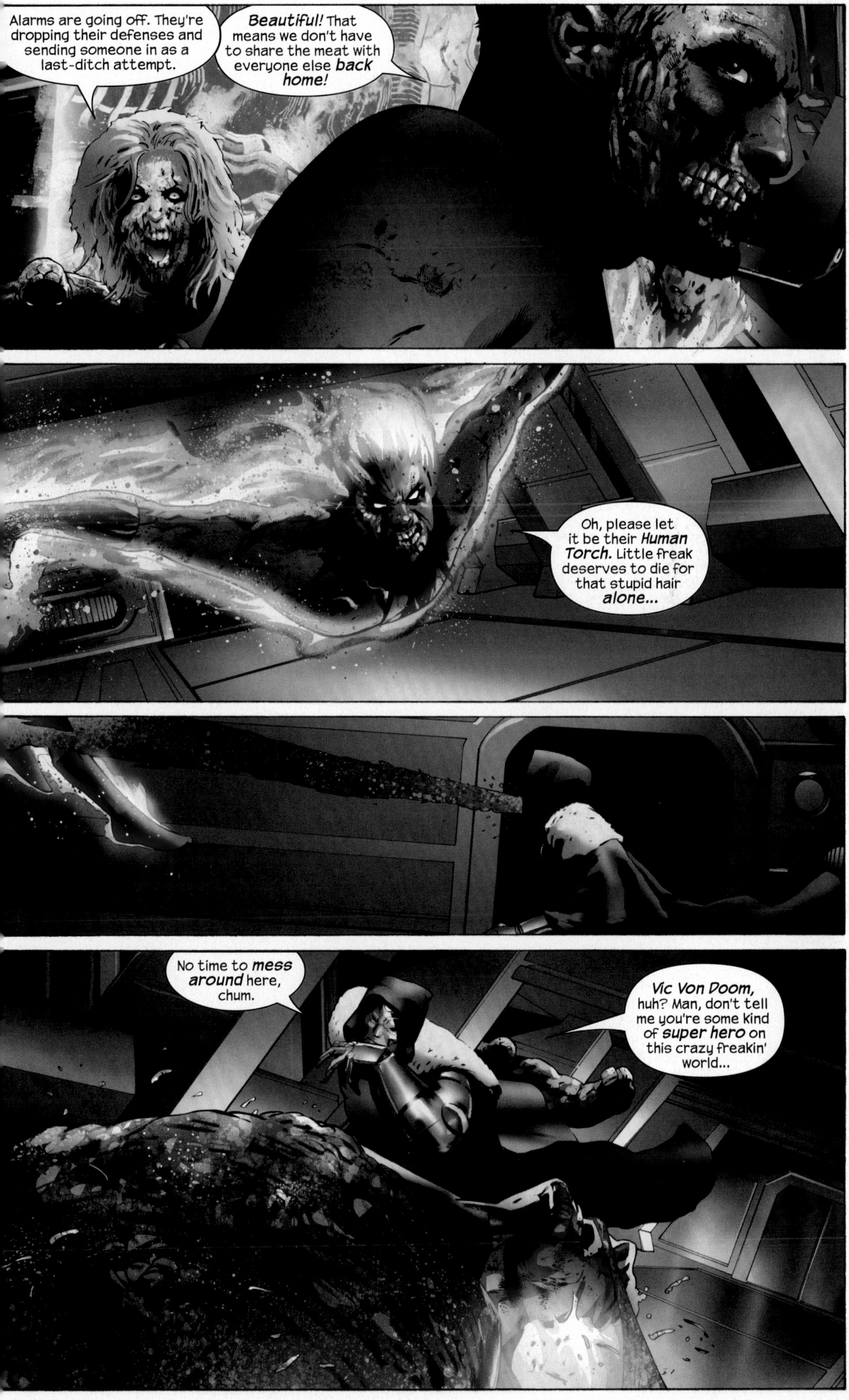
Alarms are going off. They're dropping their defenses and sending someone in as a last-ditch attempt.
Beautiful! That means we don't have to share the meat with everyone else *back home!*
Oh, please let it be their *Human Torch.* Little freak deserves to die for that stupid hair *alone...*
No time to *mess around* here, chum.
Vic Von Doom, huh? Man, don't tell me you're some kind of *super hero* on this crazy freakin' world...

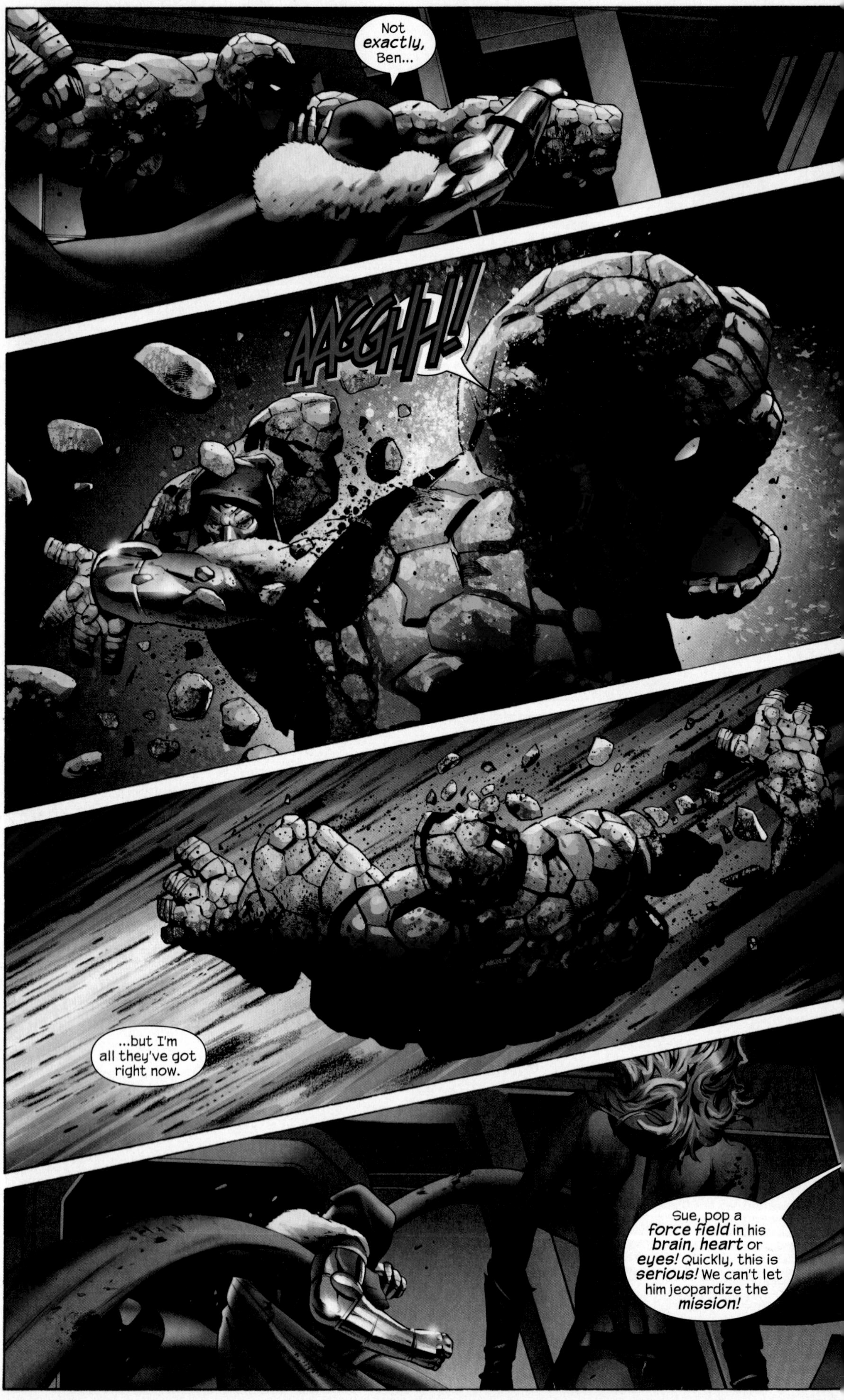
Not exactly, Ben...
AAGGHH!!
...but I'm all they've got right now.
Sue, pop a force field in his brain, heart or eyes! Quickly, this is serious! We can't let him jeopardize the mission!

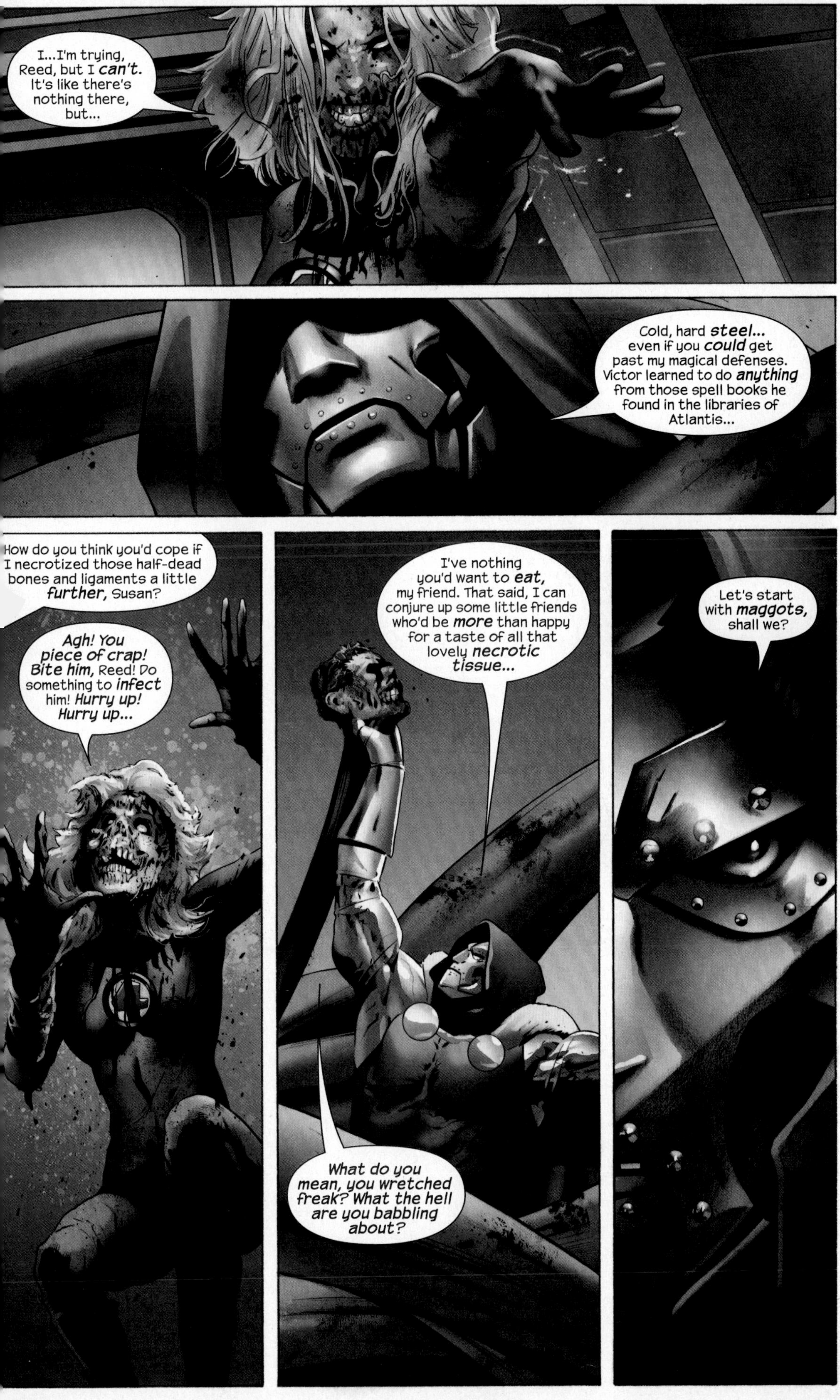
I...I'm trying, Reed, but I can't. It's like there's nothing there, but...
Cold, hard steel... even if you could get past my magical defenses. Victor learned to do anything from those spell books he found in the libraries of Atlantis...
How do you think you'd cope if I necrotized those half-dead bones and ligaments a little further, Susan?
Agh! You piece of crap! Bite him, Reed! Do something to infect him! Hurry up! Hurry up...
I've nothing you'd want to eat, my friend. That said, I can conjure up some little friends who'd be more than happy for a taste of all that lovely necrotic tissue...
What do you mean, you wretched freak? What the hell are you babbling about?
Let's start with maggots, shall we?

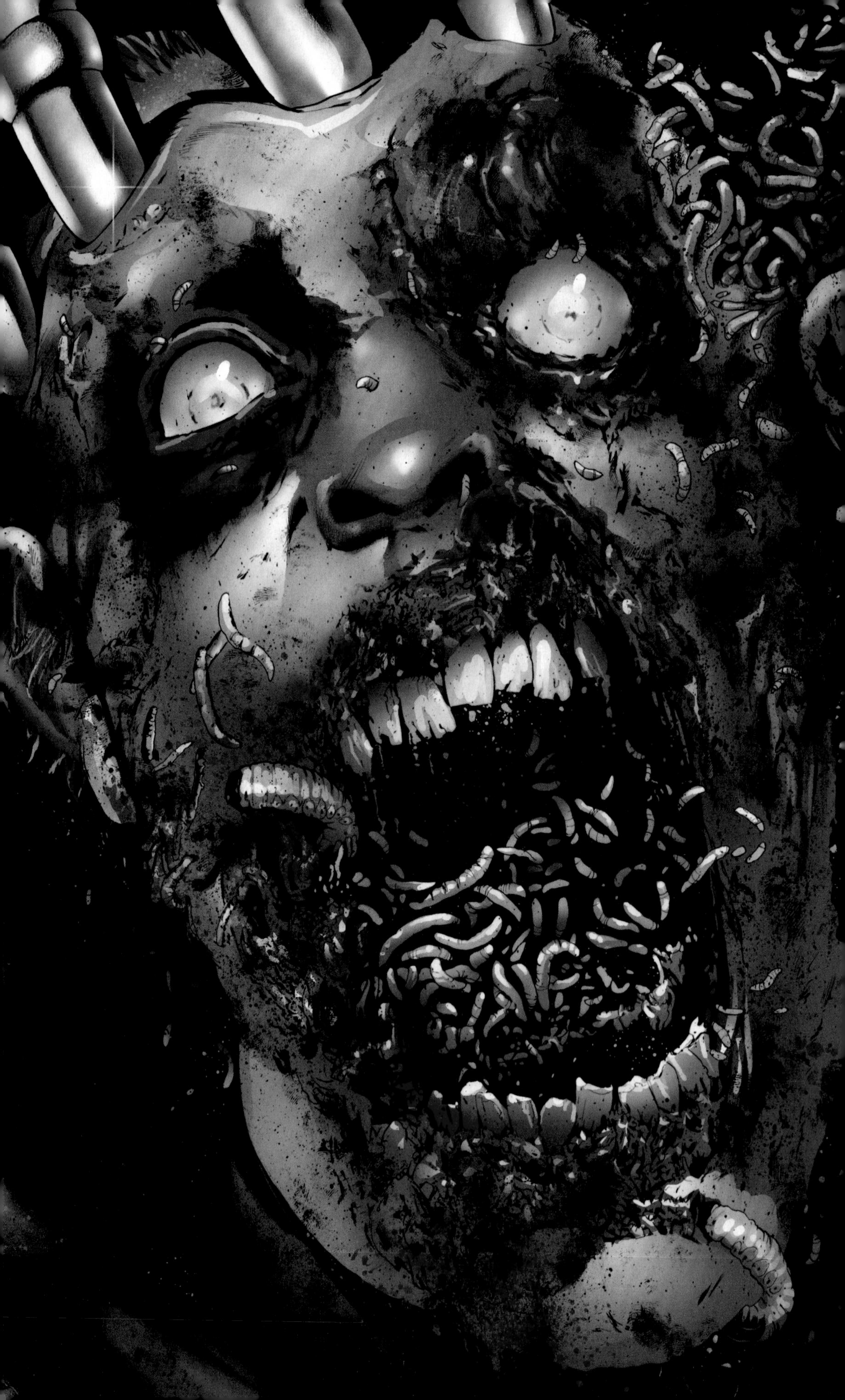

Victor, this is Franklin Storm. Audio's back, but we've still lost visual. What's *happening* in there? Have you managed to get the entity to the *teleporter*?

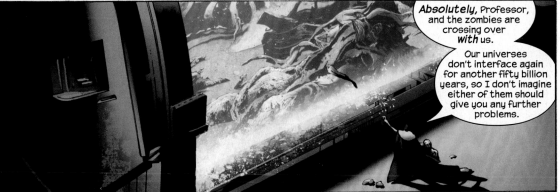

Absolutely, Professor, and the zombies are crossing over *with* us.

Our universes don't interface again for another fifty billion years, so I don't imagine either of them should give you any further problems.

Victor, I have to say... well, to be honest... I'm a little *shocked* by this sacrifice you're making on everyone's behalf.

It seems a great many of us have *misjudged* you over the years, son.

Oh, but this isn't *Victor*, sir.

Quite the opposite, actually.

Excuse me?

Do *you* want to tell him or shall I, Victor?

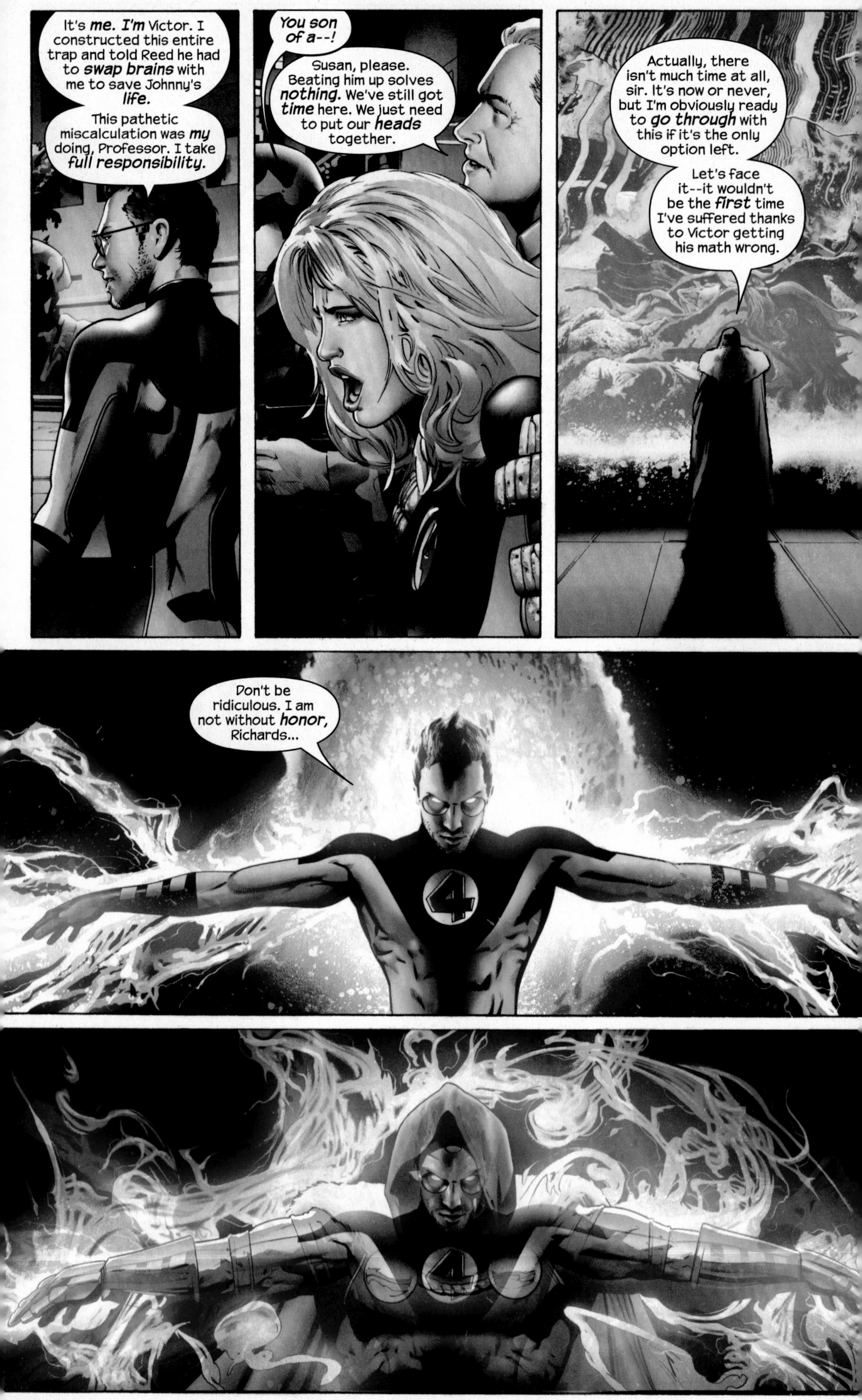
It's me. I'm Victor. I constructed this entire trap and told Reed he had to swap brains with me to save Johnny's life.
This pathetic miscalculation was my doing, Professor. I take full responsibility.
You son of a--!
Susan, please. Beating him up solves nothing. We've still got time here. We just need to put our heads together.
Actually, there isn't much time at all, sir. It's now or never, but I'm obviously ready to go through with this if it's the only option left.
Let's face it--it wouldn't be the first time I've suffered thanks to Victor getting his math wrong.
Don't be ridiculous. I am not without honor, Richards...

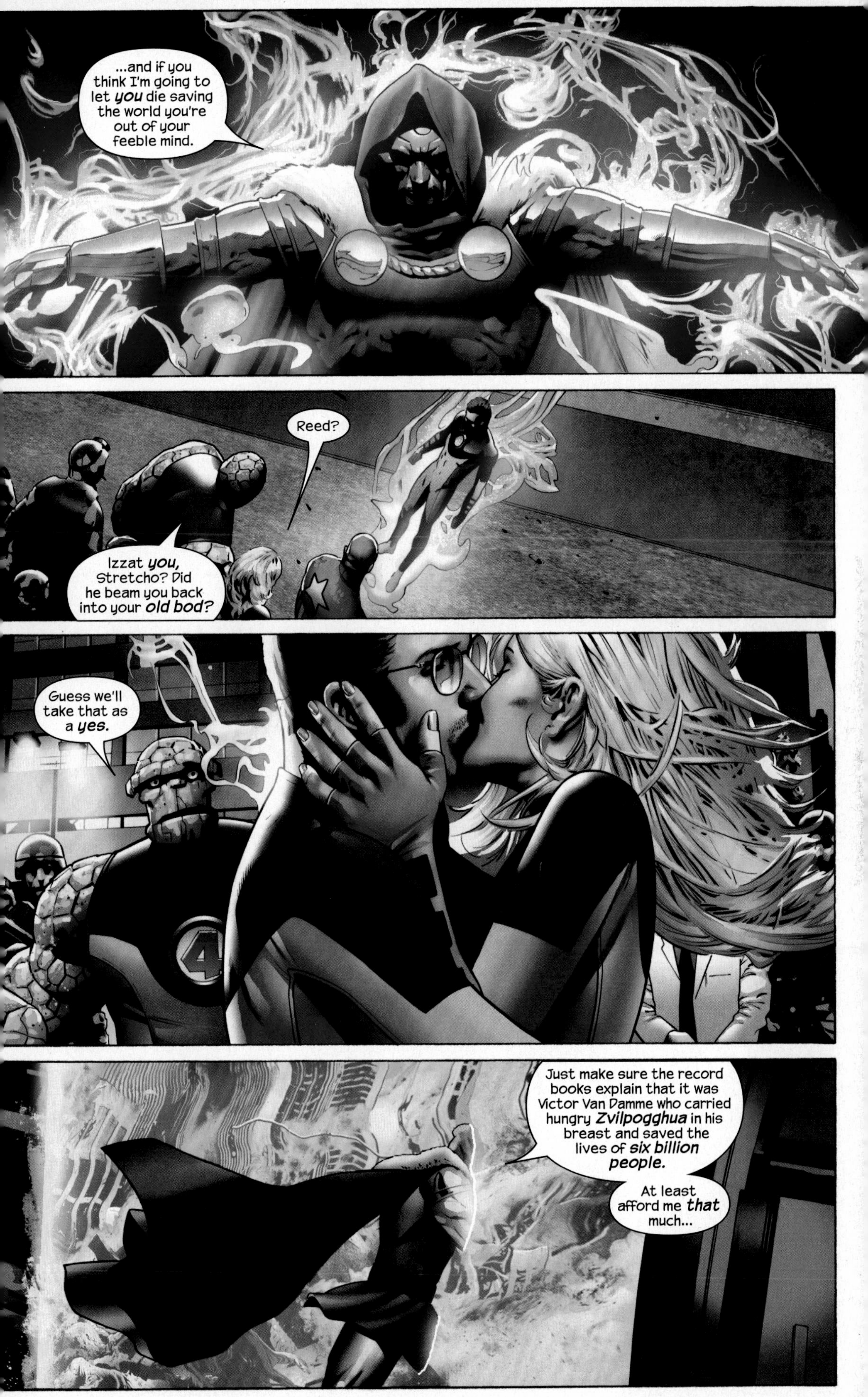
...and if you think I'm going to let *you* die saving the world you're out of your feeble mind.
Reed?
Izzat *you,* Stretcho? Did he beam you back into your *old bod?*
Guess we'll take that as a *yes.*
Just make sure the record books explain that it was Victor Van Damme who carried hungry *Zvilpogghua* in his breast and saved the lives of *six billion people.*
At least afford me *that* much...

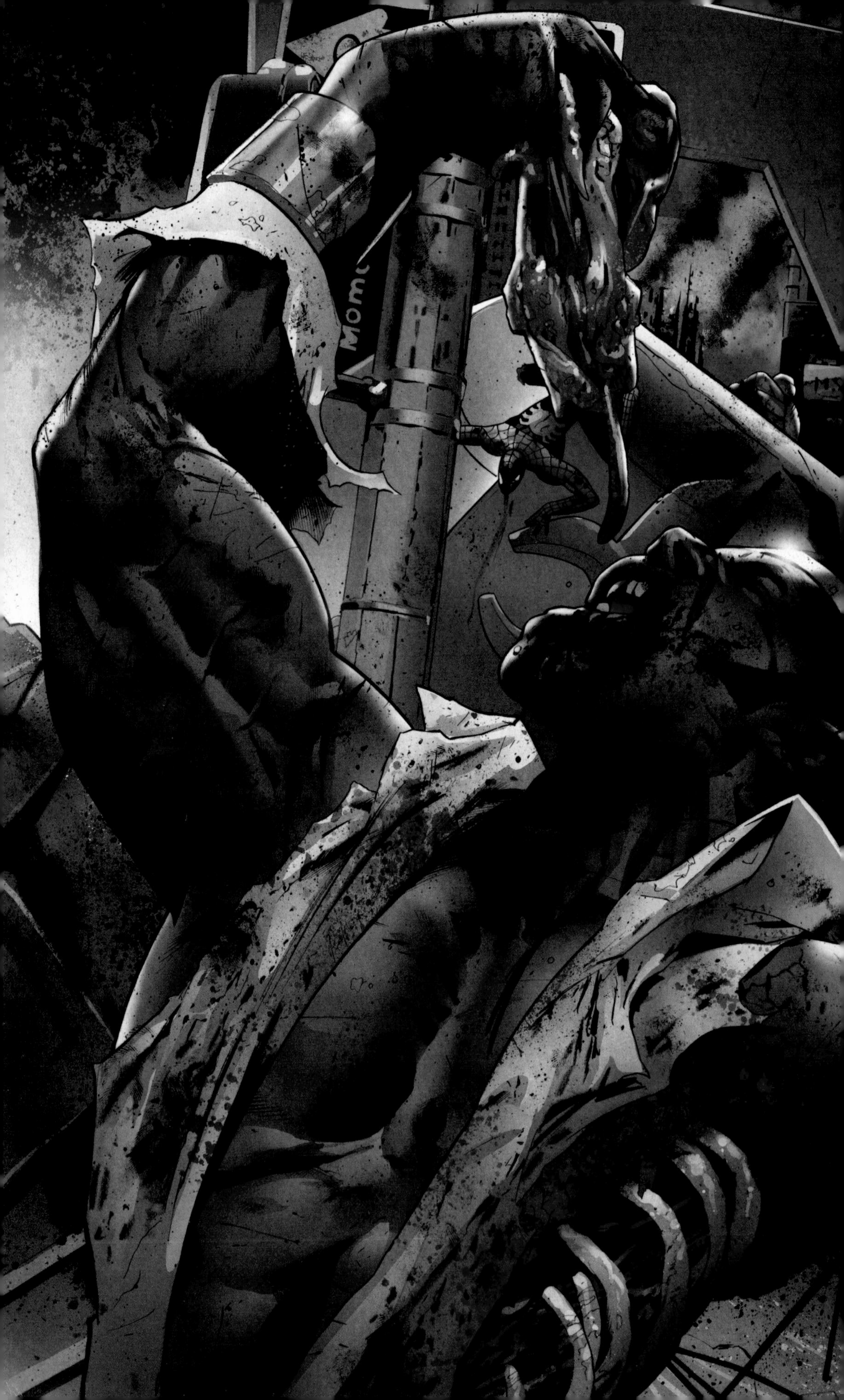

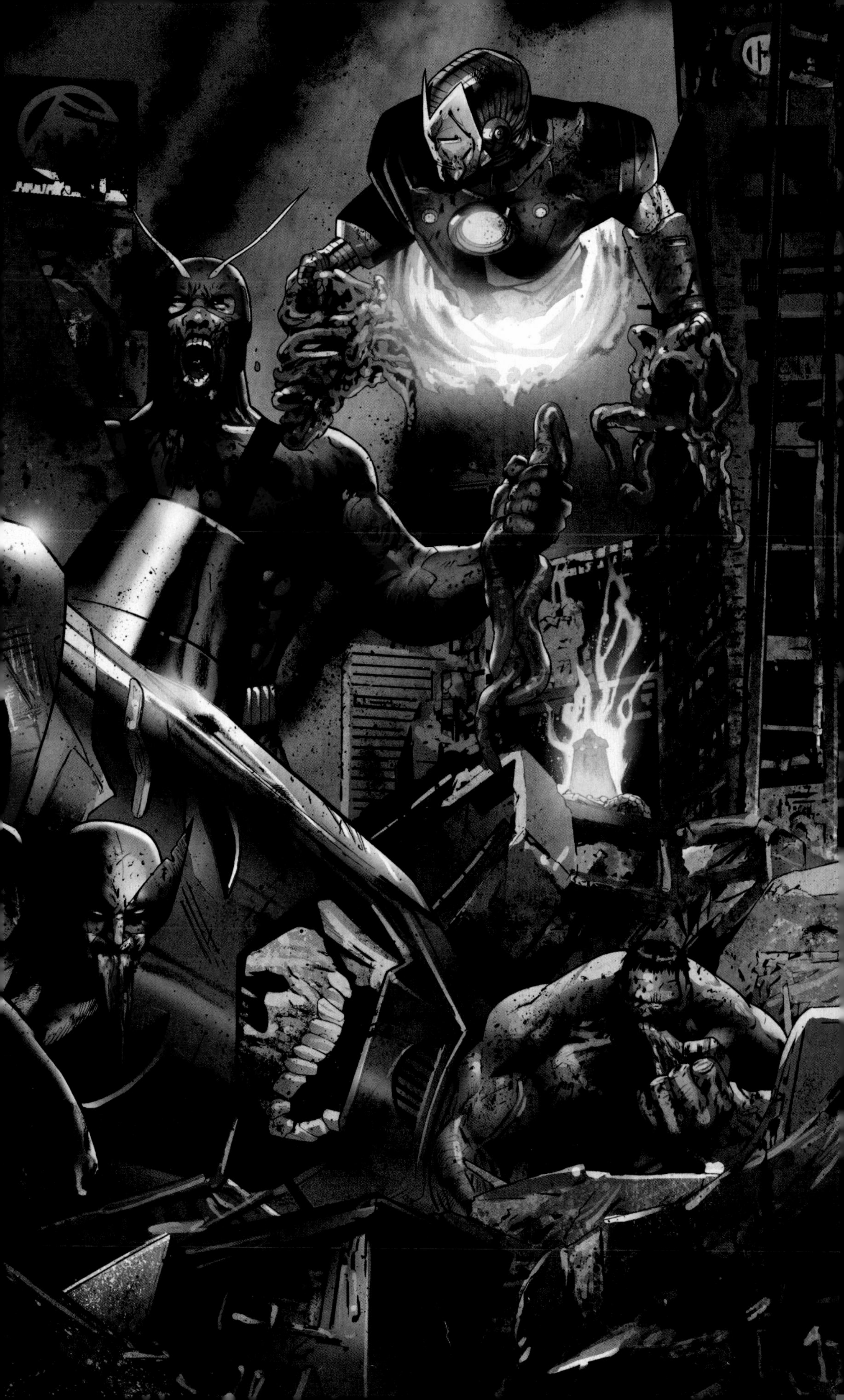

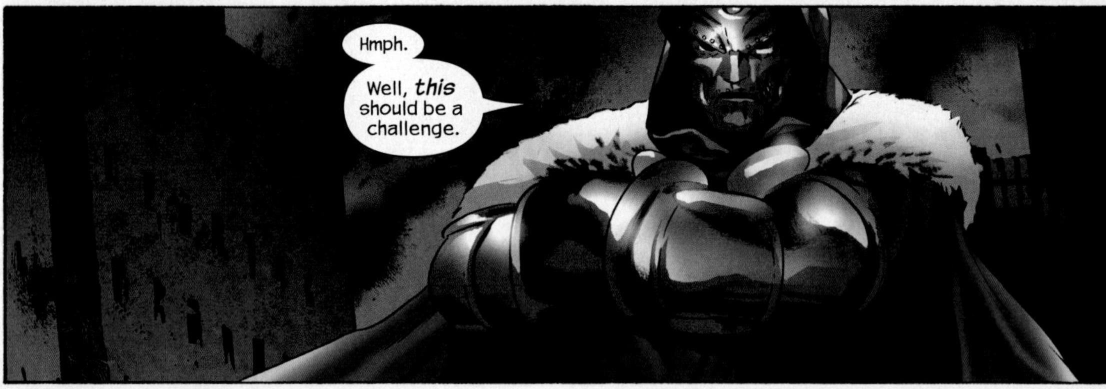
Hmph.
Well, *this* should be a challenge.

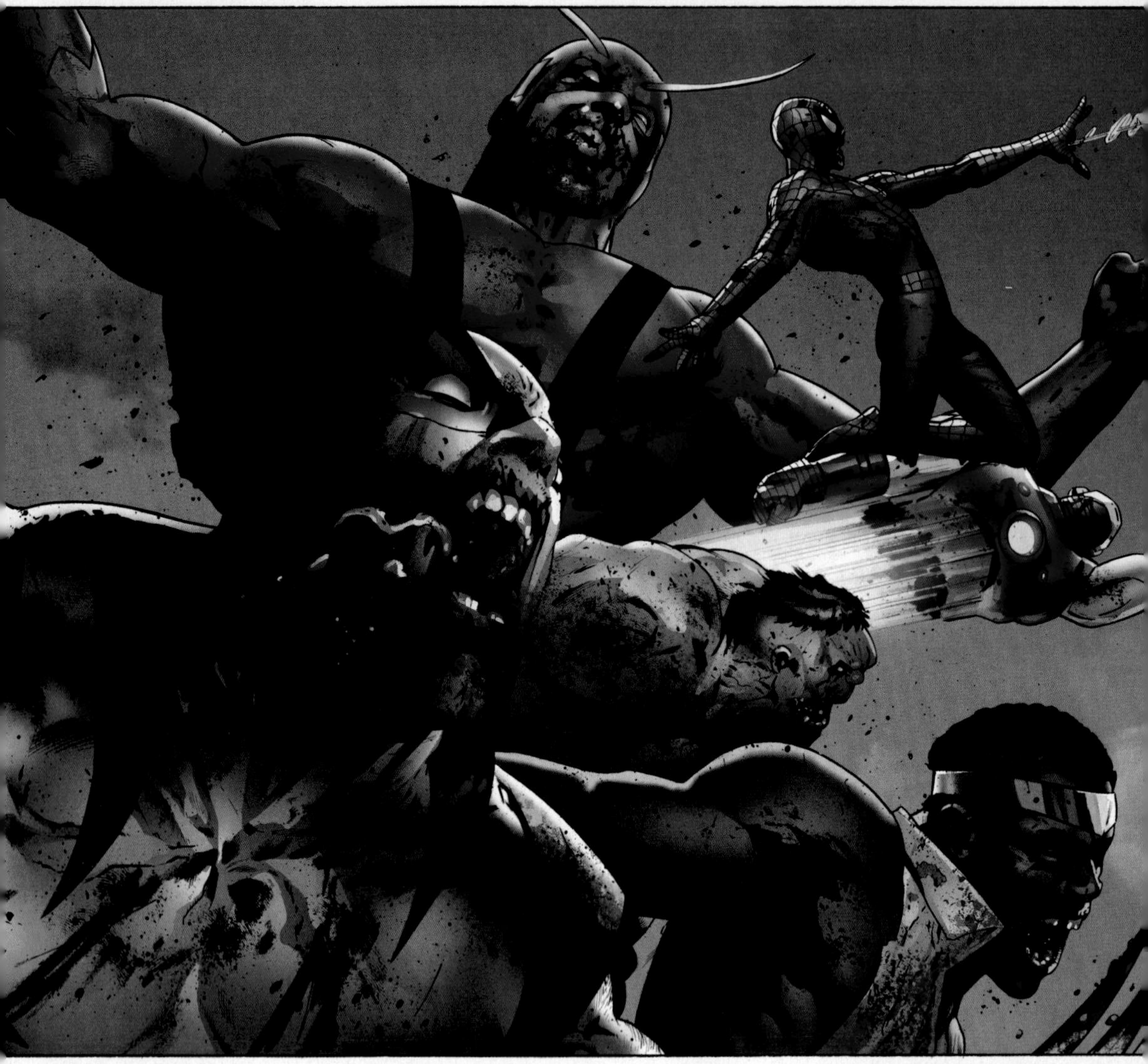

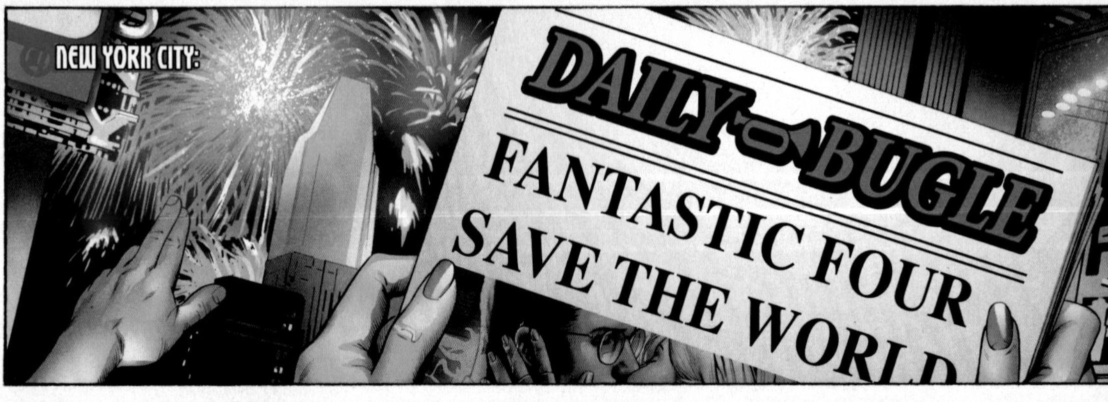
NEW YORK CITY:
DAILY BUGLE
FANTASTIC FOUR SAVE THE WORLD

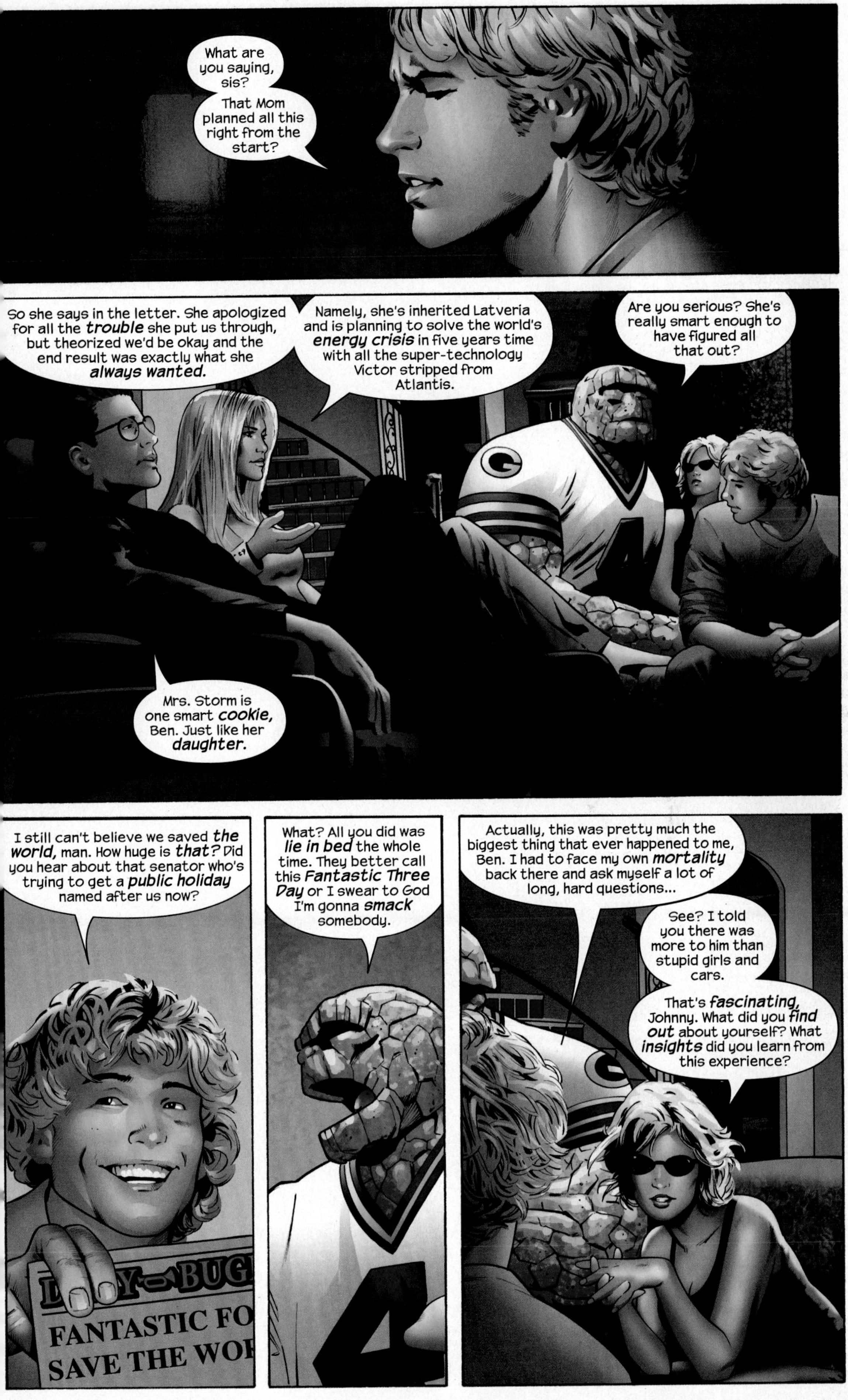
What are you saying, sis?
That Mom planned all this right from the start?
So she says in the letter. She apologized for all the trouble she put us through, but theorized we'd be okay and the end result was exactly what she always wanted.
Namely, she's inherited Latveria and is planning to solve the world's energy crisis in five years time with all the super-technology Victor stripped from Atlantis.
Are you serious? She's really smart enough to have figured all that out?
Mrs. Storm is one smart cookie, Ben. Just like her daughter.
I still can't believe we saved the world, man. How huge is that? Did you hear about that senator who's trying to get a public holiday named after us now?
FANTASTIC FO
SAVE THE WO
What? All you did was lie in bed the whole time. They better call this Fantastic Three Day or I swear to God I'm gonna smack somebody.
Actually, this was pretty much the biggest thing that ever happened to me, Ben. I had to face my own mortality back there and ask myself a lot of long, hard questions...
See? I told you there was more to him than stupid girls and cars.
That's fascinating, Johnny. What did you find out about yourself? What insights did you learn from this experience?

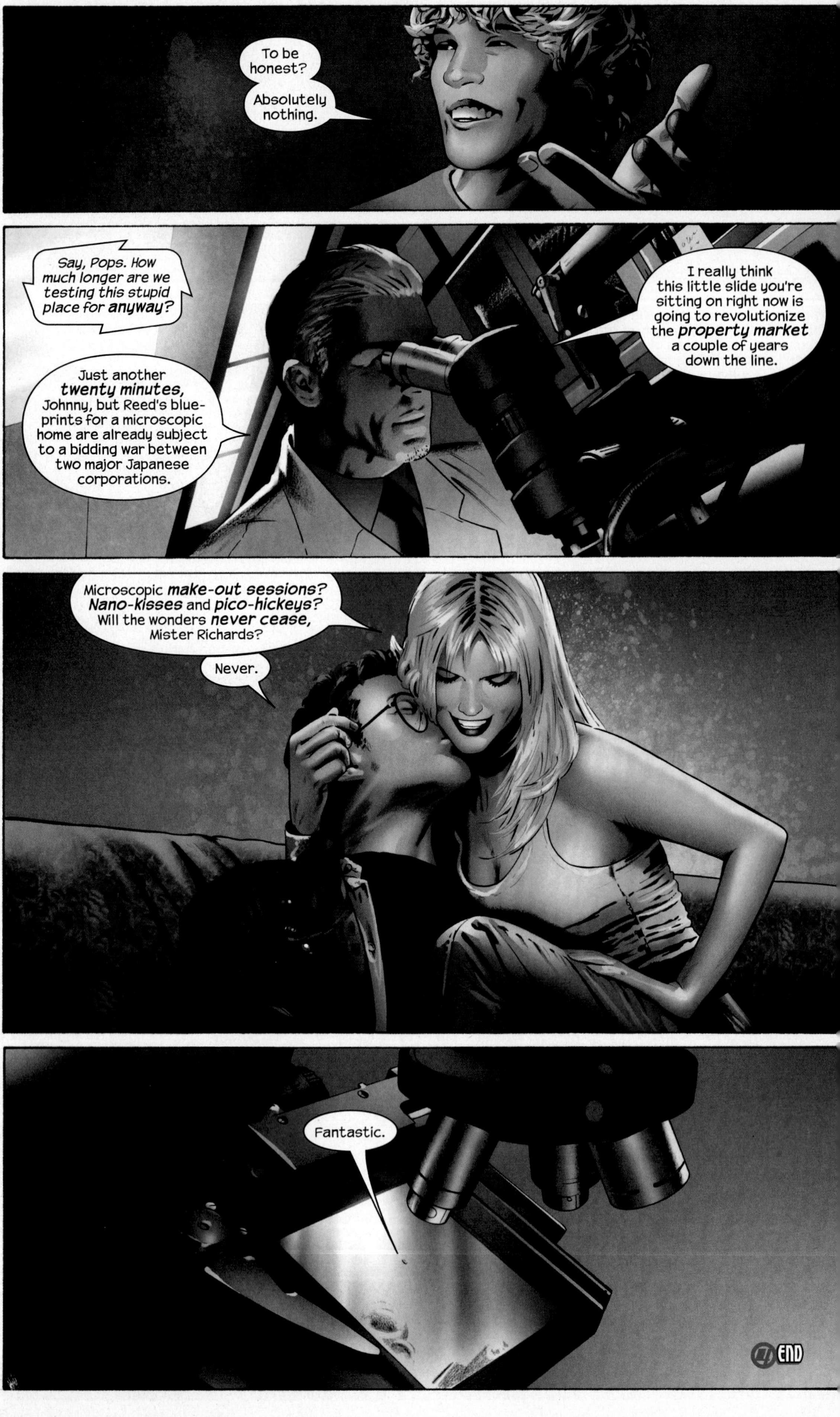
To be honest?
Absolutely nothing.
Say, Pops. How much longer are we testing this stupid place for anyway?
Just another twenty minutes, Johnny, but Reed's blue-prints for a microscopic home are already subject to a bidding war between two major Japanese corporations.
I really think this little slide you're sitting on right now is going to revolutionize the property market a couple of years down the line.
Microscopic make-out sessions? Nano-kisses and pico-hickeys? Will the wonders never cease, Mister Richards?
Never.
Fantastic.
END

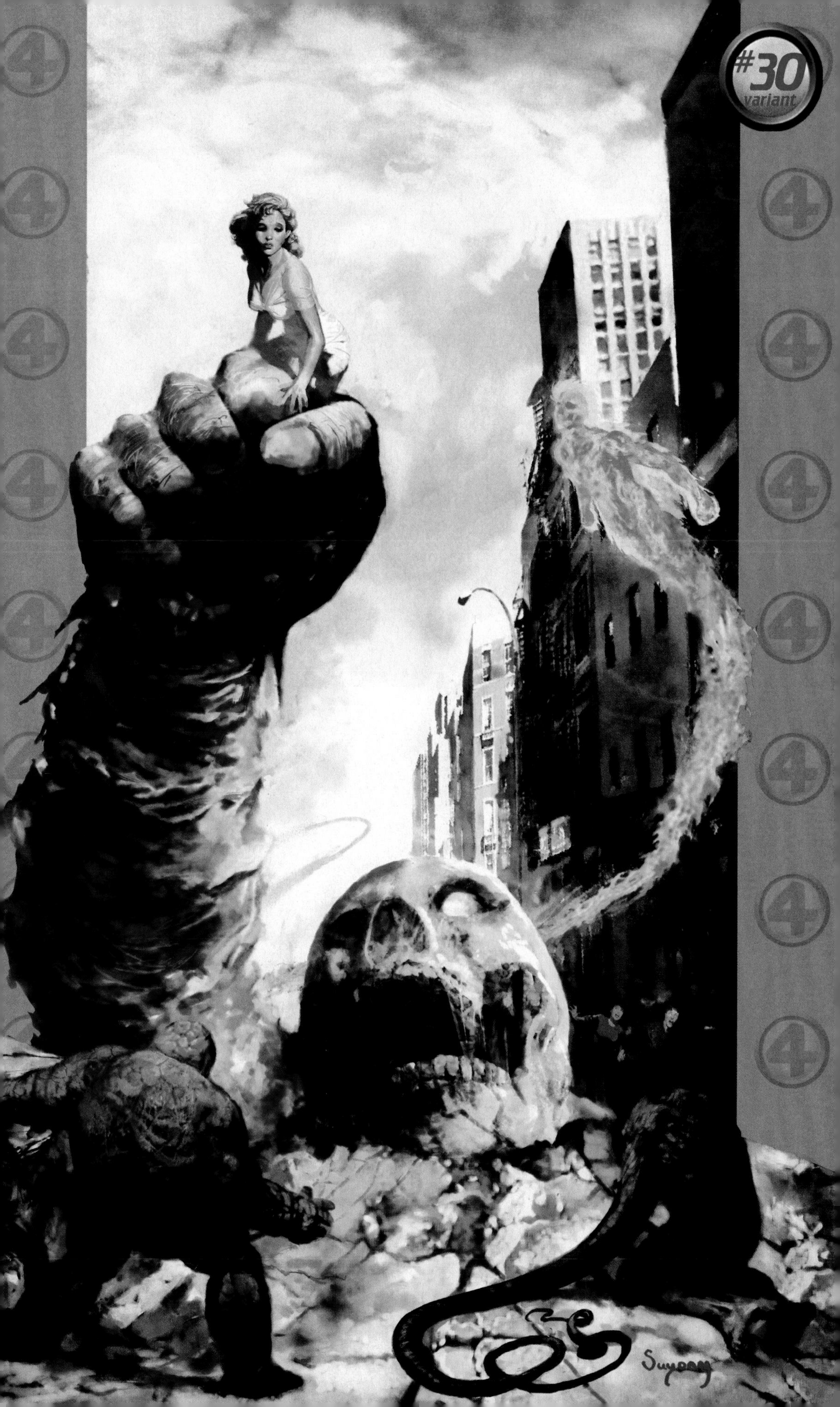
#30
variant
Suydam

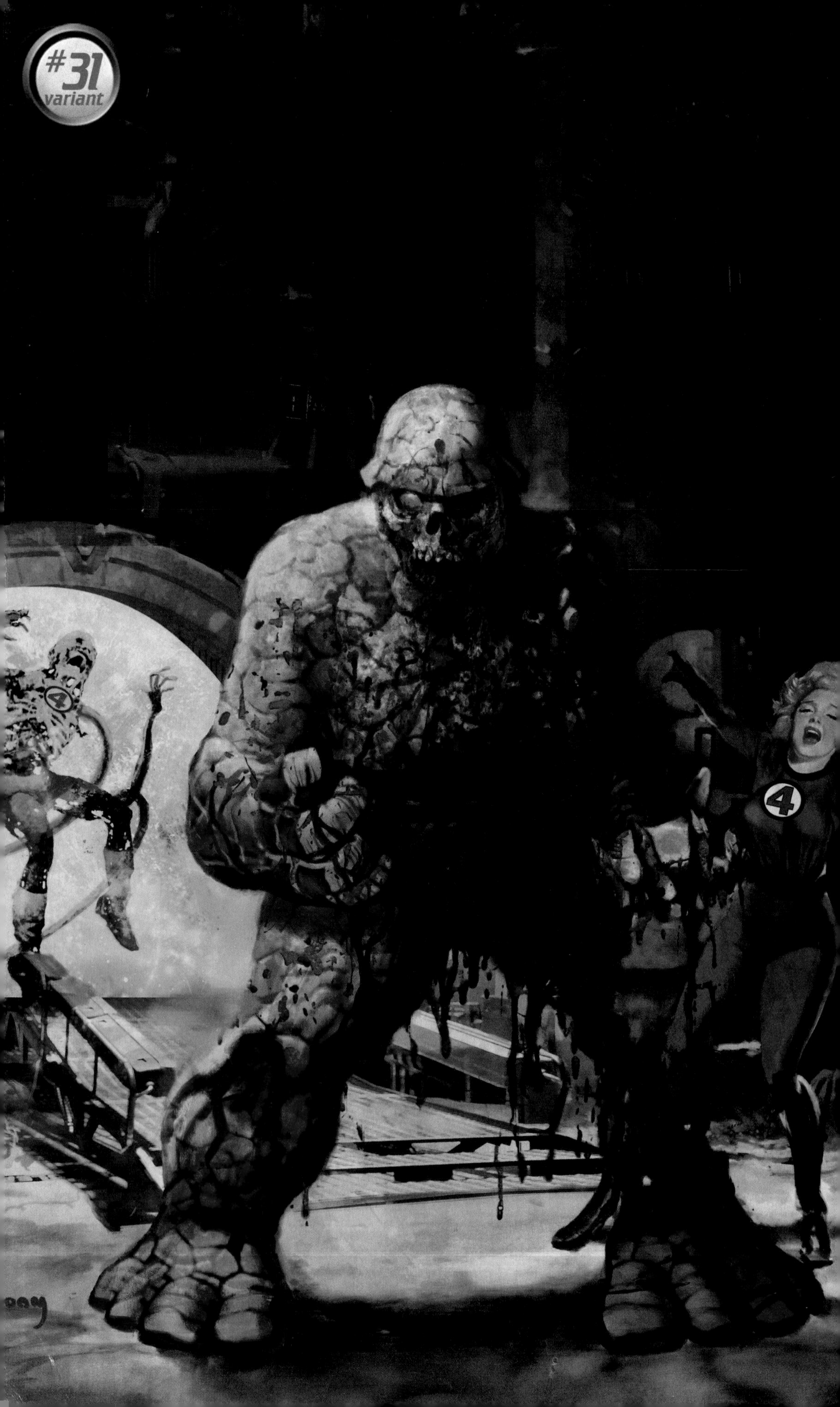
#31
variant

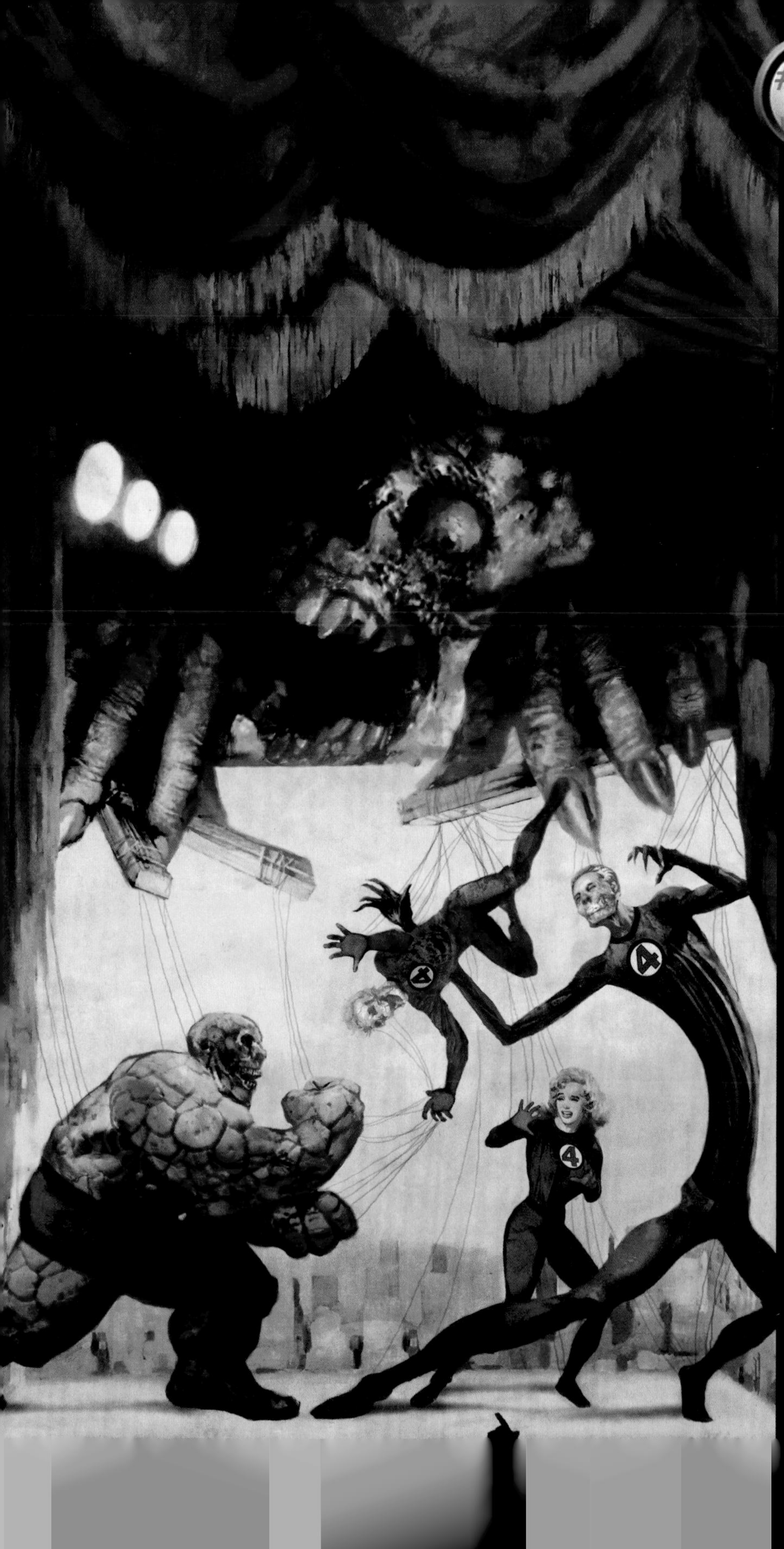
#32
variant

ISSUE #27
COVER SKETCHES
BY GREG LAND

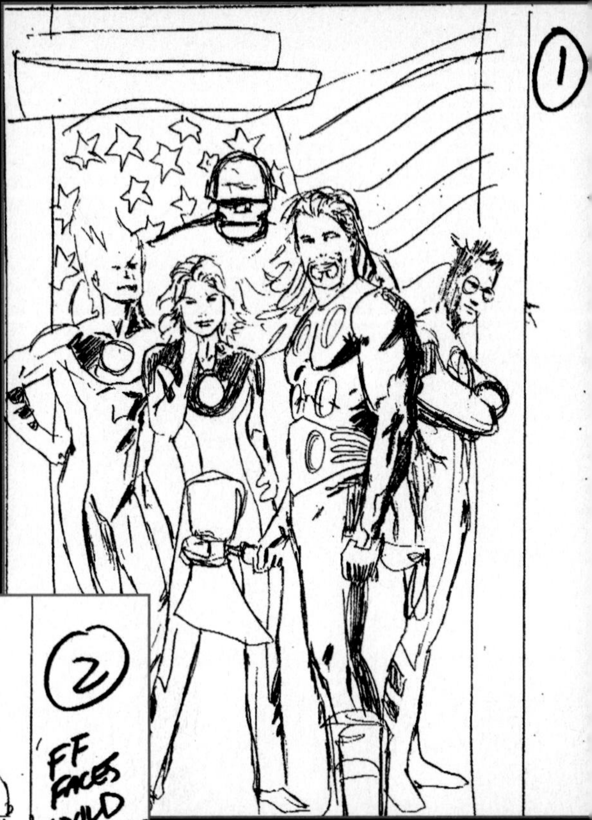
1

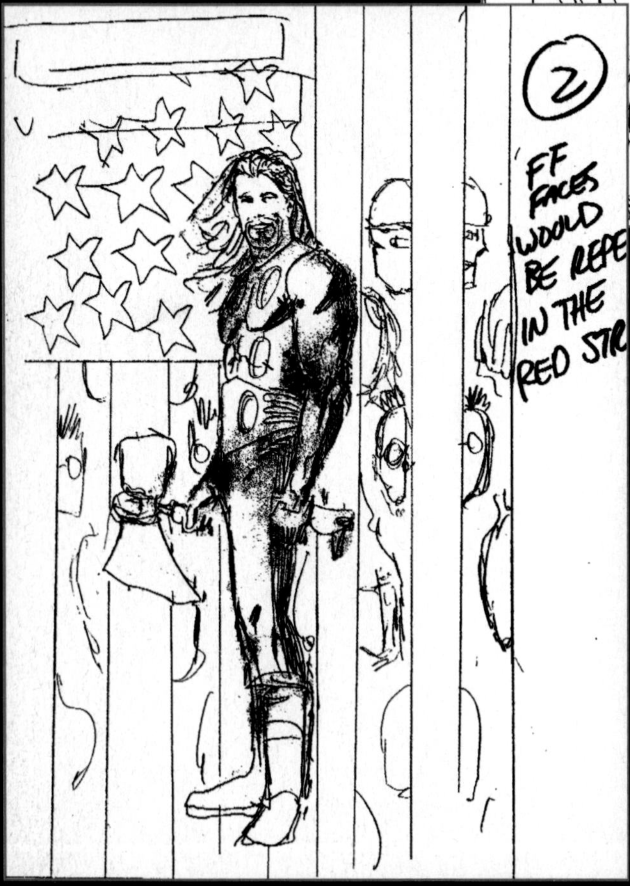
2
FF
FACES
WOULD
BE REPE
IN THE
RED STR

3
WHITE HOUSE
OR CAPITOL
BUILDING

4

5
IN FRONT
OF WHITE
HOUSE

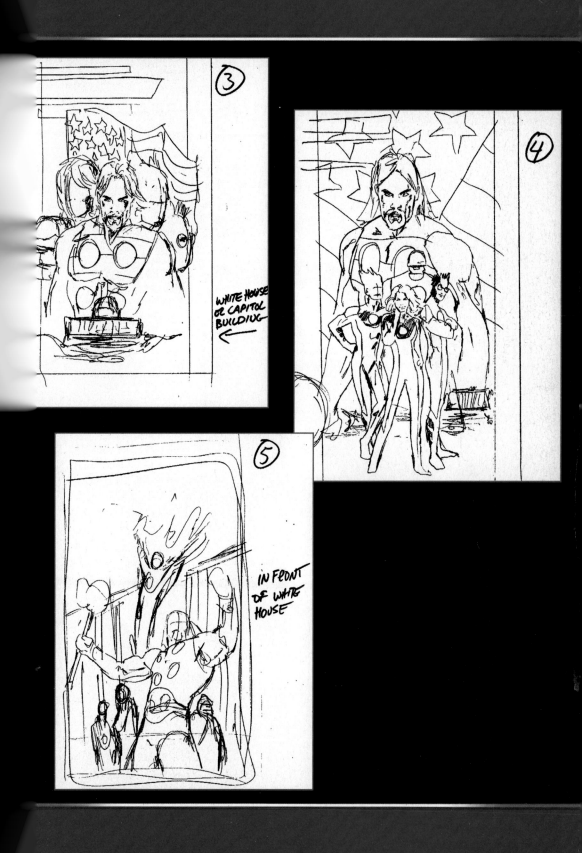